SPECTRUM SERIES
WORD STUDY
&
PHONICS
TABLE OF CONTENTS

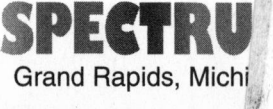

SPECTRUM
Grand Rapids, Michi

INSTRUCTIONAL CONSULTANT
Mary Lou Maples, Ed.D.
Chairman of Department of Education
Huntingdon College
Montgomery, Alabama

EDITORIAL AND PRODUCTION STAFF
Series Editor: Joyce R. Rhymer; *Project Editor:* Connie Johnson Long; *Production Editor:*
Carole R. Hill; *Senior Designer:* Patrick J. McCarthy; *Associate Designer:* Terry D. Anderson;
Project Artist: Gilda Braxton Edwards; *Artist:* Bill Roberson; *Illustrator:* Leslie Dunlap

Frank Schaffer Publications®

Send all inquiries to: Frank Schaffer Publications • 3195 Wilson Drive NW • Grand Rapids, Michigan 49534

ISBN 1-56189-944-5   6 7 8 9 10 11 VHG 09 08 07 06 05

Organized for successful learning!

The SPECTRUM PHONICS SERIES builds the right skills for reading.

The program combines four important skill strands — phonics, structural analysis, vocabulary, and dictionary skills — so your students build the skills they need to become better readers.

Four types of lesson pages offer thorough, clearly focused, systematic skills practice. That means you can focus on just the skills that need work — for the whole class, a small group, or for individualized instruction.

The SPECTRUM PHONICS SERIES is easy for students to use independently.

Although phonics may be an important part of a reading program, sometimes there just isn't enough time to do it all. That's why PHONICS offers uncomplicated lessons your children can succeed with on their own.

Colorful borders capture interest, highlight essential information, and help organize lesson structure. And your children get off to a good start with concise explanations and clear directions . . . followed by sample answers that show them exactly what to do.

In addition, vocabulary has been carefully controlled so your children work with familiar words. Key pictures and key words are used consistently throughout the series to represent specific sounds. And a sound-symbol chart at the back of the text helps your students quickly recall sound-symbol relationships.

Vowel Pairs: *AI, AY,* and *EI*

Name _____

In some words, two vowels together stand for one vowel sound. The letters **ay** and **ai** usually stand for the long-a sound, as in **hay** and **train**. The letters **ei** sometimes stand for the long-a sound, as in **eight**.

hay
train
eight

Read the words and name the pictures. Draw a line from each word to the picture it names.

sprain		tray	
spray		trail	
reindeer		sail	
rainstorm		sleigh	

Read each clue and the list of words. Find the word in the list that matches the clue. Write the word next to the clue.

1. a color ___gray___
2. a number _____
3. a path through the woods _____
4. someone in charge of a city _____
5. water that falls from clouds _____
6. blood runs through these _____
7. to lift up something _____
8. perhaps _____

trail
mayor
pay
veins
eighty
say
maybe
raise
rain
pail
gray

INSTRUCTION PAGE . . . The skill being covered is noted at the bottom of each student page for easy reference.

Vowel Pairs: *AI, AY,* and *EI*

Name _____

Read each set of sentences and its list of words. Write a word from the list that makes sense in each sentence.

1. Last summer we took a ___train___ ride on our vacation.
2. It took two _____ from beginning to end.
3. We had a little room where we _____ on the train.
4. The room had a closet and drawers where we could put our clothes _____.
5. I couldn't _____ to have supper in the dining car.
6. One of the train cars was used to carry freight and _____.
7. Riding on a train is a great _____ to travel.

sail
wait
mail
way
sleigh
train
stayed
playing
days
away

1. My brother and I lift _____ to exercise our bodies.
2. In one exercise we _____ the weights over our heads.
3. My brother can lift _____ pounds with just one arm.
4. Weight lifting helps your heart to pump blood through your _____.
5. If we try to lift too much, we get _____.
6. Then we have to _____ a while before exercising again.
7. Someday I hope I can lift as much as I _____.

veins
eighty
trail
wait
weights
sleigh
pains
rain
weigh
raise

REINFORCEMENT PAGE . . . Comprehension exercises that use context as well as phonics skills to help build the connection from decoding to comprehension.

Turn page for more information.

Easy to manage

REVIEW PAGES . . . Frequent reviews emphasize skills application.

ASSESSMENT PAGES . . . Assessment pages give you helpful feedback on how your students are doing.

PROGRESS CHECK — Prefixes and Suffixes

Name _____

Read the list of words below. Circle the prefix or suffix in each word.

treat(able)	careless	sleepy	disappear
preschool	replay	untie	misbehave
thankful	dusty	goodness	homeless
agreement	postwar	overload	teachable
distrust	babyish	incorrect	sweetly

Read the list of words below. Then read the sentences that follow. Write the word from the list that makes sense in each sentence.

pretest	mistaken	cloudy	overpaid	lightness
unlocked	rewrite	tightly	tasteless	grayish

1. I think it might rain, because the sky looks gray and

REVIEW — Prefixes and Suffixes

Name _____

Read the list of prefixes and suffixes below. Then read the clues that follow. Add one of the prefixes or suffixes to the underlined word to form a word that matches the clue.

un-	dis-	re-	pre-	-ful	-less	-y	-ly	-ness

1. the opposite of <u>continue</u>   *discontinue*
2. without <u>color</u> _____
3. every <u>year</u> _____
4. to <u>view</u> before _____
5. to <u>do</u> again _____
6. full of <u>care</u> _____
7. having <u>thirst</u> _____
8. not <u>planned</u> _____
9. a state of being <u>weak</u> _____

Read the list of prefixes and suffixes below. Then read the clues that follow. Add one of the prefixes or suffixes to the underlined base word to form a word that matches the clue.

post-	in-	mis-	over-	-able	-ish	-ment

1. somewhat <u>warm</u>   *warmish*
2. not <u>complete</u> _____
3. to <u>pronounce</u> wrongly _____
4. the act of <u>agreeing</u> _____
5. able to be <u>trained</u> _____
6. like a <u>child</u> _____
7. after the <u>season</u> _____
8. <u>pay</u> too much _____

Review of forming words with prefixes and suffixes   127

Synonyms

Teaching Suggestion 9, Page T–15   Extending Activity 14, Page T–20

Name _____

Words to use: hotel-inn, jelly-jam, meadow-field, rapid-fast, alive-living, funny-amusing, terrible-awful, started-began, boast-brag, cattle-cows, center-middle, correct-right

A synonym is a word that has the same or nearly the same meaning as another word.	rush—hurry

Read the words in each box below. Draw a line to match each word with its synonym (word that has the same meaning).

quiet — thin	raise — tell	ship — close
simple — easy	say — lift	near — yell
narrow — still	small — little	shout — boat

tale — story	stay — hear	chilly — cold
well — large	forest — remain	present — wash
big — healthy	listen — woods	clean — gift

Read the list of words below. Then read the sentences that follow. Write the word from the list that is a synonym (word that has the same meaning) for the underlined word in each sentence.

unload	skinny	sea	fix	begin
going	raw	cover	hurry	tall

1. Kara will <u>repair</u> the kitchen sink.   *fix*
2. I would like a <u>thin</u> slice of bread.   skinny
3. Don't <u>rush</u> through your homework.   hurry
4. Billy enjoyed the <u>uncooked</u> vegetables.   raw
5. The <u>ocean</u> was calm yesterday.   sea
6. Tess is unhappy that I am <u>leaving</u>.   going
7. We can <u>start</u> the game without Carlos.   begin
8. The workers wanted to <u>unpack</u> the truck.   unload
9. The cats were sitting on the <u>high</u> fence.   tall
10. Please put a <u>lid</u> on the box.   cover

ANSWER KEY . . . Gives you the help you need when you need it — including student pages with answers for quick, easy reference.

Beginning Sounds

Name _____

Read the words and name the pictures. Circle the word that names each picture.

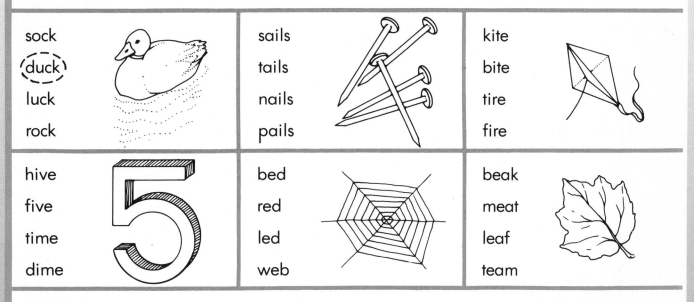

sock	sails	kite
(duck)	tails	bite
luck	nails	tire
rock	pails	fire
hive	bed	beak
five	red	meat
time	led	leaf
dime	web	team

Read each sentence and the word beside it. Change the first letter of the word to form a new word that makes sense in the sentence. Write the new word in the blank.

1. I'll need to buy another stamp to ___*send*___ this letter.   bend

2. I need to have a new _____ put on this cowboy boot.   feel

3. Our neighbor's dog likes to hide its bones in our _____.   card

4. I have just enough _____ to finish my breakfast.   dime

5. They planted tomatoes and _____ in their garden.   torn

6. The three days of rain made our cellar very _____.   camp

7. It took two hours to _____ the road in the snowstorm.   mind

8. We needed another piece of _____ to tie the boxes.   hope

Beginning Sounds

Name _____

Name the pictures. Write the missing letter to complete each picture name.

$\mathcal{L}$emon

____orn

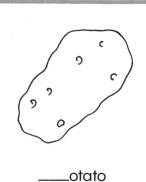
____otato

____anana

____omato

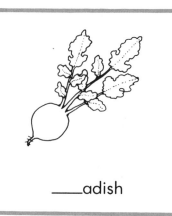
____adish

In each sentence, complete the unfinished word by writing the missing letter. The word you form must make sense in the sentence.

1. You can find almost anything in our $\mathcal{G}$____arage.

2. We have spare parts for the lawn ____ower.

3. There is a box full of empty orange ____uice cans.

4. In one corner is a set of tires for my brother's ____an.

5. The mast for our neighbor's ____ailboat is there, too.

6. There is an old movie ____amera on a shelf.

7. A roll of garden ____ose is beside it.

8. We even have a toy monkey we bought at the ____oo.

Sound-symbol association of initial consonants; Words containing initial consonants in context

Ending Sounds

Name _____

Read the words and name the pictures. Circle the word that names each picture.

chair (chain) chart cheek	boot bowl book box	broom brook brood brown
wit win wig wax	but bus bun bud	roll root room roof

Read each sentence and the word beside it. Change the last letter of the word to form a new word that makes sense in the sentence. Write the new word in the blank.

1. We went to see a traveling circus last _____*week*_____. weed

2. We _____ in a large tent and watched the show. sad

3. One of the trained animals was a _____. dot

4. It was wearing a funny cap and a _____. bit

5. They also had a trained _____ in the show. seam

6. It was able to _____ a ball on the end of its nose. keel

7. We stopped for a quick _____ after the show. mean

8. Then I _____ a nap while Dad drove home. tool

Ending Sounds

Name _____

Name the pictures. Write the missing letter to complete each picture name.

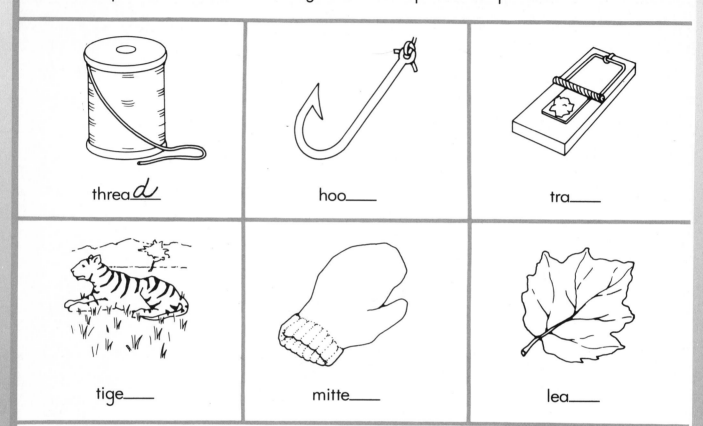

threa*d*　　　　　　hoo____　　　　　　tra____

tige____　　　　　　mitte____　　　　　　lea____

In each sentence, complete the unfinished word by writing the missing letter. The word you form must make sense in the sentence.

1. My best friend got a new kitten last wee*k*.

2. I rode the bu____ to her house to see it.

3. It's quite young and not very bi____ yet.

4. It sleeps in an old shoe bo____.

5. My friend gives it a bow____ of warm milk for supper.

6. For breakfast it eats cat foo____.

7. When it gets tired, it curls up to take a na____.

8. Playing with my friend's kitten is a lot of fu____.

Sound-symbol association of final consonants; Words containing final consonants in context

Beginning and Ending Sounds

Name _____

In each sentence, complete each unfinished word by writing the missing letter. The word you form must make sense in the sentence.

1. Some new people just _m_oved in _n_ext to us.

2. They have two boys, one ___irl, and a do___.

3. The mother is an animal ___octor at our ___oo.

4. Some of their things were tied onto the to___ of their ___an.

5. I helped carry a giant bo___ and an old cri___ upstairs.

6. They asked my mo___ if I could ___oin them for supper.

7. She said I could stay to ea___ if I wanted to.

---

1. Our class goes to the _L_ibrary each wee_k_.

2. We each get to take home a ___ook that we ___ike.

3. I like to ___ead books about space trave___.

4. Felipe likes book___ about ___ire fighters.

5. Sue likes to read about ___eople who have discovere___ things.

6. Sharon likes scary stories abou___ old ___ouses.

7. Bob and Carol both ___ook home books about race ___ars.

8. You can find almost any ___ind of book in ou___ library.

Short Vowels

Name _____

Read the words and name the pictures. Circle the word that names each picture.

fin fat fit (fan)	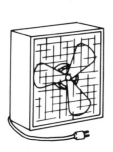	moss mop map moth		jog jag jig jug	
pun pan pen pin		lid lip led lad		map mop mitt mat	

Read the sentences and the word choices. Circle the word that best completes each sentence.

1. I like to look (at, it) the beautiful trees in the park.

2. There are a (let, lot) of different kinds of trees growing there.

3. The pine tree keeps its needles all (winter, wonder) long.

4. The oak tree (has, his) colored leaves in the fall.

5. Many birds build their (nuts, nests) in the tree branches.

6. Squirrels also like to live high (if, up) in the trees.

7. Some of the older trees have grown very (big, bag).

8. It would be (fin, fun) to climb to the tops of those trees.

9. I could (sit, sat) on a branch and watch the birds.

10. I could even take some (nets, nuts) to feed the squirrels.

Symbol-sound association of short-vowel words; Short-vowel words in context

Short Vowels

Name _____

Read each sentence and the words shown below the blank. Complete each sentence by writing the word that has a short-vowel sound.

1. Yesterday my family had a ___*picnic*___.
    (picnic, race)

2. It was the first sunny day in _____.
    (spring, June)

3. My sister and I helped Dad pack a _____ with food.
    (case, basket)

4. I made _____ and put it in a cooler.
    (punch, tea)

5. We sat near the _____ pond in the center of the park.
    (duck, wide)

6. I had fun watching the ducks _____ in the water.
    (splash, wade)

Read each clue. Find the word in the list that matches the clue. Write the word next to the clue.

1. something to cook food in	*pot*	brick
2. something used in making buildings	_____	crop
3. to knock lightly	_____	cup
4. something to drink from	_____	mop
5. a fast airplane	_____	pot
6. a large boat	_____	hat
7. something to sit on	_____	ship
8. something used to wash a floor	_____	bench
		jet
		tap
		stick

Short Vowels

Name _____

Read each sentence and the word beside it. Change the vowel of the word to form a new word that makes sense in the sentence. Write the new word in the blank.

1. I want to buy a new ____*pack*____ for camping.   pick

2. The one I already have has a giant rip in the top _____.   flip

3. It also has a burned _____ on it.   spit

4. The new one will keep out the _____ and water.   mad

5. I don't want one that is too _____.   bag

6. I don't have a _____ of things to carry in it.   let

7. I want it to _____ me just right.   fat

8. And the straps shouldn't _____ or be uncomfortable.   punch

9. I hope the _____ downtown has the one I want.   ship

Read the paragraph below. Complete each unfinished word by writing the missing vowel. The word you form must make sense in the paragraph.

Goldfish make wonderful p_e_ts. You will need a bowl or tank b___g

enough for the n___mber of fish you want. The people at the pet store

can t___ll you how large a t___nk you'll need. You will also need clean

water and fish food. Be sure the water is n___t too cold or too h___t.

Feed your fish every day. Feed th___m only what they c___n eat in

about five minutes. You will need to change the water ___nd clean the

tank about every t___n days.

Short Vowels

Name _____

Read the list of words below. Then read the sentences that follow. Write a word from the list that makes sense in each sentence.

sister	let	butterfly
has	possible	best
brush	tricks	gentle
twenty	red	box
big	strings	

1. My older _____*sister*_____ and I like to fly kites in spring and autumn.

2. We can fill a giant _____ with all the ones we own.

3. My sister has a big kite that is _____ with two yellow tails.

4. It _____ a bright rainbow painted in the middle of it.

5. Her kite is so _____ it reaches up to her eyebrows when she holds it!

6. My sister _____ me fly her big kite once.

7. The kite I like _____ is colored purple.

8. It has a tail over _____ feet long.

9. I have to use two _____ to fly it.

10. I pull on the strings to make it do _____.

11. It's _____ to make it loop and dive.

12. I can make it _____ against the ground and go back up.

13. One kite we made has wings and looks like a _____.

14. It flies best in a quiet, _____ breeze.

Long Vowels

Name _____

Read the words and name the pictures. Write each word below the picture it names.

| page | skate | cube | spider | nine | globe |

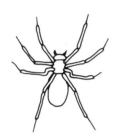

spider

_____

_____

_____

_____

_____

Read the sentences and the word choices. Circle the word that makes sense in each sentence.

1. Last year everyone in our class ((wrote), write) a book.

2. We could write about whatever we (chase, chose).

3. Someone's book was about rock (make, music).

4. My best friend wrote about the homes of (snakes, spokes).

5. I wrote about the care of (bikes, bakes).

6. I also wrote some safety (ropes, rules) that bikers should follow.

7. My book had ten (pages, poles).

8. I (like, lake) to ride my bike, and I enjoyed writing my book.

14

Long Vowels

Name _____

Read each word below and listen to its vowel sound. Write the word under the picture whose name has the same vowel sound.

vase	shape	cone	June
hive	cute	note	huge
bike	tune	code	lime
close	flame	tame	ripe
blade	dive	chose	rude

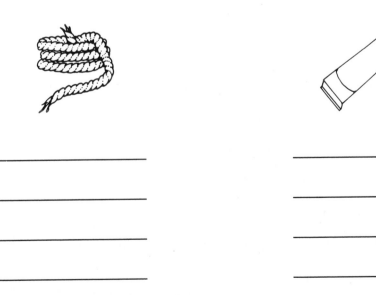

vase
_____
_____
_____

_____
_____
_____
_____

_____
_____
_____
_____

_____
_____
_____
_____

In each sentence, complete the unfinished word by writing the missing vowel or vowels. The word you form must make sense in the sentence.

1. My uncle dr_i_v_e_s one of the city buses.

2. He leaves for work at f___v___ o'clock every morning.

3. He m___k___s the first stop on his route at six o'clock.

4. M___st of his passengers are going to work.

5. Uncle Dave w___v___s to the passengers as they leave the bus.

6. They usually sm___l___ and tell him to have a good day.

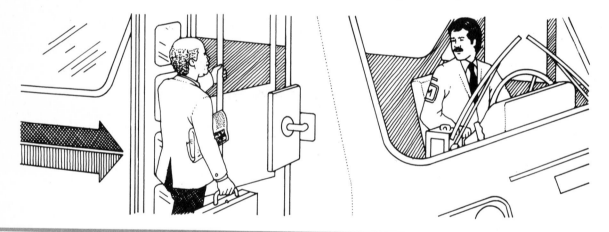

Read the paragraph below. Complete each unfinished word by writing the missing vowel or vowels. The word you form must make sense in the paragraph.

The hills in the West are filled with old silver and gold m_i_n_e_s. Some of them are very small, but others are h___g___. Mice and sp___ders now live in most of them. P___n___ trees grow in front of many mines. Some of the mines look like deep c___v___s. At one t___m___, miners worked in all these mines. All of them h___p___d to str___k___ it rich. Some did, but many went br___k___.

Long-vowel words in context

OLD and *IND*

Name _____

The letter **o** followed by **ld** usually stands for the long-**o** sound. The letter **i** followed by **nd** usually stands for the long-**i** sound.

cold
kind

Read each sentence. In the blanks below the sentence, write the words from the sentence that have the long-**o** sound.

1. I thought it was cold inside, but it was even colder outside.

   _____cold_____   _____colder_____

2. We saved a lot of very old things, such as this tin candle mold.

   _____   _____

3. I put the papers in a folder and asked my mom to hold them.

   _____   _____

4. The workers told us they had found a gold mine in the hills.

   _____   _____

5. The people at the shop just sold the last candle holder.

   _____   _____

Read each sentence. In the blank, write the word from the sentence that has the long-**i** sound.

1. We visited a place where dogs are trained to help blind people.

   _____blind_____

2. This old mill used to grind wheat and corn into flour. _____

3. This morning our sister couldn't find her shoe. _____

4. It was very kind of you to remember his birthday. _____

5. You can solve this puzzle if you put your mind to it. _____

Identifying words containing *old* and *ind* in context

OLD and IND

Name _____

Read each sentence and the words beside it. Write the word that makes sense in each sentence.

---

1. They _____*told*_____ us that the movie begins at six o'clock.

2. The paper had gotten wet and was hard to _____.

unfold
told
sold

---

3. The chest full of _____ was hidden by the lake.

4. My brother is three years _____ than you.

gold
bold
older

---

5. Do you _____ if I watch you put that toy together?

6. The machine was _____ the wheat into flour.

find
grinding
mind

---

7. We made candle _____ from empty paper tubes.

8. It almost never gets very _____ in Florida.

holders
cold
sold

---

9. How much water do you think this pan will_____?

10. The jacket I was hoping to buy has already been

   _____.

hold
told
sold

---

11. The headlights of the car _____ me for a moment.

12. I'm going to try to _____ another way to get home.

find
kind
blinded

---

13. Can we _____ the tent and fit it back into the bag?

14. Our apartment building is the _____ one in the city.

oldest
fold
told

Words containing *old* and *ind* in context

OLD and *IND*

Name _____

Read each sentence. Complete the unfinished word by writing **old** or **ind.** The word you form must make sense in the sentence.

1. How long will it take you to w_____*ind*_____ up all that string?

2. I'm teaching my dog to walk on his h_____ legs.

3. It's usually c_____er in Canada than in Mexico.

4. After you complete the order form, f_____ it in half.

5. No one t_____ me that there was no school today.

6. Thinking is a good exercise for your m_____.

7. The fancy watch was made of g_____.

8. Did you ever f_____ the key that was missing?

9. My dad has a tool h_____er he wears on his belt.

10. Please pull the bl_____ on the window to keep the sunshine out.

11. I caught two bad c_____s last winter.

12. Please h_____ the flashlight higher so I can see better.

13. I forgot to put the bread away, and now there's m_____ on it.

14. The store owner s_____ fruit and vegetables.

15. "Be k_____ to animals" is a good thought to remember.

16. I left the f_____er on my desk, but now I can't find it.

17. The kitchen is the c_____est room in the house.

18. The teacher is h_____ing the word cards.

Long Vowels

Name _____

Read each sentence and the words beside it. Write the word that makes sense in each sentence.

1. Sometimes I like to lie on my back and ___*gaze*___ at the clouds.

   gaze
   quite
   whole

2. It's an enjoyable way to rest my _____ for a while.

   mind
   old
   make

3. I _____ my best friend about all the pictures I can see.

   shape
   tape
   told

4. One time I saw a whole group of _____ trees.

   pine
   joke
   find

5. The clouds looked like a _____ forest in the sky.

   huge
   take
   find

6. There was even a winding stream and a tiny _____.

   whole
   lake
   fold

7. People's _____ are fun to look for, too.

   faces
   finds
   times

8. Some of them have big _____ or funny ears.

   names
   lakes
   noses

9. Some of them seem to be laughing and telling _____.

   jokes
   places
   homes

10. The _____ of the clouds are always changing.

    shapes
    lakes
    holds

11. There are always new pictures to _____.

    huge
    joke
    find

20

Short and Long Vowels

Name _____

Read the words and look at the pictures. Write each word below the picture it tells about.

can	hat	tape	van
plate	note	slide	cap
mat	cape	rip	cane

note

_____

_____

_____

_____

_____

_____

_____

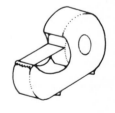

_____

_____

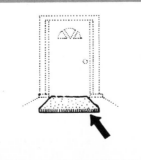

_____

_____

Short and Long Vowels

Name _____

Read the words and name the pictures. Circle the word that names each picture.

dam		deck		pile	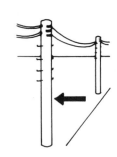
(dime)		disk		pill	
dome		dock		pole	
dim		desk		pale	
mule		sift	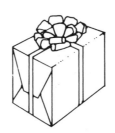	punch	
mole		gift		pitch	
mile		golf		pinch	
male		soft		patch	

Read each sentence and the word beside it. Change the first vowel of the word to form a new word that makes sense in the sentence. Write the word in the blank.

1. A loud noise _____*woke*_____ me while I was sleeping.   wake

2. It sounded a _____ like a crash.   let

3. The _____ showed it was only two o'clock in the morning.   click

4. I jumped out of _____ and ran to the window.   bid

5. The full moon _____ everything very bright.   mode

6. I could see my _____ lying on the grass.   bake

7. My lunch box _____ fallen out of the bike basket.   hid

8. I remembered leaving some _____ in my lunch box.   chaps

9. A raccoon was eating the _____ of my lunch!   rust

Symbol-sound association of short- and long-vowel sounds; Short- and long-vowel words in context

Short and Long Vowels

Name _____

In each sentence, complete the unfinished word by writing the missing vowel or vowels. The word you form must make sense in the sentence.

1. Cal and Kate h_o_p_e_d to be in the school play.

2. It was going to be about bold knights and dr___gons.

3. They had noticed a sign that t___ld about the first practice.

4. They w___nt to Miss Blanco's room after school to sign up.

5. There was a h___g___ crowd of boys and girls with Miss Blanco.

6. "I can f___nd something for each of you to do," she said.

7. Miss Blanco had everyone read a p___g___ from the play book.

8. Then she told everyone to come b___ck the next day.

9. The n___xt afternoon everyone hurried to Miss Blanco's room.

10. She started by reading the n___m___s of the queen and the king.

11. Next she read the names of each of the t___n knights.

12. Kate was going to be one of th___m.

13. Th___n she read the names of the three dragons.

14. Cal g___t to be a dragon.

15. It would be a l___t of fun to put on a play.

16. But it would also t___k___ a lot of hard work.

17. Kate would have to study her l___n___s every night.

18. Cal would have to pretend to blow sm___k___ and fire.

19. Cal and Kate ran all the way h___m___ to tell the family the news.

Short and Long Vowels

Name _____

Read each sentence and the words beside it. Write the word that makes sense in each sentence.

1.	My little sister is wearing blue pants and a ___*pink*___ skirt.	pin pine pink
2.	After I took a short nap, I felt _____.	find fine fin
3.	Last year my family flew on a jet _____ for the first time.	plate plane plans
4.	We must guess the answer after he gives us a _____.	club clock clue
5.	When Tat runs out of the house, he will _____ his backpack.	grass grab grape
6.	Would you _____ carrying these boxes to the closet?	mine mint mind
7.	When will the _____ city bus stop at this corner?	next need nest
8.	His uncle taught him how to _____ a flag.	fog fond fold
9.	Small brown birds are a _____ sight in our backyard.	common cot cold
10.	Alma _____ her puppy every time it runs to her.	hugs huge hum
11.	I was able to fix the bookshelf that I _____.	bold box broke

Assessment of short- and long-vowel words in context

Hard and Soft C and G

Name _____

The letters **c** or **g** followed by **e, i,** or **y** usually stand for their soft sounds, as in **cent** and **page.** The letters **c** or **g** followed by any other letters stand for their hard sounds, as in **can** and **wagon.**

cent   **page**
(soft **c**)   (soft **g**)

Read the words and name the pictures. Draw a line from each word to the picture it names.

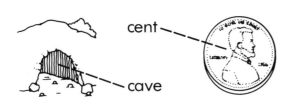
cent
cave

goat
badge

bridge
goose

camera
celery

giant
gate

picture
rice

mice
comb

tag
stage

Hard and Soft C and G

Name _____

Read the sentences. In the blanks below each sentence, write the words that have the soft **c** or **g** sound.

cent   pa**ge**
(soft **c**)   (soft **g**)

1. My Uncle Antonio gets to wear a shiny badge on his coat.

   badge

2. He works on a big bridge in the middle of the city.

   _____ _____

3. He is in charge of raising and lowering it when a barge comes by.

   _____ _____

4. He knows all the police who work nearby.

   _____

5. He says it's nice to work in a place outdoors.

   _____ _____

Read the sentences. Circle the words in each sentence that have the hard **c** or **g** sound.

1. Gary and Angela decided to plant a garden.

2. They wanted to raise corn, carrots, peas, and other vegetables.

3. They thought maybe they could can some of what they raised.

4. They began to dig in the dirt and gently put the seeds in.

5. When the work was completed, they decided they had done a good job.

6. The gardeners tried to guess how long it would be before their crops would grow.

7. They didn't want to wait until they could eat the vegetables from their garden.

Hard- and soft-c and g words in context

Hard and Soft C and G

Name _____

Read each clue. Write **c** or **g** to complete the word that matches the clue.

cent   pa**ge**
(soft **c**)   (soft **g**)

1. something that can be pinned on a coat or shirt   bad_*g*_e

2. a piece of bread   sli___e

3. someone who prepares food in a kitchen   ___ook

4. red, blue, green, and yellow   ___olors

5. how a dog's tail moves   wa___s

6. something to keep a tiger in   ca___e

7. not noisy   pea___eful

8. something that is usually red and has wheels   wa___on

Read each sentence and the words beside it. Write the word that makes sense in each sentence.

1. Put your horn in its carrying ___*case*___ .   cage
2. It's just about time to leave for the _____.   circus / case

3. There's a book of directions that tells how to play the _____.   game / page
4. But the book is missing the _____ that tells about scoring.   gave

5. Check in the kitchen to see if there is any _____ left.   cup / cent
6. Then please get me a _____ of flour from under the counter.   rice

7. We have two _____ that we milk every day.   giant / goats
8. We put the milk into a _____ can and keep it cool.   gown

Hard and Soft C and G

Name _____

Read the list of words. Notice the sound that **c** or **g** stands for in each word. Then write each word under the correct heading.

given	giant	copper	center
guide	costume	city	stage
forgot	gentle	picnic	fog
fierce	gaze	peace	became
curl	certain	judge	badge

Hard **g** as in **wagon**

given

_____

_____

_____

_____

Soft **g** as in **page**

_____

_____

_____

_____

Hard **c** as in **can**

_____

_____

_____

_____

Soft **c** as in **cent**

_____

_____

_____

_____

Review of symbol-sound association of hard- and soft-c and g words

Hard and Soft C and G

Name _____

Read each sentence and the words beside it. Write the word that makes sense in each sentence.

1.	My family likes to go *camping* when it is warm.	camping cashing circling
2.	Some of the best stories I've ever read begin with the words, "_____ upon a time."	Once Organ Office
3.	We need to have seven people to play this _____.	game germ gave
4.	My aunt enjoys her job as a _____.	juice judge jug
5.	A giant _____ is flying above our city building.	flag face fancy
6.	The guide knows the way through the dark _____.	cave cent cape
7.	The zoo just built a bigger _____ for its tigers.	came cage cities
8.	Look at the _____ tag and tell me the jacket's cost.	price prince piece
9.	After the play was over, the actors left the _____.	stage strange stack
10.	Begin by having partners stand in the _____ of the room.	cellar center circus
11.	All of the _____ were burning brightly.	camera certain candles

Seeds and Plants

Inside every seed is a tiny plant waiting to grow. What does the little seed need to grow into a plant?

Seeds

Seeds come in many shapes and sizes. Some seeds are round, and some are long and thin. Some seeds are as tiny as grains of sand; others are bigger than golf balls.

Inside every seed is a tiny plant and stored food to help the seed grow. The food part of the seed is much larger than the plant part.

What Makes Seeds Grow?

A seed needs water and heat to grow. Most seeds grow best in the spring when there is a lot of rainfall and the weather is warm. After the seed begins to grow, it is called a seedling. The little seedling needs water, air, sunlight, and food to grow.

The Parts of a Plant

Most plants have roots, stems, leaves, and flowers. The roots hold the plant in the ground and take in water and food from the soil. The stems help water travel up to the leaves and flowers. They also help the plant stand up. The leaves make and store food. The flowers of the plant make seeds for new plants to grow.

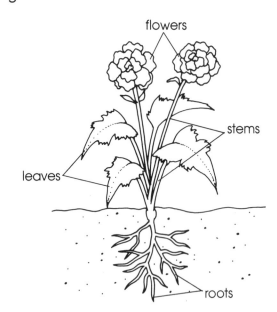

1. List the two things that are found inside every seed. _____ _____

2. When does a seed become a seedling? _____

_____

Application of reading and comprehension skills in a science context

Name _____

3. List the four most important things a seedling needs to grow into a plant.

_____   _____   _____   _____

4. List the four major parts most plants have.

_____   _____   _____   _____

5. Tell what you think would happen if you planted a seed in a cold, dark basement. Give reasons for your answer.

_____

_____

_____

6. Write a story about how a seed becomes a plant. You might decide to write your story in the form of a newspaper story. Or you might pretend to be a seed and write your story as if the seed is telling how it became a plant.

_____

_____

_____

_____

_____

_____

_____

_____

Two-Letter Blends

Name _____

In some words, two consonants appear together. To say these words, blend the sounds of the two consonants together.

stop	**tw**in
blue	**sq**ueeze
tree	

Read the words and name the pictures. Draw a line from each word to the picture it names.

flower

clown

squirrel

star

tree

frog

twenty

twelve

flag

plant

drum

truck

plate

skate

slide

globe

Symbol-sound association of words containing *tw, s, l,* and *r* blends

Two-Letter Blends

Name _____

Read each set of sentences and its list of words. Find the word in the list that matches the clue. Write the word next to the clue.

1. something used on a bed _____ *blanket* _____
2. something fluffy in the sky _____
3. happy, pleased _____
4. to put seeds into the ground _____
5. what birds do to stay in the air _____
6. a toy to use in the snow _____
7. a sharp noise or cry _____
8. the color of a clear sky _____
9. grain that has been ground into powder _____

plant
blanket
fly
blend
squeak
blue
place
glad
sled
cloud
flour

1. a small stream _____
2. a large bird that is black _____
3. doesn't cost any money _____
4. to make a picture on paper _____
5. to say hello _____
6. how much something costs _____
7. what trains run on _____
8. something to catch a mouse in _____
9. an idea that may never come true _____

greet
crow
draw
grab
tracks
dream
price
trap
free
brook
tree

Two-Letter Blends

Name _____

In each sentence, complete the unfinished word by writing **s** or **t**. The word you form must make sense in the sentence.

1. My _t_win brother and I have a lot of fun together.

2. We both like to go roller ___kating and swimming.

3. In the winter we go ___ledding down steep slopes.

4. Mom says we get into ___wice as much trouble together.

5. One time the two of us ate ___welve cookies.

6. They tasted good, but we didn't ___leep very well that night.

In each sentence, complete the unfinished word by writing **l** or **r**. The word you form must make sense in the sentence.

1. Some of my friends and I have started a c_l_ub.

2. We meet after school under a big pine t___ee.

3. Sometimes all we do is p___ay games or tell stories.

4. Other times we go for walks or swing from tree b___anches.

5. One time we helped a neighbor cut her g___ass and rake it.

6. Tomorrow we are all going to help clean up the p___ayground.

Words containing *tw, s, l,* and *r* blends in context

Two-Letter Blends

Name _____

Read each sentence and the words beside it. Write the word that makes sense in each sentence.

1. This oak tree is already _**twenty**_ feet tall.

2. Each of the tree's branches began as just a little _____.

twice
twenty
twig

3. Let's make a swing out of this _____ piece of wood.

4. We'll also need a strong piece of rope that won't _____.

snap
sting
square

5. Someday this tadpole will grow into a big _____.

6. Then it will sit by the _____ and catch flies.

creek
frog
croak

7. My aunt and uncle just had a set of _____.

8. They say it's _____ as much work but a lot more fun.

twins
twig
twice

9. My grandmother has a _____ fireplace in her new house.

10. She uses a _____ to keep the ashes off the rug.

break
brick
broom

11. A little green _____ lives under our back porch.

12. It likes to _____ through the grass in the backyard.

slide
swim
snake

13. Last summer we visited another _____.

14. I can _____ remember all the exciting things we saw.

state
still
steam

Review of words containing *tw, s, l, and r* blends in context

Three-Letter Blends

Name _____

In some words, three consonants appear together. To say these words, blend the sounds of the three consonants together.

spring **spl**it
scream **str**ip

Read the words and look at the pictures. Draw a line from each word to the picture it tells about.

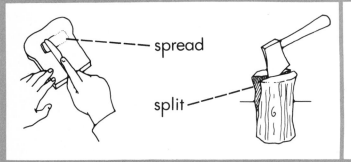

spread

split

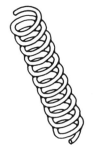 

string

spring

straw

screw

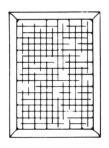

splash

strap

screen

street

stream

scream

scrape

spray

sprain

splinter

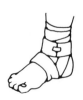

Symbol-sound association of words containing three-letter blends: *spr, scr, spl, str*

Three-Letter Blends

Name _____

Read each clue. Write **scr** or **spl** to complete the word that matches the clue.

1. to yell loudly ___*scr*___eam

2. to break something into pieces _____it

3. something used to fasten boards together _____ew

4. to rub hard while washing _____ub

5. to scatter water in all directions _____ash

6. a very thin piece of wood _____inter

7. something used on doors and windows
   to keep bugs out _____een

8. a piece of something that is left over _____ap

Read each clue. Write **str** or **spr** to complete the word that matches the clue.

1. a person you do not know ___*str*___anger

2. to make something longer by pulling _____etch

3. to lightly cover with tiny drops of water _____ay

4. a wide, straight line _____ipe

5. a small river _____eam

6. the season that comes after winter _____ing

7. how butter is put on bread _____ead

8. without any curves or corners _____aight

9. a road _____eet

Three-Letter Blends

Name _____

In each sentence, complete the unfinished word by writing **spr** or **scr.** The word you form must make sense in the sentence.

1. We clean and ___*scr*___ub everything in our apartment every spring.

2. I gather all the window _____eens and take them outside.

3. I use a hose to _____ay off all the dirt and dust.

4. When they're clean, we fasten the screens to the windows with _____ews.

5. I have to be careful not to _____atch myself while I'm working.

6. I like _____ing better than any other time of year.

In each sentence, complete the unfinished word by writing **spl** or **str.** The word you form must make sense in the sentence.

1. At summer camp, we learned how to build a bridge over a ___*str*___eam.

2. First, we had to _____it some big logs for the bridge.

3. One of the campers got a _____inter in her hand doing this.

4. Then we _____etched a rope across the water.

5. It took a lot of _____ength to move the logs into place.

6. We made the bridge very _____ong so it would last a long time.

Words containing three-letter blends in context: *spr, scr, spl, str*

Three-Letter Blends

Name _____

Read each sentence and the words beside it. Write the word that makes sense in each sentence.

1. The batter _____*struck*_____ the ball so hard that it went over the wall.

   strain
   strip
   struck

2. I had to _____ my eyes to see it.

3. We had to _____ the old paint off the door before we could repaint it.

   screws
   scrape
   scream

4. Then we put new _____ in the corners.

5. Today I got out the hose to _____ the flower garden.

   spring
   spray
   sprained

6. But I tripped over the hose and _____ my arm.

7. When my brother and I swim in the lake, we _____ each other.

   split
   splash
   splinter

8. After swimming, we rest and _____ a sandwich.

9. I couldn't find a _____ to fasten around the broken crate.

   strange
   strap
   strong

10. I tried to use string, but it wasn't _____ enough.

11. I'll need some help repairing the _____ door.

    screen
    spring
    stripe

12. I have to patch some holes, and it needs a new _____.

13. I got a _____ in my hand when I climbed the tree.

    stray
    splinter
    scrap

14. I was trying to rescue a _____ kitten that climbed up there.

Ending Blends

Name _____

At the end of some words, two consonants appear together. To say these words, blend the sounds of the two consonants together.

la**st**	ba**nk**	wo**lf**
de**sk**	fe**lt**	a**rt**
ha**nd**	sta**mp**	gi**ft**

Read the words and look at the pictures. Draw a line from each word to the picture it tells about.

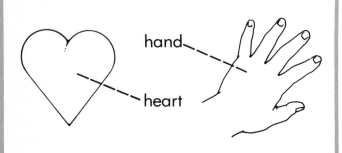 hand — heart

gift

golf

 dirt

desk

 cent

coast

 skirt

skunk

 pond

pump

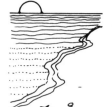

 shirt

quilt

cast

sink

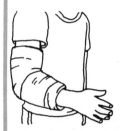

Symbol-sound association of words containing final blends: *st, sk, nd, nk, lt, mp, lf, rt, ft*

Ending Blends

Name _____

Read each clue. Write **nd, nk,** or **nt** to complete the word that matches the clue.

1. part of a minute   seco *nd*

2. to put seeds into the ground   pla_____

3. to close one eye   wi_____

4. a kind of bed   bu_____

5. to look for something   hu_____

6. a small lake   po_____

7. a place to save money   ba_____

8. to color a picture with brushes   pai_____

9. to turn grain into flour   gri_____

Read each clue. Write **lf, lt,** or **rt** to complete the word that matches the clue.

1. to have pain   hu *rt*

2. soil   di_____

3. something to put books on   she_____

4. an outdoor game played with clubs and a small ball   go_____

5. to begin   sta_____

6. something used to change the taste of food   sa_____

7. a tiny make-believe person   e_____

8. a piece of clothing a girl might wear   ski_____

9. pumps blood through your body   hea_____

Ending Blends

Name _____

In each sentence, complete the unfinished word by writing **sk** or **st**. The word you form must make sense in the sentence.

1. I have a li_*st*_ of contests I'd like to enter.

2. I enter a new contest ju_____ about every week.

3. All I ri_____ is the price of a stamp.

4. I enter so many that I have a de_____ full of entry forms.

5. The fir_____ contest I entered was run by a radio station.

6. Another one was run by a company that sells breakfa_____ food.

7. One time I wrote a short song and won a monster ma_____.

8. Another time I had to guess how fa_____ a tiger could run.

9. I guessed carefully, but I lo_____ that contest.

In each sentence, complete the unfinished word by writing **mp** or **ft**. The word you form must make sense in the sentence.

1. Have you ever floated down a river on a rubber ra_*ft*_?

2. Where the river is slow, you can just dri_____ along.

3. If you fall into the river, your clothing will be da_____ all day.

4. Sometimes you can see frogs ju_____ from the river bank.

5. The ride gets more exciting where the river is swi_____.

6. Then you bu_____ into rocks and logs as you race along.

7. At night you can ca_____ along the shore.

8. Then you can fall asleep while listening to the so_____ river sounds.

Words containing final blends in context: *st, sk, mp, ft*

Ending Blends

Name _____

Read each sentence and the words beside it. Write the word that makes sense in each sentence.

1. Many birds and animals live in the __*forest*__ .

2. You may see their footprints in the _____ .

must
forest
dust

3. Yuji's _____ has a rip in the back.

4. I think he _____ himself when he fell.

hurt
lift
shirt

5. I always do my homework at the _____ in my bedroom.

6. If I need help, I can _____ my mom or dad.

ask
desk
mask

7. We have a large _____ of fish in our living room.

8. There are _____ stones on the bottom of the tank.

tank
honk
pink

9. When we go camping, we _____ everything we need.

10. We get sleeping bags, a stove, and a big _____ .

rent
tent
spent

11. We lit an oil _____ when the lights went out.

12. We had to be careful not to _____ into it and break it.

lump
bump
lamp

13. Someone left a box in the _____ .

14. Someone had tried to _____ the lid.

sand
bend
hand

15. The cans of paint are on the top _____ .

16. Be careful not to spill any of them on _____ .

yourself
wolf
shelf

Read each set of sentences and its list of words. Write a word from the list that makes sense in each sentence.

1. There is a bicycle _____*club*_____ in the town where we live.

2. There were only ten members when the club _____.

3. Now, almost one hundred people _____ into our meeting room.

4. Sometimes the members _____ for bicycle contests.

5. One of these contests tests the rider's _____.

6. There were _____ of us who rode in that race last year.

7. These people had very _____ legs to pedal quickly.

8. We were _____ that our club took second place in the contest.

9. Now some of those riders are _____ of a world race.

speed

pleased

club

strong

started

dreaming

crowd

twelve

practice

1. People enjoy saving many _____ things as a hobby.

2. My oldest sister has a very large _____ book.

3. She keeps the stamp book on a _____ in her bedroom.

4. My uncle says it is the _____ book he's ever seen.

5. I _____ I'd like to save stamps when I get older.

6. I just hope there will still be some good ones _____.

sent

think

stamp

drink

left

shelf

different

best

sift

Assessment of words containing initial and final consonant blends in context

Silent Consonants: KN, WR, and SC

Name _____

In some words, two consonants together stand for one sound.
The letters **kn** usually stand for the sound of **n,** as in **knot.**
The letters **wr** usually stand for the sound of **r,** as in **write.**
The letters **sc** sometimes stand for the sound of **s,** as in
scissors.

knot
write
scissors

Read the words and name the pictures. Draw a line from each word to the picture it names.

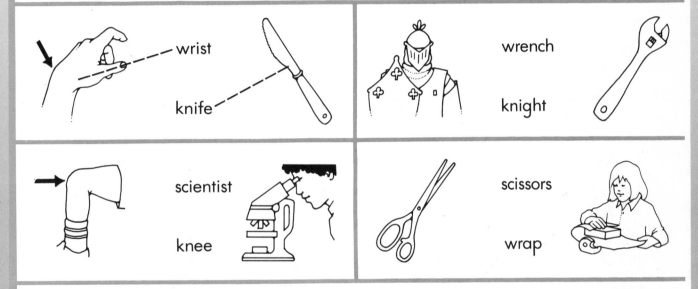

wrist

knife

wrench

knight

scientist

knee

scissors

wrap

Read each clue and the list of words. Find the word in the list that matches the clue. Write the word next to the clue.

1. to put letters and words on paper _____*write*_____

2. not right _____

3. to understand a fact _____

4. to hit a door with the hand _____

5. a nice smell _____

6. a person who does science experiments in a lab

_____

wrong

know

scent

wreck

scissors

write

knight

scientist

knock

Silent Consonants: *KN, WR,* and *SC*

Name _____

Read the riddles and the list of answers. Find the answer that matches each riddle. Write the answer next to the riddle.

a doorknob	a square knot	a flowery scent	sewing scissors
knee socks	a butter knife	a pulled muscle	a mountain scene
a pipe wrench	writing paper	wrapping paper	knitting needles

1. You'll be unhappy if you feel me. What am I? *a pulled muscle*

2. I can be used to help fix a leak under a sink. What am I?

    _____

3. You use me and send me away. What am I? _____

4. You can use me to cut thread or cloth. What am I? _____

5. You may see me on a postcard or when you travel. What am I?

    _____

6. I can help you get from one room to another room. What am I?

    _____

7. You may wear me to keep your feet and legs warm. What am I?

    _____

8. I can be made out of rope or string. I am good at holding things together.

    What am I? _____

9. I can cover a gift or a package. What am I? _____

10. You might use me when you have a piece of bread. What am I?

    _____

11. You smell me when you walk through a garden. What am I?

    _____

12. I'll help you make a sweater or a scarf. What am I? _____

Silent Consonants: *KN, WR,* and *SC*

Name _____

In each sentence, complete the unfinished word by writing **kn, wr,** or **sc.** The word you form must make sense in the sentence.

1. Shelly hurt her *wr*ist in the basketball game.

2. The doctor said she had bent it the _____ong way.

3. Shelly said her _____ee was also sore.

4. She did not _____ow how she had hurt it.

5. The doctor _____ote some directions on a piece of paper.

6. Then the doctor used _____issors to cut a bandage.

7. She showed Shelly how to _____ap her wrist and knee.

8. She also showed her how to tie a special _____ot.

9. The doctor wanted to make sure Shelly _____ew what to do.

---

1. My family and I stopped to look at the beautiful _____ene in the valley.

2. The _____ent of wild mountain flowers filled the air.

3. We had taken the _____ong road to camp.

4. My older brother said, "I thought I _____ew the way."

5. Then Dad said, "If you had _____own the right road, we might have missed this beautiful spot."

6. Everyone agreed, and then we got out the sandwiches Dad had _____apped for supper.

7. I started to _____ite a note on the map about this "wrong road."

8. On the map at this very spot, I saw the words "_____enic lookout."

Silent Consonants: *CK, MB, GN,* and *GH*

Name _____

In some words, two consonants together stand for one sound. The letters **ck** usually stand for the sound of **k,** as in **duck.** The letters **mb** usually stand for the sound of **m,** as in **lamb.** The letters **gn** usually stand for the sound of **n,** as in **sign.** The letters **gh** are usually **silent,** as in **night.**

du**ck**	si**gn**
la**mb**	ni**gh**t

Read the words and look at the pictures. Circle the word that tells about each picture.

dump (duck) luck lump	limb lamb lamp limp	flight sight night tight
fight light might right	crash trash track crack	dumb thump dump thumb
comb crumb chest chick	dock deck check clock	sick sign sigh sock
crack crown combs crumbs	back brick bright bake	sight flight right knight

Symbol-sound association of words containing silent consonants: *ck, mb, gn, gh*

Silent Consonants: *CK, MB, GN,* and *GH*

Name _____

In each sentence, complete the unfinished word by writing **ck** or **mb**. The word you form must make sense in the sentence.

1. Our family drove to my aunt's farm in our pickup tru _ck_.

2. Mom said that Aunt Ella had some baby pigs and a newborn la_____.

3. She also had a swing hanging from a tree li_____.

4. The pigs were kept in a building in ba_____ of the barn.

5. It was funny to watch the lamb su_____ milk from a bottle.

6. We remembered to lo_____ the barn when we were finished.

7. I almost pinched my thu_____ when I locked the door.

8. We hid the key under a ro_____ before we left.

In each sentence, complete the unfinished word by writing **ck, mb, gn,** or **gh**. The word you form must make sense in the sentence.

1. Bill was making a si _gn_ for the bird house.

2. The new house was going to hang from the li_____ of the oak tree.

3. Bill had painted the house with bri_____t yellow paint.

4. He wanted the birds to be able to find the house at ni_____t.

5. Bill also had painted a flower desi_____ on the front of the house.

6. Bill hoped the large birds wouldn't pe_____ at the wood.

7. He said that would wre_____ the house.

8. When Bill was finished, he put cru_____s of bread in a small dish for the house's first visitors.

Silent Consonants: *CK, MB, GN,* and *GH*

Name _____

Read each sentence and the words beside it. Write the word that makes sense in each sentence.

1. I could find only one blue ___*sock*___ this morning.

luck
sock
neck

2. Manny kept his _____ in his pocket.

comb
lamb
crumb

3. We watched the bird _____ at the small piece of bread.

pest
part
peck

4. My _____ in the small airplane was very smooth.

bright
flight
tight

5. Please _____ your name at the bottom of the letter.

sign
design
assign

6. Our neighbor usually raises a _____ each spring.

comb
lamb
thumb

7. The house was a _____ after the bad storm.

wrap
wrist
wreck

8. The brave _____ fought the terrible dragon.

knight
known
knock

9. Troy _____ visit us next month.

might
tight
night

10. The giraffe has the longest _____ of any animal.

check
neck
tuck

Words containing silent consonants in context: *ck, mb, gn, gh*

Silent Consonants

Name _____

Read the list of words below. Then read the sentences that follow. Write a word from the list that makes sense in each sentence.

knife	scissors	sign	lambs
wrench	light	crumbs	track
check	knot	written	delighted

1. Please _____ *check* _____ each answer carefully before you hand in your paper.

2. We left some bread _____ on the lawn for the birds.

3. I was _____ with the gift you sent.

4. The barber used a pair of _____ and a comb to cut my hair.

5. A spoon and _____ go on the right side of the plate.

6. This story was _____ by a woman who lived long ago.

7. We wrote a colorful _____ that said "Happy Birthday."

8. Sally used a _____ to tighten the pipe.

9. Don't forget to turn off the _____ before you leave.

10. Two of our _____ have black, fuzzy faces.

11. Railroad trains don't use this _____ anymore.

12. You'll need a tighter _____ to tie the ribbon on the package.

Review of words containing silent consonants: *kn, wr, sc, ck, mb, gn, gh*

Read each sentence and the words beside it. Write the word that makes sense in each sentence.

1. My grandmother _____*knitted*_____ the sweater for my birthday.

known
knitted
knew

2. This blanket has a beautiful _____ on it.

design
signing
assigned

3. I think my answer to the question was _____.

wrist
wrong
wring

4. Last _____ storm blew a lot of sticks into our yard.

night's
light's
fight's

5. Please hold your _____ on this ribbon while I tie it.

crumb
thumb
number

6. Grandfather likes to _____ on raw vegetables.

snack
smack
stack

7. A well-known _____ will teach us about the planets.

scene
scientist
sciences

8. The three shirts I packed in the trunk are _____.

wreck
wrinkled
wrapping

9. We saw beautiful _____ when we were in Maine.

scenery
sciences
scent

10. Our apartment building is the _____ one in the city.

highest
tighter
brightly

11. We will watch the workers build a new _____ wall.

chick
brick
sticker

Assessment of words containing silent consonants in context: kn, wr, sc, ck, mb, gn, gh

Vowel Pairs: *AI, AY,* and *EI*

<u>Name</u> _____

In some words, two vowels together stand for one vowel sound. The letters **ay** and **ai** usually stand for the long-**a** sound, as in **hay** and **train**. The letters **ei** sometimes stand for the long-**a** sound, as in **eight**.

h**ay**   **ei**ght
tr**ai**n

Read the words and name the pictures. Draw a line from each word to the picture it names.

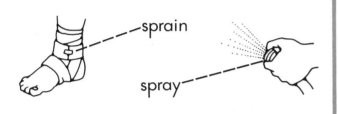

sprain

spray

tray

trail

reindeer

rainstorm

sail

sleigh

Read each clue and the list of words. Find the word in the list that matches the clue. Write the word next to the clue.

1. a color _____ *gray* _____

2. a number _____

3. a path through the woods _____

4. someone in charge of a city _____

5. water that falls from clouds _____

6. blood runs through these _____

7. to lift up something _____

8. perhaps _____

trail
mayor
pay
veins
eighty
say
maybe
raise
rain
pail
gray

Vowel Pairs: *AI, AY,* and *EI*

Name _____

Read each set of sentences and its list of words. Write a word from the list that makes sense in each sentence.

1. Last summer we took a ___*train*___ ride on our vacation.

2. It took two _____ from beginning to end.

3. We had a little room where we _____ on the train.

4. The room had a closet and drawers where we could put our clothes _____.

5. I couldn't _____ to have supper in the dining car.

6. One of the train cars was used to carry freight and _____.

7. Riding on a train is a great _____ to travel.

sail

wait

mail

way

sleigh

train

stayed

playing

days

away

1. My brother and I lift _____ to exercise our bodies.

2. In one exercise we _____ the weights over our heads.

3. My brother can lift _____ pounds with just one arm.

4. Weight lifting helps your heart to pump blood through your _____.

5. If we try to lift too much, we get _____.

6. Then we have to _____ a while before exercising again.

7. Someday I hope I can lift as much as I _____.

veins

eighty

trail

wait

weights

sleigh

pains

rain

weigh

raise

Words containing vowel digraphs in context: *ai, ay, ei*

Vowel Pairs: *AI, AY,* and *EI*

Name _____

Read the list of words below. Then read the sentences that follow. Write a word from the list that makes sense in each sentence.

train	clay	weight	weighed
may	rained	sleigh	afraid
eight	trail	spray	playground

1. When I was very young, I was _____*afraid*_____ of the dark.

2. The fire fighters used four hoses to _____ water on the fire.

3. I took my brother to the _____, where there were new swings and a sliding board.

4. I think it would be fun to take a _____ ride through the snow.

5. We can follow this _____ made by the deer through the forest.

6. In some parts of the desert, it hasn't _____ for three years.

7. I _____ all the fish I caught.

8. My brother's dog had _____ puppies yesterday.

9. The puppet's head is made from hardened _____.

10. We _____ travel to another state next summer.

11. When I go to the doctor, she always checks my_____.

12. We'll have to wait at the crossing until the_____ goes by.

Words containing vowel digraphs in context: *ai, ay, ei*

Vowel Pairs: *EE, EA, OA,* and *OW*

Name _____

In some words, two vowels together stand for one vowel sound. The letters **ee** usually stand for the long-**e** sound, as in **bee**. The letters **ea** can stand for the long-**e** sound, as in **bean,** or the short-**e** sound, as in **bread**. The letters **oa** and **ow** often stand for the long-**o** sound, as in **coat** and **window**.

b**ee**   c**oa**t
b**ea**n   wind**ow**
br**ea**d

Read the words and name the pictures. Draw a line from each word to the picture it names.

 soap

sheep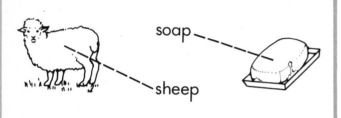

boat

bowl

 bread

beach

beetle

beaver

 window

wheel

seeds

seal

 toast

toad

road

row

Symbol-sound association of words containing vowel digraphs: *ee, ea, oa, ow*

Vowel Pairs: *EE, EA, OA,* and *OW*

Read each set of sentences and its list of words. Write a word from the list that makes sense in each sentence.

1. We like to walk on the _____*beach*_____ in the summer.
2. We also like to play in the sand or swim in the

    _____.
3. The water gets very _____ when waves come in.
4. Sometimes, pieces of _____ wash up onto the sand.
5. Usually we take a picnic lunch along to_____.
6. We also bring a large jug of iced _____ to drink.
7. We all _____ that we have a good time at the beach.

please

seaweed

agree

beach

peace

eat

deep

free

sea

tea

---

1. My grandfather will be sixty years old _____.
2. Our whole family will _____ up at our house for dinner.
3. My sister is cooking a giant _____ to feed everyone.
4. My aunt and uncle are bringing four _____ of vegetables.
5. My brother has baked a _____ of special bread.
6. I get to look out the _____ to watch for Grandfather.
7. I'll be able to see him when he drives down our

    _____.

bowls

road

bow

window

tomorrow

boat

roast

show

loaf

soap

Vowel Pairs: *EE, EA, OA,* and *OW*

Name _____

Read the sentences. Circle the key word that has the sound of **ea** heard in the underlined word.

1. Our basketball <u>team</u> won all of its games this year.   (bean)   bread

2. I had a <u>dream</u> about my summer vacation.   bean   bread

3. I need a needle and <u>thread</u> to put this button on.   bean   bread

4. Please <u>spread</u> butter on each slice of bread.   bean   bread

5. Bob and Joyce spent some time <u>cleaning</u> their messy rooms.   bean   bread

6. The painting is so good, you can almost count the <u>feathers</u> on the duck.   bean   bread

Read each sentence and words beside it. Write the word that makes sense in the sentence.

1. Where is the _____*soap*_____ to clean the dishes?   soap
                                                          windows
2. I put it on the shelf under the kitchen _____.   sleep

3. Our _____ didn't give us any homework tonight.   needed
                                                              team
4. He said we _____ to have an evening off.   teacher

5. See if this purple hat fits your _____.   heel
                                                       coat
6. Then try on that _____ with the yellow trim.   head

Symbol-sound association of words containing *ea*; Words containing vowel digraphs in context: *ee, ea, oa, ow*

Vowel Pairs: *OO, AU, AW,* and *EW*

Name _____

In some words, two vowels together stand for one sound. The letters **oo** can stand for the sound you hear in the middle of **moon** or **book**. The letters **au** and **aw** usually stand for the sound you hear in **auto** and **saw.** The letters **ew** usually stand for the sound you hear in the middle of **news.**

m**oo**n   **au**to
b**oo**k   s**aw**
n**ew**s

Read the words and look at the pictures. Write each word below the picture it tells about.

claw	foot	broom
balloon	jewel	launch
screw	jaw	hook

jaw	_____	_____
_____	_____	_____
_____	_____	_____

Symbol-sound association of words containing vowel digraphs: *oo, au, aw, ew*

Vowel Pairs: OO, AU, AW, and EW

Name _____

Read each clue. Write **oo** or **au** to complete the word that matches the clue.

1. an animal that has a pouch   kangar_oo_

2. a building where you go to learn   sch_____l

3. to send a rocket into space   l_____nch

4. what people eat   f_____d

5. a person who prepares food   c_____k

6. where you can swim   p_____l

7. the kind of hair a sheep has   w_____l

8. to carry or to pull   h_____l

9. another word for car   _____to

Read each clue. Write **aw** or **ew** to complete the word beside it to match the clue.

1. how a baby gets around   cr_aw_ls

2. the feet of dogs and cats   p_____s

3. a thick soup with meat in it   st_____

4. not old   n_____

5. something to drink through   str_____

6. the time of day when the sun rises   d_____n

7. a group of people who work on a ship   cr_____

8. not very many   f_____

9. a cutting tool   s_____

Words containing vowel digraphs: oo, au, aw, ew

Vowel Pairs: OO, AU, AW, and EW

Name _____

Read each sentence and the words beside it. Write the word that makes sense in the sentence.

1.	Please get the dustpan and _____*broom*_____, and help me clean this mess.	too broom noon
2.	I'm going to _____ a picture of this pretty flower.	claw saw draw
3.	Gina and I _____ each other in second grade.	dew few knew
4.	Put up your _____ before going outside in the snow.	hood look good
5.	One of our best players _____ the ball to win the game.	auto caught because
6.	Which of these _____ will you need to do the repair work?	tools cool roof
7.	We'll have to stand _____ there aren't enough chairs.	taught auto because
8.	We built our house with _____ from this forest.	look wood good
9.	Very _____ people showed up for the meeting.	few knew dew
10.	A _____ flew high above our heads.	hawk dawn jaw

Vowel Pairs

Name _____

Read the list of words below. Then read the sentences that follow. Write a word from the list that makes sense in each sentence.

balloon	spread	below	books	caught
paw	gray	wheel	sleighs	news
toad	teaching	maid	stream	bloom

1. Ms. Holly has been _teaching_ us about Mexico.

2. Our dog can open the screen door with her _____.

3. Do these flowers _____ early in the summer?

4. My sister has a summer job as a hotel _____.

5. One _____ of my bicycle has a very noisy squeak.

6. Did you know that a brown _____ lives in our flower garden?

7. Mom and Dad like to listen to the _____ on television.

8. This little _____ looks like a good place to go fishing.

9. The sky got dark and very _____ just before the storm.

10. My shirt got ripped when I _____ it on a nail.

11. People used to travel in _____ in the wintertime.

12. The library has more _____ than I could ever read.

13. We put the bowl in the cabinet _____ the sink.

14. Use this knife to _____ the peanut butter on the bread.

15. Have you ever had a ride in a hot-air _____?

Review of words containing vowel digraphs in context: *ai, ay, ei, ee, ea, oa, ow, oo, au, aw, ew*

Vowel Pairs: *IE*

Name _____

In some words, two vowels together stand for one vowel sound. In the word **tie,** the letters **ie** stand for the long-**i** sound. In the word **shield,** the letters **ie** stand for the long-**e** sound.

 tie

 sh**ie**ld

Read the list of words. Notice the sound that **ie** stands for in each word. Then write each word under the correct heading.

died	cries	field	duties
movie	piece	untie	relief
berries	chief	believe	dried
lie	pie	skies	cities
tried	thief	flies	fried

Long **i** as in **tie**

died

_____

_____

_____

_____

_____

_____

_____

_____

Long **e** as in **shield**

_____

_____

_____

_____

_____

_____

_____

_____

_____

Vowel Pairs: *IE*

Name _____

Read each clue and the list of words. Find the word in the list that matches the clue. Write the word next to the clue.

		dried
1.	a kind of dog _*collie*_	field
2.	something a knight used to protect himself _____	shield
3.	to join pieces of rope or string together _____	chief
		collie
4.	small flying insects _____	pie
5.	very large towns _____	thief
6.	something to eat _____	piece
7.	an open area of land _____	cities
		tie
8.	a person who steals _____	flies

Read the sentences. In the blank beside each sentence, write the word that has the letters **ie.** Then circle the key word that has the sound of **ie** heard in the word you wrote.

1. Have you ever eaten fried grasshoppers? _*fried*_   (tie) shield

2. Would you like dried apples or bananas? _____   tie   shield

3. Do you think you'd like berries and honey? _____   tie   shield

4. These are some of the unusual foods people have tried.

   _____   tie   shield

5. Some cities have stores that sell unusual foods.

   _____   tie   shield

6. Just remember to start with a small piece of any food

   that's new to you. _____   tie   shield

Words containing *ie*; Symbol-sound association of words containing *ie*

Vowel Pairs: *IE*

Name _____

Read each sentence and the words beside it. Write the word that makes sense in each sentence.

---

1. I had _*berries*_ on my pancakes this morning.

2. They grow wild in the _____ behind our house.

shield
field
berries

---

3. My uncle _____ a big jet airplane.

4. Sometimes he takes _____ to other countries.

flies
dried
supplies

---

5. Do you need any help trying to _____ that rope?

6. We _____ to untie it yesterday.

thief
untie
tried

---

7. The tribe picks the wisest person to be its _____.

8. They _____ that person will guide them well.

believe
chief
collie

---

9. We had blueberry _____ for dinner today.

10. Dad spilled some of it on his best _____.

pie
dried
tie

---

11. We watched a very sad _____ last night.

12. At the end, the hero got sick and _____.

died
movie
flies

---

13. I helped Ned cut some potatoes into thin _____.

14. Then we _____ them until they were crisp.

pieces
fried
movie

---

15. My _____ helped me bake turnovers.

16. We used the _____ that we had bought and frozen last summer.

duties
cherries
nieces

Words containing *ie* in context

65

Vowel Pairs: *OU*

Name _____

In some words, two vowels together stand for one vowel sound. The letters **ou** can stand for the vowel sounds you hear in **soup, touch, doughnut,** and **should.**

soup **dou**ghnut
touch sh**ou**ld

Read the words and look at the pictures. Circle the word that tells about each picture.

(boulder) route shoulder bought	trouble through touchdown tough	soul sound should soup
double touch dough though	should shoulder south soup	doughnut dough through though

Read each clue and the list of words. Find the word in the list that matches the clue. Write the word next to the clue.

1. yourself _____ *you* _____

2. very well-known _____

3. uneven; not smooth _____

4. something bread is made from _____

5. a very large rock _____

6. a spoon is used to eat this _____

7. where the arm joins the body _____

8. eager to find out about things _____

rough
dough
would
you
famous
through
curious
soup
shoulder
youth
boulder

Symbol-sound association of words containing *ou;* Words containing *ou*

Vowel Pairs: *OU*

Name _____

Read the list of words. Notice the sound that **ou** stands for in each word. Then write each word under the correct heading.

though	curious	although	famous	would
rough	you	boulder	country	through
youth	could	group	shoulder	

ou as in **doughnut**

though

_____

_____

_____

ou as in **soup**

_____

_____

_____

ou as in **touch**

_____

_____

_____

ou as in **should**

_____

_____

Read each clue. Find the word in the list that matches the clue. Write the word next to the clue.

1. just the right amount _____*enough*_____

2. not easy to cut or chew _____

3. not old _____

4. small cakes shaped like rings _____

5. three or more persons or things _____

6. a word that means "ought to" _____

group
young
trouble
tough
soup
should
shoulder
doughnuts
enough

Vowel Pairs: OU

Name _____

Read each sentence and the words beside it. Write the word that makes sense in each sentence.

1. Dad and I were going to make homemade _doughnuts_.

2. First I had to be sure we had _____ flour.

3. Then Dad said we _____ begin working.

enough
doughnuts
could

4. A huge _____ of people showed up for our garage sale.

5. Many of them were just _____ about the sale.

6. I knew many of the people _____ not buy anything.

group
would
curious

7. We saw a baby camel that is _____ than my little sister.

8. The baby camel seemed _____ and hid behind its mother.

9. Not even the zookeeper could _____ it.

younger
touch
nervous

10. Can _____ help me carry this heavy log?

11. It will be easier if you can get it on your _____.

12. Be careful not to hurt your hand on the _____ bark.

shoulder
you
rough

13. I'm making something to eat I think you _____ like.

14. We have to roll this _____ into little balls.

15. Then we will put them into this special _____.

soup
dough
should

Words containing *ou* in context

Vowel Pairs

Name _____

Read each sentence and the words shown below the blank. Write the word that makes sense in each sentence.

1. Carmen and Juan are newspaper carriers with a ___*tough*___ job.
    (tough, though)

2. At first, the papers came _____ in a big bundle.
    (tied, tried)

3. The children _____ untie the papers and put them into the bag.
    (would, young)

4. Now the bundle comes with _____ plastic bags for each paper.
    (although, enough)

5. The papers stay dry even if they _____ in a puddle.
    (fried, lie)

6. Carmen and Juan have always _____ to do a good job.
    (tried, dried)

7. They _____ win an award.
    (should, shoulder)

1. On Saturdays, I go to a cooking class for _____ people.
    (through, young)

2. Last week we learned to bake apple _____.
    (pie, berries)

3. Two weeks ago we made a big pot of vegetable _____.
    (should, soup)

4. Perhaps you _____ like to join the class, too.
    (would, curious)

5. Next week our _____ is planning to make pizza.
    (ground, group)

Two Sounds of Y

Name_____

When **y** comes at the end of a word that has no other vowel, the **y** usually stands for the long-**i** sound. When **y** comes at the end of a word that has another vowel, the **y** usually stands for the long-**e** sound.

fl**y**   pon**y**

Read the list of words. Notice the sound that **y** stands for in each word. Write the words that have the long-**i** sound under the word **fly.** Write the words that have the long-**e** sound under the word **pony.**

sky	twenty	city	fry
sticky	fly	any	pry
easy	sly	try	many
happy	berry	carry	why
by	very	cry	dry

long **i** as in **fly**

sky

_____

_____

_____

_____

_____

_____

_____

_____

long **e** as in **pony**

_____

_____

_____

_____

_____

_____

_____

_____

_____

Symbol-sound association of words containing y as a vowel

Two Sounds of Y

Name _____

Read each clue and the list of words. Find the word in the list that matches the clue. Write the word next to the clue.

		celery
1.	a green vegetable _celery_	slowly
2.	a store that sells food _____	grocery
3.	an insect with wings _____	carry
4.	not wet _____	dry
5.	afraid to talk to people _____	shy
6.	not ill _____	my
		fly
		healthy

Read the list of words below. Then read the sentences that follow. Write the word from the list that makes sense in each sentence.

why	very	firefly	snowy
my	carry	Try	easy

1. Did you ever catch a _firefly_ in a glass jar?

2. First, punch some _____ small holes in the lid.

3. Then _____ the jar outside in the evening.

4. It will be _____ to see the fireflies when they flash.

5. _____ to scoop one out of the grass with the jar.

6. Then you can try to guess _____ they flash their lights.

Two Sounds of Y

Name _____

Read each sentence. Circle the key word that has the sound of **y** heard in the underlined word.

		fly	pony
1.	I just finished writing a <u>scary</u> story.	fly	(pony)
2.	I thought about it a lot before I wrote <u>any</u> words.	fly	pony
3.	I decided I wanted the story to have a <u>happy</u> ending.	fly	pony
4.	When I was <u>ready</u> to write, I sat down at my desk.	fly	pony
5.	The first time I wrote the story, I wrote it too <u>quickly</u>.	fly	pony
6.	Mom said I should change some parts and <u>try</u> again.	fly	pony
7.	I wrote the whole <u>story</u> two more times.	fly	pony
8.	Each time I wrote it, <u>my</u> story got better.	fly	pony
9.	One <u>tricky</u> part was hard to write.	fly	pony
10.	The people had to fight a dragon that flew through the <u>sky</u>.	fly	pony

1.	My birthday is in the month of <u>February</u>.	fly	pony
2.	My friend <u>Danny</u> has his birthday in June.	fly	pony
3.	It's usually <u>icy</u> when I have my birthday.	fly	pony
4.	But it's always <u>very</u> hot for my friend's birthday.	fly	pony
5.	<u>Why</u> couldn't he and I trade for one year?	fly	pony
6.	Then he could get gifts for cold, <u>snowy</u> days.	fly	pony
7.	<u>My</u> gift could be a great big kite to fly.	fly	pony
8.	I wonder if he would like to <u>try</u> my idea?	fly	pony

Symbol-sound association of words containing *y* as a vowel

Read each sentence and the words beside it. Write the word that makes sense in each sentence.

1. This is the biggest pine _____*tree*_____ I have ever seen.

2. I wonder why it is growing in the middle of this_____.

field
tree
bead

3. The team members are having _____ and sandwiches for lunch.

4. I hope there are enough _____ for everyone.

soup
should
spoons

5. Last night we had to _____ the basement.

6. I bumped my _____ on an old pipe.

head
clean
scream

7. Bananas don't _____ well in this country.

8. They used to be sent here on large _____.

boats
snow
grow

9. It _____ all day long yesterday.

10. Our _____ ducks had a great time at the pond.

play
rained
eight

11. My grandfather _____ me how to use his tools safely.

12. He said that I can't use the power _____ until I'm older.

saw
taught
claw

13. The weather was very _____ last summer.

14. Everything in our garden grew very _____.

dry
slowly
heavy

15. My little cousin _____ that picture with her new crayons.

16. It shows a horse eating _____ in a barn.

drew
took
hay

Your Bones

Have you ever broken a bone in your body? If you have, you know how important healthy bones are to a healthy body.

Bones are made of living cells. Blood runs through tiny vessels in your bones and supplies your bones with food to help them grow. Bones also have nerves in them. Nerves are what cause feeling. When you break a bone, the nerves in the bone make you feel pain.

Your bones also protect parts of your body. Your ribs protect your heart and lungs. The bones in your back protect many nerves that run through them.

Your bones are a frame that helps hold up your body. Your muscles are connected to your bones. Between your bones are joints so you can bend. Your bones, muscles, and joints work together. They help you walk, run, swim, roller skate, ride a bicycle, and do many other things.

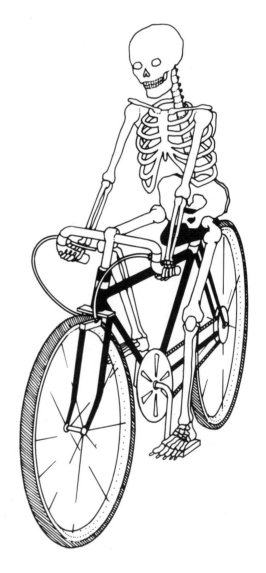

A.   Name the three parts of your body that work together to help you move.

_____   _____   _____

B.   What does blood do for your bones?

_____

Application of reading and comprehension skills in a health context

Name _____

C. Check each group of words that describes a job your bones do.

    _____ feed your body   _____ help you sleep

    _____ protect parts of your body   _____ support your body

D. Finish each sentence with the correct word or words.

    1. Bones are made of _____.

    2. A broken bone hurts because of the _____ inside it.

E. Draw a line from each word on the left to the word or words on the right that have the same meaning.

    protect   keep safe
    support   joined
    connected   hold up

F. If you broke a rib, what other part of your body might be hurt? _____

G. Imagine that you have broken a bone in your left arm. Tell why it hurts. Explain how you would have to change your way of doing certain things because of your broken bone.

    _____

    _____

    _____

    _____

    _____

    _____

Beginning Consonant Pairs

Name _____

Two consonants together can stand for one sound. Some consonants that stand for one sound are **sh, th,** and **wh.** At the beginnings of some words, three consonants together stand for special sounds, as in **three** and **shrug.**

shoe	**thr**ee
thin	**shr**ug
wheel	

Name the pictures. Write the letters that stand for the beginning sound of each picture name.

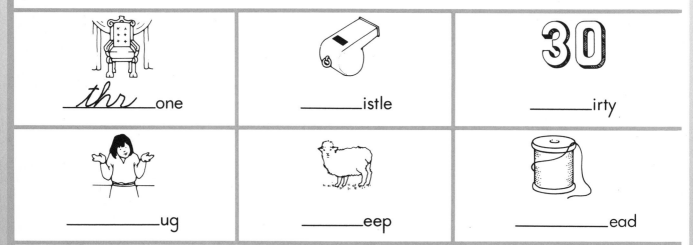

*thr*___one   _____istle   _____irty

_____ug   _____eep   _____ead

Read each clue. Write **sh, th, wh, thr,** or **shr** to complete the word that matches the clue.

1. not fat   *th*_in

2. to get smaller   _____ink

3. to talk very quietly   _____isper

4. you swallow with this   _____oat

5. a place for books   _____elf

6. what you do with your mind   _____ink

7. a tool used for digging   _____ovel

8. a bicycle has two of them   _____eels

Sound-symbol association of words containing initial consonant digraphs;
Words containing initial consonant digraphs: *sh, th, wh, thr, shr*

Ending Consonant Pairs

Name _____

Two or three consonants together can stand for one sound. Some consonants that stand for one sound are **sh, th,** and **ng.**

| wi**sh** | ri**ng** |
| wi**th** | |

Name the pictures. Write the letters that stand for the ending sound of each picture name.

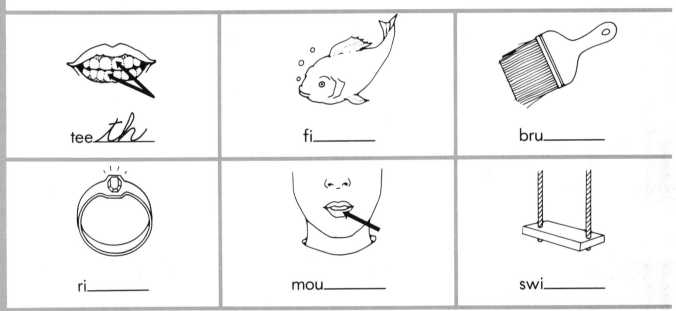

tee_th_   fi_____   bru_____

ri_____   mou_____   swi_____

Read each clue. Write **sh, th,** or **ng** to complete the word that matches the clue.

1. something to put food on   di_sh_

2. a loud noise   ba_____

3. what a shirt is made of   clo_____

4. a trail   pa_____

5. how a bee can hurt you   sti_____

6. able to lift heavy things   stro_____

7. unwanted things that are thrown away   tra_____

8. not stale   fre_____

Sound-symbol association of words containing final consonant digraphs;
Words containing final consonant digraphs: *sh, th, ng*

77

Consonant Pairs

Name _____

Read each sentence and the list of words. Write the word from the list that makes sense in each sentence.

1. My dad owns a bicycle repair _____*shop*_____.

2. Sometimes I get to help _____ some of the work.

3. I use a _____ to clean off the workbench.

4. One time Dad let me oil all the squeaky bicycle _____.

5. There were no noisy bicycles when I was _____ working.

6. One time I made a mistake and put a pair of handlebars on _____.

7. They looked really funny, but I was able to fix _____.

path
with
through
wrong
wish
brush
them
flight
wheels
shop

Read the list of words below. Then read the paragraph that follows. Write the word from the list that makes sense in each sentence.

three	health	spring	shrugged
thread	shrubs	wishes	pushed
shovel	with	them	which

We planted new _____*shrubs*_____ around our house yesterday. We placed _____ small ones on each side of the front door. I used a _____ to dig the holes. We decided _____ shrub should go into each hole. Then, using a hoe, Mom _____ dirt around the trunk of each shrub. I watered each one _____ the garden hose. Then we gave _____ all some special plant food. We'll give them more plant food in the _____. When we were done, I _____ my shoulders and said, "What do we do now?"

Words containing initial and final consonant digraphs in context: *sh, th, wh, ng, thr, shr*

Consonant Pairs

Name _____

Two or three consonants together can stand for one sound. The letters **ch** and **tch** usually stand for the sound you hear at the beginning of **chair** and the end of **catch**. The letters **ch** sometimes stand for the sound of **k,** as in **chemist**. The letters **ch** can also stand for the sound of **sh,** as in **chef**.

chair   **ch**emist
ca**tch**   **ch**ef

Read the key word shown at the left of each sentence. Then read the sentence. Circle the word in the sentence that has the same sound of **ch** as the key word.

chair | 1. | Look at the chart that shows the parts of the new machine.

catch | 2. | Yoko and Cheryl stayed up late to watch a scary movie on television.

chef | 3. | Can you teach me how to parachute from an airplane?

chemist | 4. | I ate too much, and now my stomach hurts.

chair | 5. | The chef served us a plate of cheese and fruit.

chef | 6. | Could you teach me how to use this new machine?

catch | 7. | The chemist lit the match to heat the oil.

chemist | 8. | Chad and I have parts singing in the chorus for our next music show.

Consonant Pairs

Name _____

Read each clue and the list of words. Find the word in the list that matches the clue.
Write the word next to the clue.

1. something used to light a fire *match*

2. something that tells the time _____

3. the part of the face beside your nose and mouth

     _____

4. a person who prepares food _____

5. a pain _____

6. a meal that is eaten at noon _____

7. a large box or trunk _____

8. a farm on which sheep, cattle, or horses are

     raised _____

9. to look or hunt for something _____

chain

lunch

match

chef

ranch

search

ache

cheek

chemist

watch

chest

latch

Read the sentences and the word choices. Circle the word that makes sense in each
sentence.

1. My uncle works in a place in which wooden (benches, each) are made.

2. When he started working, his job was to clean up the wood (chips, chef).

3. That is quite a (chose, chore) in a big place.

4. Now he has a job as a (chose, mechanic).

5. He repairs any of the (catch, machines) that break down.

6. Sometimes he has to (watch, chorus) a machine very carefully.

7. Then he can find out (couch, which) part isn't working.

8. One time a machine kept making (aches, scratches) on the benches.

9. Someone had left a (cheese, each) sandwich inside it.

Words containing consonant digraphs in context: *ch, tch*

Consonant Pairs

Name _____

Read the sentences. Circle **yes** or **no** to tell whether the letters **ch** and **tch** in the underlined words stand for the same sound.

1. Isn't it your turn to <u>choose</u> where we go for <u>lunch</u>?　　(yes)　　no

2. I sunburned my <u>stomach</u> while I was at the <u>beach</u> yesterday.　　yes　　no

3. This <u>machine</u> slices <u>peaches</u> and puts them into cans.　　yes　　no

4. I had to <u>watch</u> my baby sister while Dad fixed <u>lunch</u>.　　yes　　no

5. We used to raise <u>chickens</u> when we lived on a <u>ranch</u>.　　yes　　no

6. <u>Which</u> movie would you and <u>Chris</u> like to watch tonight?　　yes　　no

7. We have only one <u>match</u> left to light the <u>torch</u>.　　yes　　no

8. The <u>mechanic</u> said he could <u>change</u> the tires on our car.　　yes　　no

9. The <u>coach</u> was <u>cheering</u> louder than anyone else for the team.　　yes　　no

10. How <u>much</u> will a new <u>couch</u> and <u>chair</u> cost?　　yes　　no

11. We can <u>chop</u> the <u>branches</u> off this dead <u>birch</u> tree.　　yes　　no

12. The <u>chef</u> used just a <u>pinch</u> of salt in this soup.　　yes　　no

13. I was trying to <u>catch</u> <u>each</u> <u>cherry</u> that fell from the tree.　　yes　　no

Consonant Pairs

Two consonants together can stand for one sound. The letters **gh** sometimes stand for the sound of **f,** as in **laugh.** The letters **ph** usually stand for the sound of **f,** as in **elephant.**

lau**gh**
ele**ph**ant

Read the words and look at the pictures. Write each word below the picture it tells about.

| cough | elephant | telephone | photo | trophy | laugh |

elephant

_____

_____

_____

_____

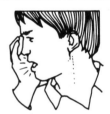

_____

Read each clue and the list of words. Find the word in the list that matches the clue. Write the word next to the clue.

1. a picture taken with a camera ___*photo*___

2. a very large animal _____

3. what you do when something is funny _____

4. a prize for winning a contest _____

5. not easy to cut or break _____

6. not smooth _____

elephant
photo
enough
laugh
telephone
rough
cough
trophy
tough

Consonant Pairs

Name _____

Read each sentence. In the blank that follows the sentence, write the word that contains the sound of **f** spelled by **gh** or **ph.**

1. I like to watch the tigers and the elephants at the zoo.

    _____*elephants*_____

2. The tigers walk around their cages, looking mean and tough.

    _____

3. Sometimes they'll reach through the bars with their rough paws.

    _____

4. The elephants never look very mean, though. _____

5. I took a photo of them the last time we were there. _____

6. I laughed when one tried to grab my camera with its trunk.

    _____

7. I think I'll go back next week if I have enough money. _____

8. Maybe this time I will look at the dolphins, too. _____

Identifying words containing consonant digraphs in context: *gh, ph*

Consonant Pairs

Name _____

Read each sentence and the words beside it. Write the word that makes sense in each sentence.

1. A _*microphone*_ makes your voice sound much louder.

2. A _____ lets you hear people who are far away.

microphone
telephone
trophy

3. The _____ is one of the largest animals.

4. Its skin is very _____ and thick.

rough
cough
elephant

5. I won a silver _____ in the bicycle race today.

6. Mom took a _____ of me holding it beside my bike.

photo
trophy
nephew

7. I learned the _____ when I was young.

8. My parents have a _____ of me studying the letters.

laughter
alphabet
photo

9. This wood was very _____ when I began sanding it.

10. Is it smooth _____ now for us to use?

enough
phone
rough

11. My little brother had a very bad _____.

12. My father _____ the doctor about it.

photo
cough
phoned

13. This piece of meat is so _____, I can't chew it.

14. Maybe I should give it to my _____ dog.

graph
nephew's
tough

Words containing consonant digraphs in context: *gh, ph*

Consonant Pairs

Name _____

Read the sentences. Choose and write the letters needed to complete the unfinished word in each sentence. The word you form must make sense in the sentence.

1. We planted some new trees and _*shr*_ubs in our yard.   shr, thr

2. Have you ever made a wi_____ and had it come true?   th, sh

3. Mom says I cook so well I should become a _____ef.   shr, ch

4. The whistle made a very _____ill sound.   th, shr

5. Did you know that _____ales are not really fish?   th, wh

6. Will there be enou_____ chairs for everyone at the party?   gh, ng

7. The person who just called had the wro_____ number.   ng, gh

8. I don't think the piano will fit _____ough that door.   shr, thr

9. Does this pa_____ go to the beach or to the woods?   th, sh

10. Mom needed only one ma_____ to light the campfire.   tch, sh

11. I keep some paper and a pencil by the tele_____one.   th, ph

12. My legs a_____e from running so hard in that race.   sh, ch

13. I'm trying to _____ink of the answer to your question.   th, wh

Review of words containing initial and final consonant digraphs in context   85

Consonant Pairs

Name _____

Read each set of sentences and its list of words. Write a word from the list that makes sense in each sentence.

1. Do you think we ___*should*___ wait here any longer?

2. I scraped my _____ when I fell on the ice.

3. How far can you _____ a football?

4. I forgot to _____ my hands before coming to dinner.

5. We had to _____ the hole in our tent to keep the bugs out.

6. The cat in the pet store window has a black nose and long white _____.

7. This sidewalk is too _____ for roller skating.

8. My cousin raises horses on a _____.

patch
square
should
ranch
match
throw
chin
bush
whiskers
wash
rough

1. The puppies are still too _____ to leave their mother.

2. There were over _____ people at the family picnic.

3. My throat was so sore, I could only _____.

4. I hope this shirt doesn't _____ when I wash it in warm water.

5. The _____ is going to practice singing on Friday afternoon.

6. The dentist checked my _____ during my last visit.

7. The _____ that makes peanut butter is broken.

8. The nearest _____ booth is on the next corner.

whale
teeth
whisper
machine
elephant
shrink
telephone
chorus
thirty
young
thief

Assessment of words containing consonant digraphs in context

Vowels With R

Name _____

A vowel that is followed by **r** stands for a special sound that is neither long nor short.	j**ar** h**or**n f**er**n b**ur**n b**ir**d

Name the pictures and read the sentences. Circle the word in each sentence that has the same vowel sound as the picture name.

1. The farmer is going to plow the (corn) field today.

2. We will study about the stars later this month.

3. There will be a short meeting here on Thursday.

4. The windows have dirt on them from the dust storm.

5. The clown was wearing an orange wig with curls.

6. My friends and I made a snow fort in the park.

7. Adela has a small part in the school play.

8. Tat used a long fork to stir the vegetable stew.

Vowels With R

Name _____

Read each clue and the list of words. Find the word in the list that matches the clue. Write the word next to the clue.

1. a person who cuts hair _____*barber*_____

2. to break open _____

3. soft hair on an animal _____

4. not tall _____

5. an animal that flies _____

6. a meal that is eaten in the evening _____

7. a round shape _____

8. the outside covering of a tree _____

fur

short

sir

barber

circle

hurt

burst

bark

tar

supper

bird

Read the sentences. Choose and write the letters needed to complete the unfinished word in each sentence. The word you form must make sense in the sentence.

1. Our neighbors painted their p___*or*___ch last week.

ar, or

2. F_____st, they got paint, brushes, and rags.

ir, or

3. Then they borrowed our ladd_____ to climb to the roof.

ar, er

4. I helped Jack carry the ladder into their y_____d.

ar, ur

5. We had to be careful not to h_____t any of the shrubs.

or, ur

6. Jack's mother painted the really h_____d parts.

ar, er

7. His younger brother helped st_____ each can of paint.

ir, or

8. Because Jack and I are short, we painted the bottom

   p_____t of the door.

ar, ur

Words containing r-controlled vowels; Words containing r-controlled vowels in context

Vowels With *R*

Name _____

Read each sentence and the words beside it. Write the word that makes sense in each sentence.

1. My best friend is very ____*smart*____ in math and reading.

2. She finishes _____ homework before anyone else.

her
horn
smart

3. Try to ride your bicycle along this _____ line.

4. You will win _____ prize if you can do it.

curved
first
carved

5. The store was having a sale on _____ .

6. It was the _____ sale I've been to this year.

part
purses
first

7. This is the _____ bath I've given my dog today.

8. He chased a skunk under the back _____ last night.

porch
third
perch

9. The artist drew many _____ in the pattern.

10. Then she glued the design onto a heavy piece of _____ .

paper
sort
circles

11. The knives we use in the kitchen are very _____ .

12. We are careful not to _____ ourselves when we use them.

shirt
sharp
hurt

13. My _____ clock didn't wake me up this morning.

14. Mom had to bring me to school in the _____ .

alarm
cord
car

15. We don't have any photos of Tom's _____ party.

16. Judy forgot to bring her new _____ .

camera
birthday
border

Vowels With R

Name _____

Read each sentence and the words beside it. Write the word that makes sense in each sentence.

1. I take my dog to the _____*park*_____ to exercise.

park
pork
perk

2. The _____ in the photo looks like my cousin.

purse
part
person

3. My brother is too _____ to reach the table.

sharp
shirt
short

4. Our cat always gets stickers caught in his _____.

far
for
fur

5. We watched a woman _____ a bird out of wood.

carve
curve
curl

6. I'm trying to find the brightest _____ in the sky.

star
stir
store

7. We saw a _____ of buffalo out West.

herd
hard
horn

8. Do you like to play any _____ besides basketball?

spurts
sports
sparks

9. I haven't been able to wash all the _____ off myself.

dark
dart
dirt

10. Yesterday we chopped wood to _____ in our fireplace.

born
burn
barn

Review of words containing r-controlled vowels in context

Vowels With *R*

Name _____

Read the list of words below. Then read the sentences that follow. Write a word from the list that makes sense in each sentence.

forest	birds	hard	before	for
driver	teacher	orange	march	harp
shirt	river	turtle	burn	circle

1. Mr. Campa is the best ___*teacher*___ I've ever had.

2. The dancers joined hands and formed a _____.

3. I caught a _____ in the pond behind our house.

4. In the winter, we put seeds out for the _____.

5. I have to finish my homework _____ I can play.

6. Our high-school band will _____ in the parade.

7. Our school bus _____ is always very careful.

8. The ice isn't _____ enough to skate on yet.

9. Be careful not to _____ your fingers on the hot stove.

10. The bright _____ flowers in the yard are very pretty.

11. I enjoy watching the big ships sail up the _____.

12. Have you seen the man who is wearing a gray hat and orange _____?

13. I would like to learn to play the flute and the _____.

14. Our scout troop took a hike through the _____.

15. Have you ever sent away _____ something from a catalog?

OI, OY, OU, and OW

Name _____

The letters **oi** and **oy** stand for the vowel sounds in **coin** and **toys.** The letters **ou** and **ow** often stand for the vowel sounds in **cloud** and **cow.**

co**i**n	cl**ou**d
t**oy**s	c**ow**

Read the words and look at the pictures. Write each word below the picture it tells about.

point   oil   cow   boy   mouse   mouth

boy	_____	_____
_____	_____	_____

Read each clue. Write **oi** or **ou** to complete the word that matches the clue.

1. dirt   s _oi_ l

2. a place where people live   h_____se

3. a piece of furniture to sit on   c_____ch

4. a round piece of money   c_____n

5. to make water very hot   b_____l

6. sixty minutes   h_____r

7. a small animal   m_____se

8. what you speak with   v_____ce

Symbol-sound association of words containing diphthongs; Words containing diphthongs: *oi, oy, ou, ow*

OI, OY, OU, and OW

Name _____

Read the sentences and the word choices. Circle the word that makes sense in each sentence.

1. I enjoy spring and summer in our (**town**, proud).
2. It's fun to do things (outdoors, powder) when the weather is nice.
3. I (join, enjoy) going for a hike in the forest.
4. Swimming is fun when the weather is (boiling, boy) hot.
5. Sometimes I like to just watch the (clouds, clowns) float by.
6. In the spring we plant (choice, flowers) all around our house.
7. I like to read under a tree for an (hour, joy) sometimes.
8. In the evening we can listen to the (toys, owls) in the forest.
9. There are so many things to do, it's sometimes hard to make a (loud, choice).

Read each clue. Write **oy** or **ow** to complete the word that matches the clue.

1. a male child   b _oy_
2. something a queen wears   cr_____n
3. something to play with   t_____
4. a large bird that hoots   _____l
5. a dark color   br_____n
6. to like something; to have a good time   enj_____
7. a large group of people   cr_____d
8. something to dry yourself with   t_____el
9. a farm tool   pl_____

OI, OY, OU, and OW

Name _____

Read each sentence and the words shown below the blank. Write the word that makes sense in each sentence.

1. A new boy ___*joined*___ our class today.
    (joined, joy)

2. Ping dropped some _____ on her way to buy a toy.
    (coins, coiled)

3. Some oil had leaked into the _____ and spoiled the grass.
    (soybean, soil)

4. The chef served _____ to the royal family.
    (oily, oysters)

5. This _____ will destroy the bugs that are in the house.
    (pointed, poison)

6. The farmer keeps the cows in that _____ field.
    (mountain, mounds)

7. The quick rain _____ cooled off the hot ground.
    (show, shower)

8. It took the _____ an hour to get ready for the show.
    (clown, crown)

9. The owl made a _____ noise as it swooped down.
    (loyal, loud)

10. Behind that board is where the _____ mouse lives.
    (brown, bought)

11. As the clouds covered the moon, Kenji heard a dog _____.
    (howl, hour)

12. Be careful not to get the white _____ on your eyebrows.
    (powder, pound)

13. You have the _____ of any of the blouses on this rack.
    (coil, choice)

14. We enjoyed looking at the city from the top of the _____.
    (towel, tower)

Words containing diphthongs in context: *oi, oy, ou, ow*

Name the pictures and read the sentences. Circle the word in each sentence that has the same vowel sound as the picture name.

 1. Can you (bounce) the basketball and throw it through the hoop?

 2. I think you'll enjoy this movie about a tiger.

 3. From this tower, we can see corn growing in the farthest fields.

 4. My first choice is the blue blouse, but I also like the green one.

 5. My father saves coins from all over the world.

 6. We could put the new couch by the big window.

 7. I'm not allowed to play in the snow unless I wear boots.

 8. Let's look for a rainbow when this rain shower stops.

OI, OY, OU, and OW

Name _____

Read each sentence and the words beside it. Write the word that makes sense in the sentence.

1. The Indians built huge _____*mounds*_____ of dirt in a circle.

2. They were far from any cities or _____.

    mounds
    towns
    round

3. First, we need to _____ this kettle of water.

4. Then we'll put the _____ in and let them cook.

    oysters
    boil
    point

5. I want to buy a _____ lawn mower for my brother.

6. He can use it _____ when we work in the yard.

    towel
    outdoors
    toy

7. I kept hearing a strange scratching _____ all night long.

8. In the morning I found a _____ in the drawer.

    moist
    noise
    mouse

9. Our garden has the best _____ anywhere around.

10. It's dark _____ and doesn't have many stones.

    soil
    spoil
    brown

11. Floating along in the hot-air balloon was very

    _____.

12. But coming back _____ to earth was a good feeling, too.

    brown
    enjoyable
    down

Assessment of words containing diphthongs in context: *oi, oy, ou, ow*

Endings: -ED and -ING

Name _____

When a word ends with one vowel followed by a consonant, double the consonant before adding **-ed** or **-ing.** When a word ends in **e,** drop the **e** before adding **-ed** or **-ing.** When a word ends in a consonant followed by **y,** change the **y** to **i** before adding **-ed.**

snap	snap**ped**
save	sav**ing**
hurry	hurr**ied**

Read the words below. Add **-ed** and **-ing** to each word. Write the new words in the blanks.

		Add -ed	**Add -ing**
1.	whistle	*whistled*	*whistling*
2.	try	_____	_____
3.	watch	_____	_____
4.	skip	_____	_____
5.	bake	_____	_____
6.	copy	_____	_____

Read the list of words below. Then read the sentences that follow. Add **-ed** or **-ing** to a word from the list to complete each sentence. Write the new word in the blank. The word you form must make sense in the sentence.

wash   use   tape   stir   lean   carry   search   plan

1. Joyce was *planning* to paint a picture of the park.

2. The student artist _____ her paper, paint, and brushes with her.

3. When she arrived, she began _____ her paint.

4. Joyce _____ the paper onto a board to keep it from moving.

5. She then _____ her homemade easel against a large tree.

6. The artist _____ the park bench to hold the paint and brushes.

Endings: -S and -ES

Name _____

Often new words can be formed by adding **-s** or **-es** to other words. To change many words, add the ending **-s**. When a word ends in **s, ss, sh, ch, x,** or **z**, add **-es**. When a word ends in a consonant followed by **y**, change the **y** to **i** and add **-es**.	laugh laugh**s** rush rush**es** copy cop**ies**

Read each sentence and the word beside it. Add **-s** or **-es** to the word to complete the sentence. Write the new word in the blank.

1. Mei ___*hurries*___ through breakfast every morning.   hurry

2. She _____ the bus on the corner at eight o'clock.   catch

3. On the way to school, she _____ talking to friends and classmates.   enjoy

4. Mei always _____ to do her best in school.   try

5. She _____ most of the tests and quizzes.   pass

6. One of her friends _____ schools often because her family moves often.   switch

7. Mei _____ that she would not like to change schools.   say

8. Whenever she is ill, she _____ her classes and her friends.   miss

9. Mei _____ to catch up on the work she misses.   want

Adding -s or -es to verbs in context

Base Words and Endings

Name _____

A word to which an ending can be added is called a base word.

roasting   **watch**es

Read the words below. Write the base word for each one.

1. learned   _learn_

2. buzzes   _____

3. raking   _____

4. planned   _____

5. teaches   _____

6. fries   _____

7. swinging   _____

8. hurried   _____

9. writes   _____

10. fixes   _____

11. swimming   _____

12. cried   _____

Read the list of base words below. Then read each sentence that follows. Add the ending shown beside each sentence to a word from the list. Write the new word in the blank. The word you form must make sense in the sentence.

cook	join	scrape	play	watch
think	toss	teach	win	study

1. Lucy _joined_ the soccer team this year.   -ed

2. Her team is _____ every game they play.   -ing

3. The coach _____ the players the correct ways to kick the soccer ball.   -es

4. Lucy has _____ the rule book the coach gave each team member.   -ed

5. The team _____ at five o'clock every Monday and Thursday.   -s

6. Sometimes Lucy's brother _____ the games and cheers from the sidelines.   -es

7. He is _____ about starting another soccer team in the neighborhood.   -ing

Endings: -ER and -EST

Name _____

In many words, the ending **-er** means "more." It is used to compare two things. The ending **-est** means "most." It is used to compare three or more things.

deep	deep**er**
deep	deep**est**

Read each sentence and the word beside it. Add **-er** or **-est** to the word to complete the sentence. Write the new word in the blank.

1. Selma is _____*older*_____ than I am.   old

2. It is _____ today than it was yesterday.   warm

3. The kitchen is the _____ of all the rooms in our apartment.   bright

4. The freight train was _____ than the last train.   long

5. The road runner is one of the _____ animals in the world.   fast

6. Pedro is the _____ player on the team.   tall

7. The bowl filled with noodles was much _____ than the platter of meat.   light

8. The blue package is the _____ birthday gift on the table.   small

9. This winter weather is _____ than the weather we had last winter. cold

10. Casey is the _____ boy in our class.   young

11. The hill in Forest Park is _____ than the one near school.   steep

12. The knot on that package was the _____ knot I've ever untied.   tight

13. The sky was _____ in the morning than it was in the afternoon.   clear

Adding -er or -est to adjectives in context

Endings: *-ER* and *-EST*

Name _____

When a word ends with one vowel followed by a consonant, double the consonant before adding **-er** or **-est**. When a word ends in **e**, drop the **e** before adding **-er** or **-est**. When a word ends in a consonant followed by **y**, change the **y** to **i** before adding **-er** or **-est**.

wet	wett**est**
wise	wis**er**
cloudy	cloud**ier**

Read the words below. Add **-er** and **-est** to each word. Write the new words in the blanks.

		Add **-er**	Add **-est**
1.	pretty	_prettier_	_prettiest_
2.	short	_____	_____
3.	fat	_____	_____
4.	funny	_____	_____
5.	fine	_____	_____

Read the list of words below. Then read the sentences that follow. Add **-er** or **-est** to a word from the list to complete each sentence. Write the new word in the blank. The word you form must make sense in the sentence.

friendly   dark   thick   few   funny   close   wide   sticky

1. I think this is the _____*funniest*_____ show on television.

2. Because our doctor's office is _____ to home than our dentist's office, it takes less time to get there.

3. The shade of blue in your coat is _____ than the shade of blue in your hat.

4. We had _____ than thirty people at the party.

5. The white cat is the _____ of the three cats.

Endings: -ER and -EST

Name _____

Read the paragraph below. Complete each sentence by adding **-er** or **-est** to the base word shown below the blank.

Shiny Wax is _____*easier*_____ to use than the
(easy)

best-selling wax. It is the _____ wax you can buy,
(smooth)

and it makes your floors look _____ and
(clean)

_____ than other waxes did. Hurry to the
(shiny)

_____ supermarket! Buy Shiny Wax and enjoy
(close)

having the _____ floors in town.
(bright)

Read each sentence and the word beside it. Add **-er** or **-est** to the word to complete each sentence. Write the new word in the blank.

1. Last week my family went to the ___*greatest*___ parade
   I have ever watched.   great

2. Because we were _____ than most of the crowd, we
   had a good view.   early

3. The floats were _____ than the ones in last
   year's parade.   big

4. One float carried the _____ dragon I have
   ever seen.   mean

5. Some of the _____ marching bands in the country
   took part in the parade.   fine

6. The clowns were the _____ I've seen in a long
   time.   silly

7. Because we were having a good time, my family went home at a

   _____ time than we had planned.   late

Adding -er or -est to adjectives in context

Endings

Name _____

Read each sentence and the endings shown beside it. Add the correct ending to the word shown below the blank in each sentence. Write the new word in the blank.

1. The Nile River ___*stretches*___ north for many miles
    through Africa.
    (stretch)   -s, -es

2. The Amazon River is not as long as the Nile, but it is

    _____ in parts.   -er, -est
    (wide)

3. The Mississippi River is the _____ river in
    (long)
    the United States.   -er, -est

4. It flows south and _____ much river traffic.   -s, -es
    (carry)

5. Many people are _____ near the banks of
    (live)
    these three rivers.   -ing, -ed

6. People have _____ near rivers for many years.   -ing, -ed
    (settle)

7. A river bank _____ farmers with good soil for
    (supply)
    their crops.   -s, -es

8. Farmers have _____ their crops to markets by
    (ship)
    using many kinds of boats.   -ing, -ed

9. Some of these boats have been _____
    (flat)
    than others.   -er, -est

10. Many of the world's _____ cities are
    (busy)
    built near rivers.   -er, -est

11. Many people in these cities have _____
    (use)
    the rivers for swimming and boating.   -ing, -ed

Plurals: -S and -ES

Name _____

A word that stands for one of something is a singular word. A word that stands for two or more of something is a plural word. Most plurals are formed by adding **-s** to a singular word. When a word ends in **s, ss, sh, ch,** or **x,** add **-es** to form its plural. When a word ends in a consonant followed by **y,** change the **y** to **i** and add **-es.**

plant	plant**s**
dish	dish**es**
penny	penn**ies**

Read each sentence and the word beside it. Write the plural form of the word to complete the sentence. Write the new word in the blank.

1. Making ___*lunches*___ for our family can be quite a job.   lunch

2. In some _____, each person makes his or her own lunch.   family

3. However, we take _____ working in pairs.   turn

4. Last week, I made all the _____.   sandwich

5. I used ten _____ of bread each day.   piece

6. My brother cut each sandwich into two _____.   part

7. My _____ like us to put a piece of fruit in each lunch.   parent

8. Sometimes my dad reads _____ to us while we are working.   story

9. He once read us a story about a worker who made lunch

   _____.   box

10. I enjoy making the lunches, but I don't like doing the

   _____ when I am done.   dish

Forming plurals in context: -s and -es

Plurals: Changing *F* to *V*

Name _____

To form the plural of most words that end in **f** or **fe,** change the **f** or **fe** to **v** and add **-es.**

| cal**f** | cal**ves** |
| kni**fe** | kni**ves** |

Read each sentence and the words beside it. Write the plural form of one of the words to complete the sentence, according to the rule given above. The word you write must make sense in the sentence.

1. Ms. Thomas put the dishes on ___*shelves*___ so the shoppers could see them.

self
shelf

2. Kim and her friends made two _____ of bread and a dozen rolls for the party.

loaf
leaf

3. Joe traced _____ on bright paper and cut them out to use as bookmarks.

life
leaf

4. The tale about tiny _____ and their lives in the forest was delightful.

shelf
elf

5. Matt wanted to read about the _____ of world leaders.

life
loaf

6. Please cut the small pizzas into _____ before you put them into the oven.

shelf
half

7. The farmer fed the hungry _____ early every morning.

knife
calf

8. We watched the wildlife program about _____ and learned how they travel in packs.

loaf
wolf

9. The doctor checked the horse's legs and _____ after it came back to the stable.

hoof
half

Forming plurals of nouns ending in *f* and *fe*

Irregular Plurals

Name _____

The plurals of some words are formed by changing the spellings of their singular forms.

tooth—teeth   child—children   woman—women   goose—geese
mouse—mice   man—men   foot—feet

The plural forms of some words can be the same as their singular forms.

deer   sheep   fish   moose

Read each sentence and the word beside it. Write the plural form of the word to complete the sentence. Write the new word in the blank.

1. The _____*sheep*_____ had thick coats of wool.   sheep

2. It was so cold that my _____ would not
    stop chattering.   tooth

3. Please feed the guppies and the other _____
    in the tank.   fish

4. _____ belong to the deer family and live in
    the northern fields.   Moose

5. Many women and _____ work in this building.   man

6. Beth's _____ hurt after the trail walk yesterday.   foot

7. Most of the _____ who went on the
    walk enjoyed the day.   child

8. Beth liked seeing the chipmunks and tiny field

    _____ running about.   mouse

9. Their guide pointed out two tall _____
    with antlers that were hidden behind the trees.   deer

10. The group stopped to throw bread to the ducks and

    _____ swimming on the lake.   goose

Forming irregular plurals in context

Showing Ownership

Name _____

To make most words show ownership, add an apostrophe (') and **s.** To make a plural word that ends in **s** show ownership, add just an apostrophe.

cat**'s** dishes
cats**'** dishes

Rewrite each group of words below, adding **'** or **'s** to the underlined word to show ownership.

1. the hat that <u>Judy</u> wears _____ *Judy's hat* _____

2. the pencils that the <u>pupils</u> use _____

3. the tent that belongs to <u>Jill</u> _____

4. the windows of a <u>store</u> _____

5. the toys of the <u>babies</u> _____

6. the pennies that <u>Matt</u> has _____

Read each sentence and the words beside it. Add **'s** or **s'** to one of the words to complete the sentence. The word you form must make sense in the sentence.

1. The _____ *workers'* _____ glasses protect their eyes.　　worker / world

2. The _____ speech was very long.　　matter / mayor

3. My oldest _____ friends live near us.　　brush / brother

4. All the _____ driveways have been repaired.　　neighbor / nickel

5. All the team _____ shirts stayed clean during the game.　　plate / player

6. The _____ print is large.　　book / boat

Showing Ownership

Name _____

To make a plural word that does not end in **s** show ownership, add an apostrophe (**'**) and **s**.	mice**'s** cheese children**'s** game

Rewrite each group of words below, using **'s** to form words that show ownership.

1. the cage for the mice _____ *mice's cage* _____

2. the toys for the children _____

3. the feathers of the geese _____

4. the coats that the men have _____

5. the shoes that belong to the women _____

6. the food for the geese _____

Read each sentence and the words shown below the blank. Write the word that completes the sentence. The word you form must make sense in the sentence.

1. The _____ *students'* _____ desks are arranged in rows.
    (student's, students')

2. The _____ tail was very long.
    (mouse's, mice's)

3. We will have the two _____ birthday parties this month.
    (child's, children's)

4. My _____ award was hanging on her office wall.
    (mother's, mothers')

5. The three nearest _____ schools were closed during the storm.
    (town's, towns')

6. Did you see _____ new bike?
    (Juan's, Juans')

7. The _____ pond, where they usually swam, was frozen.
    (goose's, geese's)

Forming plural possessives; Using singular and plural possessives in context

Showing Ownership

Name _____

Read each sentence and the words shown below the blank. Write the word that completes the sentence. The word you write must make sense in the sentence.

1. My favorite _____*aunt's*_____ dog sometimes stays at our house.
    (aunt's, aunts')

2. The zoo keeper cleaned all the _____ cages.
    (animal's, animals')

3. The _____ President spoke on TV and radio.
    (countries', country's)

4. The _____ noses were red from the wind.
    (child, children's)

5. I gave _____ ticket to him yesterday.
    (Fred's, Freds')

Read each sentence and the words beside it. Add **'s** or **s'** to one of the words to complete the sentence. The word you form must make sense in the sentence.

1. After the four _____*campers'*_____ boxes were unpacked, they began to set up the tents. | carton camper

2. The library _____ cover was bright and colorful. | base book

3. The two bridge _____ hats were hanging in their lockers. | worker whistle

4. My oldest _____ friend works for the mayor. | stamp sister

5. The _____ handles are all broken. | cup cut

6. The _____ playground has a new sliding board. | chalk children

REVIEW

Plurals and Showing Ownership

Name _____

Read each sentence and the singular word beside it. Change the singular word to its plural form to complete the sentence. Write the new word in the blank.

1. Ted enjoyed the story about the _____*elves*_____ and
    the shoemaker.   elf

2. Please put the _____ in the sink.   dish

3. Joyce has visited many _____.   city

4. Your _____ will get wet if you step in the puddles.   foot

5. Uncle Steve heard the _____ barking in the pet shop.   puppy

6. She made the sock puppets look like woolly _____.   sheep

7. We packed the books in _____ to ship to
    another school.   box

8. There were many cars and _____ in the parking lot.   truck

Rewrite each group of words below, adding **'** or **'s** to the underlined word to show ownership.

1. the frame for the <u>photo</u> _____*photo's frame*_____

2. the parents of the <u>children</u> _____

3. the watch that belongs to <u>Don</u> _____

4. the windows of the <u>stores</u> _____

5. the colors of the <u>rainbow</u> _____

6. the gift for <u>Jessica</u> _____

7. the pupils of the <u>teachers</u> _____

8. the maps of the <u>student</u> _____

Review of forming plurals in context; Forming singular and plural possessives

Endings and Plurals

Name _____

Read each sentence and the word beside it. Add one of the endings shown below to the word to complete each sentence. The word you form must make sense in the sentence.

-ed   -ing   -s   -es   -er   -est

1. Bill ___*hurried*___ to catch the train yesterday.   hurry

2. Sally _____ TV after she does her homework.   watch

3. Lisa used the _____ ribbon in the box to tie the bow.   long

4. The child was _____ the pages of the book.   flip

5. The twins _____ the dishes and set them on the table.   dry

6. Mom came home at a _____ time than she
   usually does.   late

7. My brother _____ me every morning and talks
   for a few minutes.   call

8. Many people were _____ on the frozen pond.   skate

9. Sue's joke was _____ than Terry's.   funny

10. Andy was _____ all his friends to the party.   invite

Read the sentences below. Complete each sentence by changing the singular word shown below the blank to its plural form. Write the new word in the blank.

1. I enjoyed watching the ___*puppies*___ in the pet show.
   (puppy)

2. The _____ will meet on Monday.
   (mayor)

3. We watched the _____ leave their den.
   (fox)

4. The _____ on the trees are bright orange.
   (leaf)

5. The backpackers saw the tracks of two _____.
   (deer)

6. Tess painted the set of _____.
   (bench)

Showing Ownership

Name _____

Read each sentence and the words beside it. Write the word that makes sense in the sentence.

1. My youngest _____*sister's*_____ cat is brown and white.

sister's
sisters'

2. The _____ pencil broke while she was taking notes.

writer's
writers'

3. The five _____ clubhouse was made with logs and stones.

friend's
friends'

4. _____ bike is being repaired in the shop.

Rosa's
Rosas'

5. We listened to the _____ speech on the radio.

President's
Presidents'

6. Before Frank cleaned his _____ cage, he put them in a large box.

hamster's
hamsters'

7. My _____ birthdays are both on the same day.

parent's
parents'

8. I found _____ ruler on the classroom floor.

Mike's
Mikes'

9. The pet _____ large sign flew in the air during the storm.

store's
stores'

10. The three _____ lunches were locked in the closet.

worker's
workers'

11. The _____ wig fell when she took off her pointed hat.

clown's
clowns'

12. Our _____ pilot arrived late at the airport.

plane's
planes'

Assessment of forming singular and plural possessives in context

Compound Words

Name _____

| A compound word is formed by joining two smaller words together. | rain + bow = rainbow |

Read each compound word and write the two words that form it.

1. homework   _____*home*_____   _____*work*_____

2. something   _____   _____

3. notebook   _____   _____

4. birthday   _____   _____

5. upstairs   _____   _____

6. downtown   _____   _____

7. sidewalk   _____   _____

Read the sentences below. Circle the compound words in each sentence.

1. (Grandmother) and I went to the beach last (weekend.)

2. I took suntan oil in my backpack.

3. We looked for seashells and made footprints in the sand.

4. We stopped to watch the lifeguards pull in a rowboat.

5. Then we found a starfish covered with seaweed.

6. We stayed to watch the beautiful sunset beyond the lighthouse.

7. On the way home, we munched on homemade popcorn we had brought.

Compound Words

Name _____

Read the words in each list below. Draw lines to match the words that form compound words.

wheel	meal	book	berry
any	noon	blue	book
oat	barrow	wind	case
tooth	body	fire	place
after	brush	school	mill

Read the list of compound words below. Then read the sentences that follow. Write the word from the list that makes sense in each sentence. Then draw a line under the other compound word in the sentence.

footsteps	everyone	runway	highway	newspaper
rainfall	sunrise	airport	suitcases	pancakes

1. Last month my <u>grandparents</u> and I went to the _____*airport*_____.

2. There was hardly anyone on the _____, so it did not take us long to get there.

3. When we arrived, we stopped downstairs to eat and I had

   _____.

4. When we went upstairs, I could see a plane arriving on the

   _____.

5. My grandfather then asked me to go to the gift shop to buy him a

   _____.

6. As I was walking into the shop, I heard _____ behind me.

7. I turned to see my cousin Jean and my grandparents carrying her

   _____.

8. Then _____ laughed, and Jean took a snapshot of my surprised look.

Compound Words

Name _____

Read each sentence below. Use two words from the sentence to form a compound word. Write the compound word in the blank.

1. A boat that tugs other boats is a _____*tugboat*_____.

2. A brush that is used to clean each tooth is a _____.

3. A box where mail is put is called a _____.

4. An area of ground where children play is a _____.

5. A person who tells a story is called a _____.

6. A book that tells people how to cook is a _____.

7. A place where a fire burns is called a _____.

8. A house made for a dog is a _____.

9. A coat that a person wears in the rain is called a _____.

Read the list of words below. Then read the paragraph that follows. Complete each sentence by writing one of the compound words from the list. The word you write must make sense in the sentence.

snowstorm	sidewalks	somewhere	sunshine	airplane
snowplows	downtown	railroad	snapshot	highway

The _____*snowstorm*_____ hit the city very quickly. The people who were

_____ were quite surprised. Shoppers had a hard time walking

on the snow-covered _____. People had to stand in long lines

at the _____ station. Some cars were stopped on the

_____ because of high winds and drifting snow. The city's

_____ tried to remove as much snow as possible. Most people

had not prepared for the snow because the weather forecasters had said there

would be _____ all week.

Contractions

Name _____

A contraction is a short way to write two words. It is written by putting two words together and leaving out a letter or letters. An apostrophe (') takes the place of the letters that are left out. The word **won't** is a special contraction made from the words **will** and **not.**

was + not = **wasn't**
I + have = **I've**
will + not = **won't**

Read the list of contractions below. Then read the word pairs that follow. Write a contraction from the list for each word pair.

| I've | he'd | I'm | let's | hasn't |
| she's | there's | we're | aren't | we'll |

1. has not _____*hasn't*_____

2. we are _____

3. there is _____

4. he would _____

5. we will _____

6. let us _____

7. she is _____

8. I have _____

9. are not _____

10. I am _____

Read each sentence and the pair of words shown below the blank. Complete the sentence by writing the contraction that stands for the word pair.

1. Larry thinks ___*we'll*___ win the basketball game.
   (we will)

2. _____ going to practice this morning.
   (We are)

3. Nina _____ be able to play because she is ill.
   (will not)

4. The coach said that she _____ worried.
   (is not)

5. _____ never been so excited about a game.
   (I have)

6. _____ got to come and watch the best game of the season.
   (You have)

116

Contractions

Name _____

Read each contraction below. Then write the two words for which each contraction stands.

1. didn't

   <u>*did not*</u>

2. that's

   _____

3. they've

   _____

4. here's

   _____

5. won't

   _____

6. I'd

   _____

7. hadn't

   _____

8. he'll

   _____

9. I'm

   _____

10. they're

    _____

Read each sentence and the contraction shown below the blank. Complete the sentence by writing the two words for which the contraction stands.

1. Judy: <u>*We will*</u> have to listen for your brother on the radio.
   (We'll)

2. Gary: Yes, _____ going to read ads for many different stores.
   (he's)

3. Judy: _____ have to listen to the ads more closely.
   (I'll)

4. Gary: _____ quite proud that Dan is doing the ad for The
   (I'm)
   Record Storeroom.

5. Judy: Well, _____ every reason to be proud of him.
   (you've)

6. Gary: _____ turn on the radio to listen to the ten o'clock ad.
   (Let's)

Contractions

Name _____

Read each sentence and find the two words that can be made into a contraction. Draw a line under the two words and write the contraction in the blank.

1. Dawn <u>does not</u> mind going to her trumpet lessons. *doesn't*

2. She is really enjoying learning how to play the trumpet. _____

3. Her teacher said he would like Dawn to try out for the school

    band. _____

4. Dawn's parents think that it is a good idea. _____

5. Dawn wonders if she will play well in front of people. _____

6. Her teacher told her, "You have no reason to worry." _____

Read the sentences and the list of contractions. Write a contraction from the list to complete each sentence.

1. Our car *wouldn't* start this morning.

2. _____ a stop sign at the corner.

3. Luis says that _____ coming home at five o'clock.

4. _____ be leaving for school soon.

5. I _____ seen you in a long time.

6. The twins have saved most of the money

    _____ earned together.

7. _____ not a good idea to leave during a storm.

8. Our neighbors told us that _____ going to be gone for a week.

We'll

won't

wouldn't

they're

There's

It's

haven't

they've

he's

I'm

Forming contractions in context; Using contractions in context

Compound Words and Contractions

Name _____

Read the clues below. Use two words from each clue to form a compound word. Write the compound word in the blank.

1. the bud of a rose   *rosebud*

2. work that is done in school   _____

3. a box where mail is put   _____

4. a cloth that is put on a table   _____

5. a flat pan that is used to pick up dust   _____

6. work that is done at home   _____

7. a tie that is worn around the neck   _____

8. a boat that uses steam   _____

9. a pot used to hold tea   _____

10. a burn that is caused by sitting in the
    sun for too long   _____

Read the word pairs below. Then write the contraction that stands for each word pair.

1. were not *weren't*		7. he will	_____
2. I would _____		8. you are	_____
3. she is _____		9. has not	_____
4. did not _____		10. they have	_____
5. you have _____		11. will not	_____
6. I am _____		12. it is	_____

Compound Words and Contractions

Name _____

Read the rows of words below. Then read the sentences that follow. Use a word from Row A and a word from Row B to form a compound word to complete each sentence. The word you form must make sense in the sentence.

A. book   home   bed   any   every   with

B. where   case   one   out   work   room

1. Has _____*anyone*_____ seen my notebook?

2. I thought I left it on my desk in my _____ at home.

3. I've looked _____ in the apartment.

4. I can't go to school _____ it.

5. Will someone look on the top shelf of my _____?

6. The book has all my math notes and _____ in it.

Read each sentence and the pair of words beside it. Complete the sentence with a contraction that stands for the word pair.

1. I _____*haven't*_____ been to the dentist since my last checkup.   have not

2. Dr. Lake is very nice, and _____ always pleasant.   she is

3. She usually has a story to tell _____ interesting.   that is

4. _____ probably have to sit in the waiting room for a while.   I will

5. _____ be surprised at the number of people who go to Dr. Lake's office.   You would

6. I guess _____ heard that Dr. Lake is a good doctor.   they have

Prefixes: *UN-, DIS-, RE-,* and *PRE-*

Name _____

A prefix is a letter or group of letters that can be added to the beginning of a word. The prefixes **un-** and **dis-** usually mean "not" or "the opposite of." For example, the word **untie** means "the opposite of tie." The word **dislike** means "not like."

The prefix **re-** usually means "again," so the word **rewrite** means "write again." The prefix **pre-** means "before," so the word **prepay** means "pay before."

un + tie = **un**tie
dis + like = **dis**like

re + write = **re**write
pre + pay = **pre**pay

Read each sentence and the word beside it. Add **un-** or **re-** to the word to complete the sentence. Write the new word in the blank. The word you form must make sense in the sentence.

1. Matt _unpacked_ his bags after he arrived.   packed

2. We can read the story when the newspaper _____ it.   prints

3. The building is _____ for people to use.   safe

4. The manager will _____ the carpet so we can see it.   roll

5. We saw the _____ of the touchdown.   play

Read each sentence and the word beside it. Add **dis-** or **pre-** to the word to complete the sentence. Write the new word in the blank. The word you form must make sense in the sentence.

1. Do you _distrust_ the story you heard yesterday?   trust

2. When making bread, first _____ the oven.   heat

3. The dog _____ its owner when she told it to sit.   obeyed

4. Marta _____ weeding the flower garden.   likes

5. Our school's band played during the last _____ show.   game

Forming words with prefixes in context

Prefixes: *IN-, OVER-, MIS-,* and *POST-*

Name _____

The prefix **in-** often means "not." The word **incomplete** means "not complete." The prefix **over-** means "too much" or "more than usual." The word **overeat** means "to eat too much."

The prefix **mis-** means "badly" or "wrongly." The word **mistreat** means "to treat badly." The prefix **post-** means "after." The word **postwar** means "after a war."

in + complete = **in**complete
over + eat = **over**eat

mis + treat = **mis**treat
post + war = **post**war

Read each sentence and the word beside it. Add **in-** or **over-** to the word to complete the sentence. Write the new word in the blank. The word you form must make sense in the sentence.

1. The bus took an ___*indirect*___ route to the park.   direct

2. During the summer I ate too much, and I became _____.   weight

3. Five of my test answers were _____.   correct

4. She is wearing an _____ shirt today.   sized

5. After the storm, the river _____ its banks.   flowed

Read each sentence and the word beside it. Add **mis-** or **post-** to the word to complete the sentence. Write the new word in the blank. The word you form must make sense in the sentence.

1. Yuji ___*misread*___ the price on the package.   read

2. The pilot wrote the _____ report.   flight

3. I try not to _____ people's names.   pronounce

4. Many of the drivers were at the _____ party.   race

5. The child was _____ in the store.   behaving

Forming words with prefixes in context

Prefixes

Name _____

Read each sentence and the prefixes beside it. Complete each sentence by adding one of the prefixes to the word shown below the blank. Write the new word in the blank. The word you form must make sense in the sentence.

1. The workers will ___*disconnect*___ the pipes.
    (connect)

    dis-
    over-

2. We'll go in as soon as you _____ the door.
    (lock)

    post-
    un-

3. Benito _____ the bookcase so the library
    (built)
    could use it.

    mis-
    re-

4. I couldn't find a seat because the room was _____.
    (crowded)

    over-
    re-

5. I corrected the _____ words in my story.
    (spelled)

    mis-
    post-

6. The trip's fees were _____ before we left town.
    (paid)

    dis-
    pre-

7. Lin was going to buy an _____ plant because
    (expensive)
    she didn't have much money.

    in-
    over-

8. After flying the plane, Rena finished a _____
    (flight)
    report.

    post-
    un-

9. The spoiled cheese had an _____ smell.
    (pleasant)

    un-
    post-

10. Beth will be _____ if we don't visit her.
    (pleased)

    re-
    dis-

Suffixes: -FUL, -LESS, -Y, and -LY

Name _____

A suffix is a letter or group of letters that can be added to the end of a word. The suffix **-ful** usually means "full of." For example, the word **restful** means "full of rest." The suffix **-less** usually means "without." The word **useless** means "without use."

The suffixes **-y** and **-ly** can be added to some words. For example, a car that has **rust** on it is a **rusty** car. A person who talks in a **loud** way talks **loudly.**

rest + ful = rest**ful**
use + less = use**less**

rust + y = rust**y**
loud + ly = loud**ly**

Read each sentence and the word beside it. Add **-ful** or **-less** to the word to complete the sentence. Write the new word in the blank. The word you form must make sense in the sentence.

1. The bridge across the wide bay seemed _____*endless*_____. end

2. We had a calm and _____ time at the beach. rest

3. The sun was shining and the sky was _____. cloud

4. The _____ day was just what each of us needed. wonder

5. I was _____ and left our lunches at home. forget

Read each sentence and the word beside it. Add **-y** or **-ly** to the word to complete the sentence. Write the new word in the blank. The word you form must make sense in the sentence.

1. We cleaned the house _____*quickly*_____ before the guests arrived. quick

2. We were busy and had not done our _____ jobs. week

3. Jan used oil to fix the _____ front door. squeak

4. Chung cleaned and polished the _____ tables. dust

5. Mom stacked the newspapers _____. neat

Forming words with suffixes in context

Suffixes: -ABLE, -ISH, -MENT, and -NESS

Name _____

The suffix **-able** means "can be" or "able to be." For example, the word **breakable** means "can be broken." The suffix **-ish** can mean "like" or "somewhat." The word **childish** means "like a child."

The suffixes **-ment** and **-ness** can be added to some words. For example, if you **enjoy** reading books, reading brings you **enjoyment.** If you are feeling **ill,** you have an **illness.**

break + able = break**able**
child + ish = child**ish**

enjoy + ment = enjoy**ment**
ill + ness = ill**ness**

Read each sentence and the word beside it. Add **-able** or **-ment** to the word to complete the sentence. Write the new word in the blank. The word you form must make sense in the sentence.

1. These bus seats are not very _comfortable_.   comfort

2. The flower _____ was pretty.   arrange

3. Are the books on the top shelf _____?   reach

4. The new wallpaper is _____.   wash

5. We are going to study our city _____.   govern

Read each sentence and the word beside it. Add **-ish** or **-ness** to the word to complete the sentence. Write the new word in the blank. The word you form must make sense in the sentence.

1. The _soreness_ in my hurt arm has gone away.   sore

2. The cat was _____ and would not share its treat.   self

3. The new rug is a _____ color.   green

4. Bart has been absent because of a long _____.   ill

Suffixes

Name _____

Read each sentence and the suffixes beside it. Complete each sentence by adding one of the suffixes to the word shown below the blank. Write the new word in the blank. The word you form must make sense in the sentence.

1. Preparing for the school play was _*enjoyable*_.
   (enjoy)
   -able
   -ish

2. Miss Norton told us to read our lines _____.
   (loud)
   -able
   -ly

3. Some days, our play practice seemed _____.
   (end)
   -y
   -less

4. I played a _____ person and had to practice
   (clown)
   falling without hurting myself.
   -able
   -ish

5. My costume was striped and very _____.
   (color)
   -ful
   -able

6. I also wore a _____ wig.
   (curl)
   -y
   -ment

7. All the actors were _____.
   (friend)
   -ly
   -y

8. Everyone was _____ on opening night.
   (cheer)
   -ful
   -ness

9. The _____ of the stage lights made it easy for
   (bright)
   the people in the back rows to see us.
   -ness
   -less

10. The _____ of the actors filled the stage.
    (excite)
    -able
    -ment

Forming words with suffixes in context

Prefixes and Suffixes

Name _____

Read the list of prefixes and suffixes below. Then read the clues that follow. Add one of the prefixes or suffixes to the underlined word to form a word that matches the clue.

un-   dis-   re-   pre-   -ful   -less   -y   -ly   -ness

1. the opposite of <u>continue</u> _____ *discontinue* _____

2. without <u>color</u> _____

3. every <u>year</u> _____

4. to <u>view</u> before _____

5. to <u>do</u> again _____

6. full of <u>care</u> _____

7. having <u>thirst</u> _____

8. not <u>planned</u> _____

9. a state of being <u>weak</u> _____

Read the list of prefixes and suffixes below. Then read the clues that follow. Add one of the prefixes or suffixes to the underlined base word to form a word that matches the clue.

post-   in-   mis-   over-   -able   -ish   -ment

1. somewhat <u>warm</u> _____ *warmish* _____

2. not <u>complete</u> _____

3. to <u>pronounce</u> wrongly _____

4. the act of <u>agreeing</u> _____

5. able to be <u>trained</u> _____

6. like a <u>child</u> _____

7. after the <u>season</u> _____

8. <u>pay</u> too much _____

Review of forming words with prefixes and suffixes

Prefixes and Suffixes

Name _____

Read the list of words below. Circle the prefix or suffix in each word.

treat(able)	careless	sleepy	disappear
preschool	replay	untie	misbehave
thankful	dusty	goodness	homeless
agreement	postwar	overload	teachable
distrust	babyish	incorrect	sweetly

Read the list of words below. Then read the sentences that follow. Write the word from the list that makes sense in each sentence.

pretest	mistaken	cloudy	overpaid	lightness
unlocked	rewrite	tightly	tasteless	grayish

1. I think it might rain, because the sky looks gray and

   _____*cloudy*_____ .

2. Because the soup had too much water, it was almost

   _____ .

3. The _____ of the box made it easy to carry.

4. I must _____ the letter I wrote yesterday.

5. The suit was _____ blue.

6. Harry is often _____ for his twin brother, Barry.

7. The bank teller _____ the safe.

8. Mario held the bike's handlebars _____ as he raced down the hill.

9. The math _____ had five problems.

10. The job was so easy that I felt I was _____ .

Assessment of identifying prefixes and suffixes; Words containing prefixes and suffixes in context

Syllables

Name _____

Words are made of small parts called syllables. Because each syllable has one vowel sound, a word has as many syllables as it has vowel sounds. The word **desk** has one vowel sound, so it has one syllable. The word **cabin** has two vowel sounds, so it has two syllables.

Look at the pictures and read the picture names. Write the number of syllables you hear in each picture name.

2 candle	___ butterfly	___ jelly
___ kite	___ sixteen	___ banjo
___ calendar	___ window	___ leaf
___ camel	___ bench	___ potato

Identifying the number of syllables in a word

Syllables

Name _____

A compound word should be divided into syllables between the words that make it compound.	high/way

Read the words below. Circle each compound word. Then write each compound word and draw a line between the syllables.

1. (bookcase) *book/case*

2. downtown _____

3. running _____

4. rainbow _____

5. replay _____

6. notebook _____

7. airplane _____

8. driveway _____

9. pencil _____

10. sunshine _____

11. into _____

12. mailroom _____

13. steamboat _____

14. camper _____

15. blend _____

16. someone _____

17. footprint _____

18. greenhouse _____

19. soapy _____

20. place _____

21. rainfall _____

22. snowplow _____

23. sprinkle _____

24. cookbook _____

25. birthday _____

26. railway _____

27. dustpan _____

28. school _____

29. tells _____

30. oatmeal _____

Identifying and dividing compound words into syllables

Syllables

Name _____

Many two-syllable words have prefixes or suffixes. These words can be divided into syllables by dividing the word between the prefix or suffix and the base word.

re/pay

cheer/ful

Read the list of words. Divide each word into syllables by drawing a line between the syllables. Then read the story and write a word from the list that makes sense in each sentence.

cloud/less   cheerful   dislikes   harmful   remind
softly   quickly   returned   snowy   unhook

It was a cold, ___*snowy*___ day when my friends and I went

sledding. The blue sky was _____. The white flakes

had fallen slowly and _____ the night before. I had to

carefully _____ my sled from the hook on the basement

wall. Then I listened to Dad _____ me of all the

sledding rules that he and Mom had set last year.

All my friends were excited and _____ when I met

them at the top of Spark's Hill. Even Jan, who _____

cold weather, was there. She and Jack had removed any

_____ things that might be in the path of our sleds. I

guess I seemed fearless on my first ride down the hill, but I was a bit

afraid. I had forgotten how steep the slope was! But when I reached the

bottom of the hill, I _____ forgot my fears. I

_____ to the top of the hill for another fun-filled ride.

Syllables

Name _____

When a two-syllable word has two consonants between two vowels, the word usually is divided between the two consonants.

but/ter
VC/CV

pic/nic
VC/CV

Read the list of words. Write each word and draw a line between its syllables.

1. napkin *nap/kin*

2. corner _____

3. worry _____

4. dentist _____

5. mistake _____

6. whisper _____

7. tunnel _____

8. contest _____

9. invent _____

10. pencil _____

Read each sentence and the word choices shown below the blank. Complete each sentence by writing the word that has the VC/CV pattern.

1. Yesterday Dad and I made the salad for _____*dinner*_____.
   (lunch, dinner)

2. We bought lettuce and pickles at the _____ vegetable stand.
   (closest, corner)

3. When we _____ home, I was very hungry.
   (arrived, got)

4. I put some rolls in a large _____ while he tossed the salad.
   (basket, bowl)

5. I also put _____, plates, and forks on the table.
   (spoons, napkins)

6. When Dad was finished, he set the salad bowl on the _____ of the table.
   (center, end)

7. Then everyone helped themselves to the cool _____ salad.
   (crisp, summer)

Dividing words with the VC/CV pattern into syllables; Identifying words with the VC/CV pattern in context

Syllables

Name _____

Words that have one consonant between two vowels can be divided into syllables in two ways. When you see a word that has one consonant between two vowels, say the word. If the first vowel sound is long, divide the word after the first vowel. If the first vowel sound is short, divide the word after the consonant that follows the vowel.

1
fā/mous
V/CV
mū/sic
V/CV

2
wăg/on
VC/V
fĭn/ish
VC/V

Read the list of words. Write each word. Mark the first vowel of the word with ˘ if it stands for the short sound or ¯ if it stands for the long sound. Then draw a line between its syllables.

1. later   _lā/ter_
2. broken   _____
3. tiger   _____
4. river   _____
5. finish   _____
6. paper   _____
7. punish   _____
8. robin   _____
9. item   _____
10. closet _____

11. lemon   _____
12. minus   _____
13. pedal   _____
14. cozy   _____
15. pilot   _____
16. fever   _____
17. moment _____
18. travel _____
19. second _____
20. motor   _____

Dividing words with the V/CV and VC/V patterns into syllables

133

Syllables

Name _____

Read the list of words. Write each word and draw a line between its syllables. Then mark the first vowel of the word with ˘ if it stands for the short sound or ¯ if it stands for the long sound.

1. acorn _ā/corn_

2. planet _____

3. petal _____

4. spider _____

5. secret _____

6. model _____

7. lemon _____

8. minus _____

9. robot _____

10. even _____

Read the list of words and the sentences. Divide each list word into syllables by drawing a line between the syllables. Then write the word from the list that makes sense in each sentence.

e/vent
broken
robin
driver
river
palace
table
medal
moment
flavor

1. The _____robin_____ was making a nest in the tree in our backyard.

2. I can't decide what _____ of oatmeal I would like for breakfast.

3. The last _____ of the picnic was the potato sack race.

4. Ray won a _____ for swimming.

5. Ruth tried to fix the _____ chain on her bicycle.

6. The narrow _____ gets a little wider at Cliff's Bend.

7. The _____ of the large truck needed a rest after his trip.

8. Will you please set ten places at the _____?

Dividing words with the V/CV and VC/V patterns into syllables;
Words with the V/CV and VC/V patterns in context

Syllables

Name _____

Read the list of words. Write each word and draw a line between its syllables.

1. wagon   *wag/on*

2. hotel _____

3. doctor _____

4. closet _____

5. retell _____

6. painless _____

7. open _____

8. airplane _____

9. tiger _____

10. useful _____

11. pupil _____

12. later _____

13. second _____

14. unlike _____

15. iron _____

16. favor _____

17. thankful _____

18. driveway _____

19. famous _____

20. never _____

21. slowly _____

22. blanket _____

23. downtown _____

24. into _____

25. cabbage _____

26. planet _____

27. toothbrush _____

28. normal _____

29. preview _____

30. replace _____

Review of dividing words into syllables

Syllables

Name _____

Read the list of words. Write each word and draw a line between its syllables.

1. metal _____*met/al*_____

2. unripe _____

3. kindly _____

4. railroad _____

5. dislike _____

6. silent _____

7. carpet _____

8. cloudy _____

9. invite _____

10. replay _____

Read the list of words and the sentences. Divide each list word into syllables by drawing a line between the syllables. Then write the word from the list that makes sense in each sentence.

q u i c k l y

r e j o i n

e n d l e s s

b o r d e r

r e p l a y

h e l p f u l

h o m e w o r k

t i g e r

b a k e r

u n z i p

1. The _____*border*_____ around the edge of the wallpaper was bright blue.

2. Lee puts away the dishes and is _____ in many other ways.

3. The children of the city were asked to name the baby _____ at the city zoo.

4. Our teacher gave us _____ in geography and spelling.

5. Last week seemed _____ to the workers who were tired.

6. The young child could not _____ his new winter coat.

7. The runners started to race _____ around the track.

8. The coach for the other team asked to see a film _____ of the swim meet.

Assessment of dividing words into syllables

Antonyms

Name _____

An antonym is a word that has the opposite meaning of another word.	early—late

Read the words in each box below. Draw a line to match each word with its antonym (opposite).

strong false	full after	early wide
true weak	before	over late
loose tight	tame empty	narrow under

win spend	cool warm	dirty heavy
save few	easy dull	light clean
many lose	sharp hard	youn old

Read the list of words below. Then read the sentences that follow. Write the word from the list that is an antonym (opposite) for the underlined word in each sentence.

correct	light	dry	never	thin
slowly	awake	deep	open	smiling

1. The water was <u>shallow</u> during the low tide. _deep_

2. I wrote down the <u>wrong</u> telephone number. _____

3. We <u>always</u> use this road to go to school. _____

4. Clara, why are you <u>frowning</u>? _____

5. The runner moved <u>swiftly</u> around the track. _____

6. The rug was <u>wet</u> after we cleaned it. _____

7. Mark dropped the <u>heavy</u> box on the floor. _____

8. I was <u>asleep</u> in the softest chair. _____

9. The pillows on the couch were <u>fat</u>. _____

10. Please <u>close</u> the car windows. _____

Identifying antonyms

Synonyms

Name _____

| A synonym is a word that has the same or nearly the same meaning as another word. | rush—hurry |

Read the words in each box below. Draw a line to match each word with its synonym (word that has the same meaning).

quiet	thin	raise	tell	ship	close
simple	easy	say	lift	near	yell
narrow	still	small	little	shout	boat

tale	story	stay	hear	chilly	cold
well	large	forest	remain	present	wash
big	healthy	listen	woods	clean	gift

Read the list of words below. Then read the sentences that follow. Write the word from the list that is a synonym (word that has the same meaning) for the underlined word in each sentence.

| unload | skinny | sea | fix | begin |
| going | raw | cover | hurry | tall |

1. Kara will <u>repair</u> the kitchen sink. _____*fix*_____

2. I would like a <u>thin</u> slice of bread. _____

3. Don't <u>rush</u> through your homework. _____

4. Billy enjoyed the <u>uncooked</u> vegetables. _____

5. The <u>ocean</u> was calm yesterday. _____

6. Tess is unhappy that I am <u>leaving</u>. _____

7. We can <u>start</u> the game without Carlos. _____

8. The workers wanted to <u>unpack</u> the truck. _____

9. The cats were sitting on the <u>high</u> fence. _____

10. Please put a <u>lid</u> on the box. _____

Antonyms and Synonyms

Name _____

Read the words below. Circle the two words in each row that are antonyms (opposites).

1. (loose)	empty	(tight)	new	pretty
2. write	sing	sell	buy	mix
3. receive	tie	send	draw	clean
4. slow	tall	noisy	raw	quiet
5. in	buy	near	after	before
6. slowly	happily	fondly	quickly	carefully

Read each sentence and the words beside it. Write the word that is a synonym (word that has the same meaning) for the word shown below the blank.

1. There is a small ____*tear*____ in the lamp shade.
   (rip)

   tear
   spot

2. Rita will _____ it tomorrow.
   (fix)

   repair
   sell

3. She knows about a special _____ that she can use to fix the shade.
   (paste)

   patch
   glue

4. Rita also wants to replace the _____ light bulb with one that burns more brightly.
   (dim)

   dull
   bright

5. She will probably go to the store _____ her house.
   (closest)

   farthest
   nearest

6. Rita will _____ to the owner about which light bulbs to buy.
   (speak)

   write
   talk

Antonyms and Synonyms

Name _____

Read each pair of sentences. In the blanks, write a pair of antonyms (opposites) from the sentences.

1. The young children wanted to play baseball.

   They were going to use the old school's field.

   young

   old

2. It was a very warm day in the spring.

   Sam brought ice and water for cool drinks.

   _____

   _____

3. One team wore dark blue shirts.

   The other team's players wore light green shirts.

   _____

   _____

4. Many people came to watch the first inning.

   Only a few stayed for the whole game.

   _____

   _____

Read each pair of sentences. In the blanks, write a pair of synonyms (words that have the same meaning) from the sentences.

1. Have you heard The Tuners' new song?

   I listened to it ten times last night.

   heard

   listened

2. This poem tells a story about John Henry.

   The tale has been told in many different ways.

   _____

   _____

3. Luke, you seem jolly today.

   Are you happy because it's your birthday?

   _____

   _____

4. I have discovered a wonderful store.

   I've found many bargains in its basement.

   _____

   _____

Review of identifying antonyms and synonyms

Antonyms and Synonyms

Name _____

Read the list of words below. Then read the sentences that follow. Write the word from the list that is an antonym (opposite) for the underlined word in each sentence.

bright	short	asleep	light
ugly	boring	late	same

1. Tom was <u>awake</u> most of the night. _____*asleep*_____

2. He was thinking about all the <u>beautiful</u> sights he and his parents would see. _____

3. They wanted to get an <u>early</u> start on the road. _____

4. Tom's parents didn't want to drive through <u>heavy</u> rush-hour traffic. _____

5. The Smiths were going to visit friends whom they had not seen in a <u>long</u> time. _____

6. Traveling to another city would be <u>exciting</u>. _____

Read the list of words below. Then read the sentences that follow. Write the word from the list that is a synonym (word that has the same meaning) for the underlined word in each sentence.

waving	happy	shining	pretty
place	dull	like	tiny

1. The scene in the painting was <u>beautiful</u>. _____*pretty*_____

2. The wings of butterflies were <u>fluttering</u> in the breeze. _____

3. The drops of dew on the leaves were <u>sparkling</u> in the sunlight. _____

4. Lidia was <u>pleased</u> that she had taken the picture. _____

5. She decided to <u>put</u> the photo in a frame. _____

6. She thought her friends would <u>enjoy</u> looking at the butterflies and leaves. _____

Reading and Writing Wrap-Up

Name _____

Homes Around the World

What kind of house do you live in? Would your house be the same if you lived in a desert or in Alaska? Would your house be the same if you often had to travel from place to place?

Weather and Houses

In the hot, dry New Mexico desert, some people build their houses out of bricks made of mud, clay, straw, and water. These houses have very thick walls to keep out the heat in summer.

In the coldest parts of Alaska, some people build their houses out of thick blocks of ice. The thick walls of ice help to keep the people comfortable during the long, cold winters.

Building Supplies and Houses

When the first settlers came to America, they found large stretches of forests, so they built their houses out of wood.

In some parts of the world there is not much wood, but there are rocks and mountains. Some people in Turkey live in houses carved into the side of stone mountains.

Movable Houses

In some countries, people have one job in the summer and another job in the winter. These people like to have houses they can take with them. In the deserts of Africa, people often live in tents, which they can carry with them when they travel from one place to another.

In the United States and other countries, many people live in trailers. Such homes allow them to live in different places during the year in order to work at different jobs.

1. How are some houses in New Mexico and Alaska alike?

_____

2. Name two kinds of movable houses. _____   _____

Application of reading and comprehension skills in a social studies context

Name _____

3. Check the sentence that tells the main idea.

    _____ Houses can be made of wood, brick, stone, or cloth.

    _____ Houses in deserts and mountains are different from houses in cities.

    _____ Houses around the world are different because of weather, building supplies, and people's jobs.

4. One reason people live in houses is to protect themselves from the weather.

    What other reasons can you think of? _____

    _____

    _____

5. Invent a new kind of house and draw a picture of it. Describe your house and tell how it will fit the weather and building supplies where you will build it.

_____   Use the space below for your drawing.

_____

_____

_____

_____

_____

_____

_____

Homophones

<u>Name</u> _____

Homophones are words that sound the same but have different spellings and different meanings.	would—wood

Read the words in each box. Draw a line to match each word with its homophone.

nose	buy	son	here	knew	deer
bare	knows	break	brake	dear	sail
by	bear	hear	sun	sale	new

one	eight	weight	peace	see	hour
beat	beet	piece	pail	our	blew
ate	won	pale	wait	blue	sea

Read each pair of sentences. In the blanks, write a pair of homophones (words that sound the same) from the sentences.

1. The flower in the vase was bright yellow.

    Dad used whole wheat flour to make the bread.

    flower
    flour

2. The heel of my shoe is loose.

    My sister's cuts should heal quickly.

    _____

    _____

3. Joe will write a letter to his grandparents.

    Make a right turn onto Hunter Street.

    _____

    _____

4. Her niece threw the last pitch of the inning.

    We couldn't find our way through the crowd.

    _____

    _____

5. There was only one piece of pizza on the platter.

    Grandma won third prize in the bicycle race.

    _____

    _____

6. The road near the bridge is being repaired.

    Yesterday was the first time I rode in a jeep.

    _____

    _____

Identifying homophones

Homographs

Name _____

Homographs are words that have the same spelling but different meanings. Sometimes they are pronounced differently.

The plumber checked the building's **lead** pipes.

The van will **lead** the group of cars.

Read each pair of sentences and circle the homographs (words that have the same spelling). Then draw a line from each sentence to the picture it tells about.

David will (wind) his new watch.

The winter (wind) was cold and biting.

A tear fell from the little boy's eye.

Lily will tear strips of newspaper for her project.

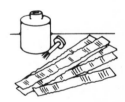

Mother stood close to the desk.

The last person to leave should close the door.

The square dancers will bow to each other.

Carlos made a large bow for the package.

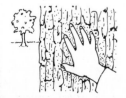

Tracy touched the rough bark of our tallest tree.

Our neighbor's dog might bark at the squirrels.

Identifying homographs; Determining meanings of homographs

145

Homophones and Homographs

Name _____

Read the words below. In each row, circle two words that are homophones (words that sound the same).

1.	saw	(sea)	side	(see)	sound
2.	pass	pail	past	pale	part
3.	meat	made	meet	mess	mouth
4.	brakes	brings	breaks	bright	breeze
5.	west	weep	week	well	weak
6.	block	blast	blew	blade	blue

Read the list of homographs (words that have the same spelling) and their meanings below. Then read the sentences that follow. In each sentence, decide the meaning of the underlined homograph. Write the letter of the correct meaning in the blank.

wind	**A.** to turn or twist	**B.** fast-moving air
close	**A.** to shut	**B.** near
bark	**A.** sound made by a dog	**B.** the covering of a tree

1. The <u>wind</u> blew all the leaves from the tree.   _B_

2. Ms. Watkins lives <u>close</u> to her office.   ___

3. Connie will show us the piece of <u>bark</u> she found.   ___

4. Please <u>close</u> the kitchen windows.   ___

5. The new highway will <u>wind</u> around the mountain.   ___

6. I called Jack when I heard Patches' <u>bark</u>.   ___

7. The kites were tossed about in the <u>wind</u>.   ___

Identifying homophones; Determining meaning of homographs

Homophones and Homographs

Name _____

Read each pair of sentences. In the blanks, write a pair of homophones (words that sound the same) from the sentences.

1. Martín knew the answer to the difficult question.

   knew

   The new airport is larger than the old one.

   new

2. My parents chopped wood for the fireplace.

   _____

   Karen said she would try to visit us soon.

   _____

3. Our cousins do not know us very well.

   _____

   The hour hand of the clock is broken.

   _____

4. Kenny will wait for the next bus.

   _____

   She read the weight label on the turkey.

   _____

5. I don't know who won the game last night.

   _____

   At one time, we lived in a small town.

   _____

Read the list of homographs (words that have the same spelling) below. Then read each pair of meanings. Write a homograph from the list that matches both meanings.

| wind | lead | tear |
| close | bow | bark |

1. **A.** near **B.** to shut *close*

2. **A.** a kind of metal **B.** to guide; to be in front _____

3. **A.** sound made by a dog **B.** the covering of a tree _____

4. **A.** a fancy knot made with ribbon **B.** to bend the body at the waist _____

5. **A.** water from the eye **B.** to rip; to pull apart _____

6. **A.** a stream of air **B.** to turn or twist _____

Homophones and Homographs

Name _____

Read each pair of sentences. Write a pair of homophones (words that sound the same) from the sentences.

1. I was walking by the store window when I saw the coat display.

   I went into the store to buy a warm winter coat.

   _by_
   buy

2. Jesse took the last piece of paper in the stack.

   He asked for peace and quiet while he was working.

   _____

   _____

3. The sail on the boat was bright blue and yellow.

   She had bought the boat at a toy sale.

   _____

   _____

4. Our telephone is not working.

   The repair person will be here in an hour.

   _____

   _____

5. Leo threw the old letters into the basket.

   He had just gone through the week's mail.

   _____

   _____

Read the homographs (words that have the same spelling) and their meanings below. Then read the sentences that follow. In each sentence, decide the meaning of the underlined homograph. Write the letter of the correct meaning in the blank.

wind
A. to turn or twist
B. a stream of air

close
A. to shut
B. near

tear
A. to rip; to pull apart
B. water from the eye

1. Jennifer, please <u>close</u> the front door. _a_

2. As I peeled the onion, a <u>tear</u> fell from my eye. _____

3. The <u>wind</u> was blowing the snow across the street. _____

4. I'm glad I live <u>close</u> to school. _____

5. The road will <u>wind</u> around the steep hill. _____

6. The thin paper will <u>tear</u> easily. _____

Assessment of identifying homophones; Determining meanings of homographs

Guide Words

Name _____

The two words at the top of a dictionary page are called guide words. The first guide word is the same as the first word listed on the page. The second guide word is the same as the last word listed on the page. To find a word in the dictionary, decide if it comes in alphabetical order between the guide words on a page. If it does, you will find the word on that page. For example, the word **home** falls between the guide words **hollow** and **hop.**

Read each pair of guide words and the words that are listed below them. Circle the words in each list that could be found on a page that has that pair of guide words.

deep / feast	**gas / hole**	**ill / knot**	**melt / noise**
dark	grease	ice	meet
(drip)	garage	jar	mountain
fog	heart	kitchen	metal
false	hold	know	needle
different	guide	knife	nobody
fast	hurry	jelly	notice

paint / pond	**reward / search**	**telephone / town**	**water / yellow**
piano	rooster	teach	wisdom
package	sale	taste	wash
people	silver	ticket	wrap
porch	special	today	wander
paste	ruler	test	weak
pencil	ribbon	toast	yard

Guide Words

Name _____

Read the lists of words below. Then read the guide words that follow. Write each list word below the correct pair of guide words. Then number each list of words to show how they would be listed in alphabetical order.

roast	cliff	power	brush	climb	sad
print	cheek	company	safe	remain	butter
cage	calf	rush	copy	quick	row
quack	rabbit	below	rose	cave	cabin

1. **bell / camera**

cage   _5_

_____ ___

_____ ___

_____ ___

_____ ___

_____ ___

2. **candle / curtain**

_____ ___

_____ ___

_____ ___

_____ ___

_____ ___

_____ ___

3. **porch / right**

_____ ___

_____ ___

_____ ___

_____ ___

_____ ___

_____ ___

4. **ripe / sail**

_____ ___

_____ ___

_____ ___

_____ ___

_____ ___

_____ ___

    Using guide words; Alphabetizing by first, second, and third letters

Guide Words

Name _____

Read the six pairs of guide words and their page numbers. Then read the lists of words that follow. Write the page number on which each list word would be found.

arm / bear—p. 8   **call / curl**—p. 11   **glove / heel**—p. 15
moon / ninety—p. 23   **pay / plow**—p. 29   **still / team**—p. 35

1. basket _p. 8_

2. peach _____

3. grain _____

4. swallow _____

5. coach _____

6. tea _____

7. moose _____

8. clever _____

9. pillow _____

10. ax _____

11. motor _____

12. half _____

13. beach _____

14. pleasant _____

15. night _____

16. carry _____

17. guest _____

18. straw _____

19. arrange _____

20. tame _____

21. heavy _____

22. sting _____

23. contest _____

24. napkins _____

25. pencil _____

26. nickel _____

Entry Words

Name _____

The word or phrase that you look up in a dictionary is called an entry word. An entry word shows the spelling of the word. It also shows the number of syllables in the word. A space is left between the syllables. Entry words are printed in dark type at the left of each column on a dictionary page. An entry word together with its meanings is called an entry.

cit y /sit′ ē/ *n, pl* **cit ies** a large town: *The city is a very busy place.*

di vide /də vīd′/ *v* **di vid ed; di vid ing** to cut into parts or to separate: *Divide the apple into three pieces.*

When you look for a word in the dictionary, look for the base word. For example, if you want to know the meaning of the word **dividing,** look for the base word **divide.** If you want to know the meaning of **cities,** look for its base word **city.** Any spelling changes for the entry word are usually listed in the entry. In the example above, **divided** and **dividing** are listed in the entry for the word **divide. Cities** is listed in the entry for the word **city.**

Read the words below. Beside each word, write the entry word (base word) you would look for in the dictionary.

1. baking _*bake*_
2. foxes _____
3. saddest _____
4. walked _____
5. planned _____
6. slipping _____
7. passes _____
8. hurried _____
9. prettier _____

10. knives _____
11. beaches _____
12. steepest _____
13. helped _____
14. happier _____
15. babies _____
16. liked _____
17. laughing _____
18. faster _____

Identifying entry words

Dictionary Meanings

Many dictionary entry words have more than one meaning. Most dictionaries show the different meanings of a word by numbering them. Some dictionaries also give an example sentence for each meaning. These sentences help to make each meaning clear.

be long /bə lòng′/ v **1** to be owned by someone or something: *Does that hat belong to Kelly?* **2** to be in the right place: *Your coats belong in the closet.*

clear /klir/ adj **1** with nothing in the way: *The road is clear now.* **2** not cloudy or foggy: *It looks as if it will be a clear day.* **3** easy to understand: *The directions on the map were clear.*

Read the sentences below. Use the entry words above to decide the meaning of each underlined word. In the blank, write the number of the correct meaning.

1. The forks and spoons <u>belong</u> in the top drawer.   *2*

2. The puppies <u>belong</u> to Jose.   ____

3. The birthday gifts <u>belong</u> to Nancy Lopez.   ____

4. These folders <u>belong</u> in my school desk.   ____

5. I hope we have a <u>clear</u> day for the picnic.   ____

6. The driveway is <u>clear</u> of snow and ice.   ____

7. The dictionary lesson was <u>clear</u> to her.   ____

8. On a <u>clear</u> day, you can see for many miles out to sea.   ____

9. The driver wanted the car windows to be <u>clear</u>.   ____

10. Ron's plan was <u>clear</u> to his friends.   ____

Determining word meaning from context

Entry Words and Dictionary Meanings

Name _____

Read the words below. Beside each word, write the entry word you would look for in the dictionary.

1. weighing *weigh*

2. happier _____

3. waved _____

4. laughs _____

5. wrapping _____

6. traveled _____

7. tracks _____

8. climbing _____

Read the dictionary entries. Then read the sentences that follow. Use the dictionary entries shown below to decide the meaning of each underlined word. In the blank, write the number of the correct meaning.

track /trak/ *n* **1** a line of metal rails for trains to travel on: *The engine pulls the train along the track.* **2** a place to run races: *I ran four miles on the track.* **3** a mark left by something that has passed by: *We saw a raccoon track near the tree.*

weigh /wā/ *v* **1** to have a certain weight: *I weigh 110 pounds.* **2** to find out how heavy something is: *Please weigh the grapes for me.*

1. The <u>track</u> was clear for the runners. _2_

2. The workers were loading fruit into the freight car on the <u>track</u>. ____

3. The campers left a <u>track</u> from their tents to the river. ____

4. The joggers used the park path as a <u>track</u>. ____

5. I am going to <u>weigh</u> the potatoes. ____

6. The apples <u>weigh</u> five pounds. ____

7. The salesperson will <u>weigh</u> the corn. ____

Identifying entry words; Determining word meaning from context

Guide Words, Entry Words, and Meanings

Name _____

Read each pair of guide words and the words that are listed below them. Circle the words in each list that could be found on a page that has that pair of guide words.

fear / give	**keep / lean**	**name / one**	**trade / vine**
face	kind	old	tire
game	lap	nail	travel
guide	joy	nose	understand
front	learn	o'clock	tunnel
fur	lamb	only	valley
giant	knife	nobody	visit

Read the dictionary entries below. Then read the sentences that follow. Use the dictionary entries to decide the meaning of each underlined word. In the blank, write the number of the correct meaning.

> **join** /join/ v **1** to become a member of a group: *Lisa would like to join the record club.* **2** to bring together: *The two roads join at the bottom of the hill.*
>
> **spend** /spend/ v spent **1** to use money to buy things: *Try not to spend too much when you're shopping.* **2** to pass time or stay: *We are going to spend our vacation at home.*

1. The artist will <u>join</u> the lines together to form a triangle. _____2_____

2. Russ might <u>spend</u> three hours on his homework. _____

3. Janet <u>joined</u> the writing class yesterday. _____

4. The farmer did not <u>spend</u> too much money for the plow. _____

5. The new bridge <u>joins</u> the two large islands. _____

6. I want to <u>join</u> the library because I like to read a lot. _____

Pronunciation Key and Respellings

Name _____

A dictionary can show you how words are pronounced. Each entry word is followed by a respelling. The respelling is made up of letters and special symbols. The words in the dictionary's pronunciation key show you how to pronounce each letter or symbol. By combining the sounds for each symbol and letter, you can pronounce the word.

Pronunciation Key

/a/ = apple, tap	/k/ = kick, can	/th/ = thing, both
/ā/ = ate, say	/l/ = laugh, pail	/u/ = up, cut
/är/ = car, heart	/m/ = mouse, ham	/ü/ = soon, rule
/ãr/ = hair, care	/n/ = nice, ran	/u̇/ = look, put
/b/ = bat, cab	/ng/ = ring, song	/v/ = vine, live
/ch/ = chain, chair	/o/ = father, hot	/w/ = wet, away
/d/ = door, sad	/ō/ = old, so	/y/ = yes, you
/e/ = get, egg	/ȯ/ = ball, dog	/yü/ = use, cute
/ē/ = even, bee	/oi/ = boy, oil	/yu̇/ = cure, pure
/f/ = fan, off	/ou/ = house, cow	/z/ = zoo, zero
/g/ = goat, big	/p/ = pan, nap	/zh/ = pleasure, beige
/h/ = her, happy	/r/ = ran, race	/ə/ = a (around)
/hw/ = wheel, why	/s/ = sun, mess	e (better)
/i/ = is, fit	/sh/ = she, rush	i (rabbit)
/ī/ = ice, tie	/t/ = toy, mat	o (doctor)
/j/ = jump, gentle	/ᵺh/ = they, smooth	u (upon)

Read each respelling below. Write the words from the key that show how to pronounce the underlined letters.

1. /chās/ *ate, say*

2. /thik/ _____

3. /tōld/ _____

4. /spün/ _____

5. /trezh′ər/ _____

6. /ᵺhəm/ _____

7. /rās/ _____

8. /klam/ _____

9. /nou/ _____

10. /kē/ _____

Pronunciation Key and Respellings

Name _____

In most dictionaries, a short form of the pronunciation key can be found on each page.

Pronunciation Key

/a/ = apple, tap; /ā/ = ate, say; /är/ = car, heart; /âr/ = hair, care; /ch/ = chain, chair; /e/ = get, egg; /ē/ = even, bee; /hw/ = wheel, why; /i/ = is, fit; /ī/ = ice, tie; /ng/ = ring, song; /o/ = father, hot; /ō/ = old, so; /ô/ = ball, dog; /oi/ = boy, oil; /ou/ = house, cow; /sh/ = she, rush; /ŧh/ = they, smooth; /th/ = thing, both; /u/ = up, cut; /ü/ = soon, rule; /u̇/ = look, put; /yü/ = use, cute; /yu̇/ = cure, pure; /zh/ = pleasure, beige; /ə/ = a (around), e (better), i (rabbit), o (doctor), u (upon)

Use the key to pronounce the symbol shown at the beginning of each row. Then read the words in the row. Circle each word that contains the sound for which the symbol stands.

1. /ē/	(team)	bread	sleep	best	shield
2. /ī/	shine	my	fish	rain	tie
3. /ō/	boat	boil	took	phone	flow
4. /ü/	moon	tube	rust	to	stew
5. /ch/	ranch	chorus	chair	chef	match
6. /ou/	soup	plow	hour	enough	outside

Use the pronunciation key shown above to pronounce the respelling shown at the beginning of each row. Then read the words in the row. Circle the word that matches the respelling.

1. /nīf/	night	(knife)	kite	knight
2. /skül/	scoop	skate	scale	school
3. /plou/	play	pound	plow	proud
4. /sāl/	said	sail	salt	seal
5. /prīz/	price	prince	pies	prize
6. /sent/	scent	scene	send	seat

Pronunciation Key and Respellings

Name _____

Use the key shown above to help you pronounce the respelling shown at the beginning of each row. Then read the words in the row. Circle the word that matches the respelling.

1.	/hōz/	house	(hose)	home
2.	/rīt′ər/	writer	written	walker
3.	/pik/	pick	pitch	pit
4.	/chüz/	cheese	choose	shoes
5.	/fòl/	false	fail	fall
6.	/ə buv′/	about	above	aboard
7.	/yüth/	you	young	youth
8.	/spred/	spray	spend	spread

Use the key to pronounce each respelling in List A. Then read the words in List B. Write the word from List B that the respelling stands for.

List A

List B

1. /stāj/   _stage_   famous

2. /ə genst′/ _____ harm

3. /laf/   _____ stage

4. /härm/   _____ laugh

5. /fā′məs/   _____ oak

6. /ōk/   _____ against

Reading dictionary respellings; Using a pronunciation key

Accent Marks

Name _____

Some words have more than one syllable. The respellings of these words show the syllables with a space or mark between them. One syllable is usually said with more stress than the others. In the respelling /fin'ish/, the mark after the first syllable shows that **fin** is said with more stress than **ish.** The mark is called an accent mark.

/fin'ish/
  fin ' ish
/traf 'ik/
  traf'fic
/ə gen'/
  a gain'

Pronunciation Key

/a/ = apple, tap; /ā/ = ate, say; /är/ = car, heart; /ãr/ = hair, care; /ch/ = chain, chair; /e/ = get, egg; /ē/ = even, bee; /hw/ = wheel, why; /i/ = is, fit; /ī/ = ice, tie; /ng/ = ring, song; /o/ = father, hot; /ō/ = old, so; /ȯ/ = ball, dog; /oi/ = boy, oil; /ou/ = house, cow; /sh/ = she, rush; /ᵺh/ = they, smooth; /th/ = thing, both; /u/ = up, cut; /ü/ = soon, rule; /u̇/ = look, put; /yü/ = use, cute; /yu̇/ = cure, pure; /zh/ = pleasure, beige; /ə/ = a (<u>a</u>round), e (bett<u>e</u>r), i (rabb<u>i</u>t), o (doct<u>o</u>r), u (<u>u</u>pon)

Use the key to pronounce each respelling in List A. Then read the words in List B. Write the word from List B that matches each respelling. Leave a space between syllables. Then put an accent mark after the syllable that is said with more stress.

	List A		List B
1.	/wun'dər/	*won'der*	cac/tus
2.	/skam'pər/	_____	re/mem/ber
3.	/splen'dəd/	_____	neigh/bor
4.	/bi gan'/	_____	scam/per
5.	/kak'təs/	_____	whis/tle
6.	/bi sīd'/	_____	be/gan
7.	/ri mem' bər/	_____	won/der
8.	/pal'əs/	_____	splen/did
9.	/hwis' əl/	_____	pal/ace
10.	/nā' bər/	_____	be/side

Recognizing accented syllables and respellings

Accent Marks

Name _____

| Some words have more than one syllable. In these words, the stress, or accent, often falls on the base word. | fish′ ing
care′ less |

Read the words that have been divided into syllables below. Say each word and listen for the stressed syllable. Put an accent mark after the stressed syllable in each word.

1. good′ness
2. thank ful
3. clown ish
4. test ing
5. night ly

6. snow y
7. push ing
8. fast est
9. dust y
10. friend less

11. help ing
12. home less
13. help ful
14. smooth est
15. calm ly

Read each word below. Say each word and listen for the stress. Write the word, leaving a space between syllables. Put an accent mark after the stressed syllable in each word.

1. barking *bark′ing*
2. tightly _____
3. careless _____
4. sleepy _____
5. quicker _____
6. rusting _____
7. slowly _____
8. wanted _____

9. snapping _____
10. weekly _____
11. grayish _____
12. strongest _____
13. cloudy _____
14. foolish _____
15. weakness _____
16. friendly _____

Recognizing accented syllables

Accent Marks

Name _____

Some two-syllable words that are spelled alike may have different respellings. They may be pronounced with the stress on different syllables. Read the entries below. Use the accent marks to help you say each word. Listen for the stressed syllable.

¹**ob ject** /ob′ jikt/ *n* a thing that can be seen or touched: *I removed the object from the table.*

²**ob ject** /əb jekt′/ *v* to be against the idea of something: *We object to the building of the new highway.*

¹**pres ent** /prez′ ənt/ *n* a gift: *I received a lovely present of flowers.*

²**pre sent** /pri zent′/ *v* to hand over or to give: *Mr. James will present the awards.*

¹**rec ord** /rek′ ərd/ *n* **1** something kept in writing for future use: *I keep a record of the books I read.* **2** a round phonograph disk: *I bought the group's latest record.*

²**re cord** /ri kȯrd′/ *v* **1** to put into writing: *Record the names of the club members who are here.* **2** to put music or words on tape: *We will record the mayor's speech.*

Read each sentence below. In the blank, write the underlined word as it's shown above. Leave a space between syllables. Put an accent mark after the stressed syllable in each word. Use the entries above to help you.

1. There was a large <u>object</u> on the road.   *ob′ ject*

2. The artist will <u>present</u> his painting. _____

3. The <u>record</u> I'm listening to has an old song on it. _____

4. Shelly might <u>object</u> to our picnic plans. _____

5. Will you <u>record</u> the school band's concert? _____

6. Sam liked the <u>present</u> the twins gave to him. _____

7. Keep a <u>record</u> of how much money you spend. _____

8. Why do you <u>object</u> to our idea? _____

9. Maggie will <u>record</u> the runners' finishing times. _____

Pronunciation Key and Respellings

Name _____

Pronunciation Key

/a/ = apple, tap; /ā/ = ate, say; /är/ = car, heart; /ãr/ = hair, care; /ch/ = chain, chair; /e/ = get, egg; /ē/ = even, bee; /hw/ = wheel, why; /i/ = is, fit; /ī/ = ice, tie; /ng/ = ring, song; /o/ = father, hot; /ō/ = old, so; /ȯ/ = ball, dog; /oi/ = boy, oil; /ou/ = house, cow; /sh/ = she, rush; /ᵺ/ = they, smooth; /th/ = thing, both; /u/ = up, cut; /ü/ = soon, rule; /u̇/ = look, put; /yü/ = use, cute; /yu̇/ = cure, pure; /zh/ = pleasure, beige; /ə/ = a (around), e (better), i (rabbit), o (doctor), u (upon)

Use the key above to help you pronounce the respelling at the beginning of each row. Then read the words in the row. Circle the word that the respelling matches.

1.	/tā′ bəl/	(table)	tasted	tablet
2.	/ə pärt′/	appeal	appear	apart
3.	/kan′ dəl/	castle	canned	candle
4.	/min′ ət/	minus	minute	miner
5.	/pen′ səl/	pedal	person	pencil
6.	/sē′ zən/	second	secret	season

Use the key to help you pronounce each respelling in List A. Then read the words in List B. Write the word from List B that each respelling stands for.

List A

1. /nēd′ əl/ *needle*
2. /nir bī′/ _____
3. /plan′ ət/ _____
4. /pur′ sən/ _____
5. /ə gen′/ _____
6. /ə lȯng′/ _____

List B

again

planet

person

along

nearby

needle

Review of using a pronunciation key; Reading dictionary respellings

Dictionary Skills

Read the sample entries below. Use them and the key to answer the questions that follow.

float /flōt/ *v* **1** to rest in or on the surface of water or liquid: *The toy boat will float in the tub of water.* **2** to move through the air: *I watched the clouds float across the sky.*

writ ing /rīt′ ing/ *n* **1** the way a person forms letters and words: *Your writing is easy to read.* **2** something that is written or printed, such as a book or a letter: *This story is an example of Mark Twain's writing.*

Pronunciation Key
/a/ = apple, tap; /ā/ = ate, say; /är/ = car, heart; /ār/ = hair, care; /ch/ = chain, chair; /e/ = get, egg; /ē/ = even, bee; /hw/ = wheel, why; /i/ = is, fit; /ī/ = ice, tie; /ng/ = ring, song; /o/ = father, hot; /ō/ = old, so; /ȯ/ = ball, dog; /oi/ = boy, oil; /ou/ = house, cow; /sh/ = she, rush; /ᵺh/ = they, smooth; /th/ = thing, both; /u/ = up, cut; /ü/ = soon, rule; /u̇/ = look, put; /yü/ = use, cute; /yu̇/ = cure, pure; /zh/ = pleasure, beige; /ə/ = a (around), e (better), i (rabbit), o (doctor), u (upon)

1. Write the number of the meaning of <u>float</u> as it is used in each sentence.

   a. The plane seemed to <u>float</u> across the clear sky.   *2*

   b. This inner tube should help me <u>float</u> on the lake.   ___

   c. I watched a leaf <u>float</u> from the tree to the ground.   ___

2. Write the number of the meaning of <u>writing</u> as it is used in each sentence.

   a. The <u>writing</u> on the chart is very clear.   ___

   b. The <u>writing</u> of E. B. White includes the story <u>Stuart</u> <u>Little</u>.   ___

3. Circle the pair of words that would be guide words for each dictionary entry shown in dark print.

   a. **float**   flake / flap   fleet / flick   flip / flow

   b. **writing**   wait / white   wrap / wrong   wrote / wrung

4. Write the words from the pronunciation key that show how to pronounce the letters shown in dark print.

   a. /fl**ō**t/ _____   b. /r**ī**t′ i**ng**/ _____

Reading and Writing Wrap-Up

Name _____

Using Your Senses to Describe

How would you describe something you can't see?

Who Has Seen the Wind?

Who has seen the wind?
  Neither I nor you;
But when the leaves hang trembling
  The wind is passing through.

Who has seen the wind?
  Neither you nor I;
But when the trees bow down their heads
  The wind is passing by.
                    —*Christina Rossetti*

The Wind

I saw you toss the kites on high
And blow the birds about the sky;
And all around I heard you pass,
Like ladies' skirts across the grass.
    O wind, a-blowing all day long,
    O wind, that sings so loud a song!

I saw the different things you did,
But always you yourself you hid;
I felt you push, I heard you call,
I could not see yourself at all.
    O wind, a-blowing all day long,
    O wind, that sings so loud a song!
                    —*Robert Louis Stevenson*

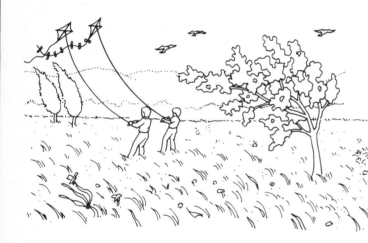

1. In "Who Has Seen the Wind?" how does the author answer the question in the

    title? _____

2. In "The Wind," what does the author say the wind is like?

    _____ a story   _____ a song   _____ a storm

3. In "The Wind," which two senses does the author say the wind affects directly?

    _____ sight   _____ sound   _____ smell   _____ taste   _____ touch

Application of reading, comprehension, and thinking skills in a literature context

Name _____

4. Even though you can't see the wind, you can see its effects. Check each statement that describes an effect caused by the wind.

_____ The leaves hang trembling on the branches of the trees.

_____ The trees bow down their heads and swing their leafy arms.

_____ Ladies in long skirts walk softly through the tall grass.

_____ The snow drifts up to the door and covers the window sills.

5. Number the following words for <u>wind</u> from **1** to **4.** Use **1** for the gentlest and **4** for the strongest.

_____ draft   _____ tornado   _____ gust   _____ breeze

6. Write a poem of your own about the wind, or about one of the topics below. Use words that will help your reader see, hear, feel, smell, or taste what you're describing.

rain   stars   trees   the sun   the moon   snow   waves

_____

_____

_____

_____

_____

_____

_____

_____

Sounds and Letters

fan

ra**ke**

tr**ai**n

j**ar**

auto

s**aw**

h**ay**

c**ar**

cent

chair

chef

chemist

du**ck**

b**e**d

b**ea**n

br**ea**d

b**ee**

eight

f**er**n

n**ew**s

Sounds and Letters

goat

pa**ge**

lau**gh**

si**gn**

b**i**b

ki**te**

sh**ie**ld

tie

b**ir**d

knot

la**mb**

ri**ng**

t**o**p

c**oa**t

b**o**n**e**

c**oi**n

m**oo**n

b**oo**k

h**or**n

cl**ou**d

Sounds and Letters

doughnut

touch

soup

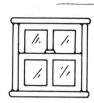

wind**ow**

c**ow**

toys

ele**ph**ant

scissors

shoe

shrug

thin

three

c**u**p

t**u**be

b**ur**n

wheel

write

fl**y**

pon**y**

Beginning Sounds

Name _____

Read the words and name the pictures. Circle the word that names each picture.

sock **(duck)** luck rock	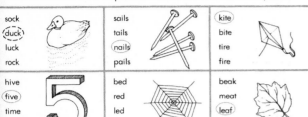	sails tails **(nails)** pails		kite bite tire fire	
hive **(five)** time dime	**5**	bed red led **(web)**		beak meat **(leaf)** team	

Read each sentence and the word beside it. Change the first letter of the word to form a new word that makes sense in the sentence. Write the new word in the blank.

1. I'll need to buy another stamp to _____*send*_____ this letter. bend

2. I need to have a new _____heel_____ put on this cowboy boot. feel

3. Our neighbor's dog likes to hide its bones in our _____yard_____. card

4. I have just enough _____time_____ to finish my breakfast. dime

5. They planted tomatoes and _____corn_____ in their garden. torn

6. The three days of rain made our cellar very _____damp_____. camp

7. It took two hours to _____find_____ the road in the snowstorm. mind

8. We needed another piece of _____rope_____ to tie the boxes. hope

---

Beginning Sounds

Words to use: banana, fan, gift, camera, hammer, kangaroo, jar, dime, leaf, needle, map, ruler, scarf, pool, teeth

Name _____

Name the pictures. Write the missing letter to complete each picture name.

_l_emon	_c_orn	_p_otato
_b_anana	_t_omato	_r_adish

In each sentence, complete the unfinished word by writing the missing letter. The word you form must make sense in the sentence.

1. You can find almost anything in our _g_arage.

2. We have spare parts for the lawn _m_ower.

3. There is a box full of empty orange _j_uice cans.

4. In one corner is a set of tires for my brother's _v_an.

5. The mast for our neighbor's _s_ailboat is there, too.

6. There is an old movie _c_amera on a shelf.

7. A roll of garden _h_ose is beside it.

8. We even have a toy monkey we bought at the _z_oo.

Ending Sounds

Name _____

Read the words and name the pictures. Circle the word that names each picture.

chair **(chain)** chart cheek		boot bowl book **(box)**		**(broom)** brook brood brown	
wit win **(wig)** wax		but **(bus)** bun bud		roll root room **(roof)**	

Read each sentence and the word beside it. Change the last letter of the word to form a new word that makes sense in the sentence. Write the new word in the blank.

1. We went to see a traveling circus last _____*week*_____ weed

2. We _____sat_____ in a large tent and watched the show. sad

3. One of the trained animals was a _____dog_____. dot

4. It was wearing a funny cap and a _____bib_____. bit

5. They also had a trained _____seal_____ in the show. seam

6. It was able to _____keep_____ a ball on the end of its nose. keel

7. We stopped for a quick _____meal_____ after the show. mean

8. Then I _____took_____ a nap while Dad drove home. tool

Ending Sounds

Words to use: (picturable) cook, deer, mail, suit, bug, chin, hoop, iron, root, soap, bread, flag, fox (additional words) coat, feel, fix, loud, shout, wag, aim, dip, fear, gas, job, lean, meal, net, plain, trap, wool, break

Name _____

Name the pictures. Write the missing letter to complete each picture name.

threa_d_	hoo_k_	tra_p_
tige_r_	mitte_n_	lea_f_

In each sentence, complete the unfinished word by writing the missing letter. The word you form must make sense in the sentence.

1. My best friend got a new kitten last wee_k_

2. I rode the bu_s_ to her house to see it.

3. It's quite young and not very bi_g_ yet.

4. It sleeps in an old shoe bo_x_.

5. My friend gives it a bow_l_ of warm milk for supper.

6. For breakfast it eats cat foo_d_.

7. When it gets tired, it curls up to take a na_p_.

8. Playing with my friend's kitten is a lot of fu_n_.

Beginning and Ending Sounds

Name _____

In each sentence, complete each unfinished word by writing the missing letter. The word you form must make sense in the sentence.

1. Some new people just *m*oved in *n*ext to us.
2. They have two boys, one g_irl, and a do_g.
3. The mother is an animal _d_octor at our _z_oo.
4. Some of their things were tied onto the to_p of their _v_an.
5. I helped carry a giant bo_x and an old cri_b upstairs.
6. They asked my mo_m if I could _j_oin them for supper.
7. She said I could stay to ea_t if I wanted to.

---

1. Our class goes to the *Library* each wee*k*.
2. We each get to take home a _b_ook that we _l_ike.
3. I like to _r_ead books about space trave_l.
4. Felipe likes book_s about _f_ire fighters.
5. Sue likes to read about _p_eople who have discovere_d things.
6. Sharon likes scary stories abou_t old _h_ouses.
7. Bob and Carol both _t_ook home books about race _c_ars.
8. You can find almost any _k_ind of book in ou_r library.

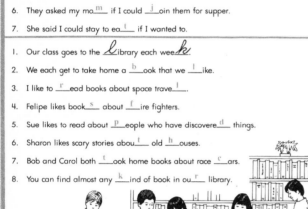

Short Vowels

Name _____

Read the words and name the pictures. Circle the word that names each picture.

fin fat fit (fan)		moss (mop) map moth

jog
jag
jig
(jug)

pun
pan
(pen)
pin

(lid)
lip
led
lad

(map)
mop
mitt
mat

Read the sentences and the word choices. Circle the word that best completes each sentence.

1. I like to look (at, it) the beautiful trees in the park.
2. There are a (let, lot) of different kinds of trees growing there.
3. The pine tree keeps its needles all (winter, wonder) long.
4. The oak tree (has, his) colored leaves in the fall.
5. Many birds build their (nuts, nests) in the tree branches.
6. Squirrels also like to live high (if, up) in the trees.
7. Some of the older trees have grown very (big, bag).
8. It would be (fin, fun) to climb to the tops of those trees.
9. I could (sit, sat) on a branch and watch the birds.
10. I could even take some (nets, nuts) to feed the squirrels.

Short Vowels

Name _____

Read each sentence and the words shown below the blank. Complete each sentence by writing the word that has a short-vowel sound.

1. Yesterday my family had a *picnic* .
   (picnic, race)
2. It was the first sunny day in ____spring____
   (spring, June)
3. My sister and I helped Dad pack a ___basket___ with food.
   (case, basket)
4. I made ___punch___ and put it in a cooler.
   (punch, tea)
5. We sat near the ___duck___ pond in the center of the park.
   (duck, wide)
6. I had fun watching the ducks ___splash___ in the water.
   (splash, wade)

Read each clue. Find the word in the list that matches the clue. Write the word next to the clue.

1. something to cook food in	*pot*	brick
2. something used in making buildings	brick	crop
3. to knock lightly	tap	cup
4. something to drink from	cup	mop
5. a fast airplane	jet	pot
6. a large boat	ship	hat
7. something to sit on	bench	ship
8. something used to wash a floor	mop	bench
		jet
		tap
		stick

Short Vowels

Name _____

Read each sentence and the word beside it. Change the vowel of the word to form a new word that makes sense in the sentence. Write the new word in the blank.

1. I want to buy a new *pack* for camping.   pick
2. The one I already have has a giant rip in the top ___flap___   flip
3. It also has a burned ___spot___ on it.   spit
4. The new one will keep out the ___mud___ and water.   mad
5. I don't want one that is too ___big___.   bag
6. I don't have a ___lot___ of things to carry in it.   let
7. I want it to ___fit___ me just right.   fat
8. And the straps shouldn't ___pinch___ or be uncomfortable.   punch
9. I hope the ___shop___ downtown has the one I want.   ship

Read the paragraph below. Complete each unfinished word by writing the missing vowel. The word you form must make sense in the paragraph.

Goldfish make wonderful p_e_ts. You will need a bowl or tank b_i_g enough for the n_u_mber of fish you want. The people at the pet store can t_e_ll you how large a t_a_nk you'll need. You will also need clean water and fish food. Be sure the water is n_o_t too cold or too h_o_t. Feed your fish every day. Feed th_e_m only what they c_a_n eat in about five minutes. You will need to change the water _a_nd clean the tank about every t_e_n days.

Short Vowels

Name _____

Read the list of words below. Then read the sentences that follow. Write a word from the list that makes sense in each sentence.

sister	let	butterfly
has	possible	best
brush	tricks	gentle
twenty	red	box
big	strings	

1. My older _____sister_____ and I like to fly kites in spring and autumn.

2. We can fill a giant _____box_____ with all the ones we own.

3. My sister has a big kite that is _____red_____ with two yellow tails.

4. It _____has_____ a bright rainbow painted in the middle of it.

5. Her kite is so _____big_____ it reaches up to her eyebrows when she holds it!

6. My sister _____let_____ me fly her big kite once.

7. The kite I like _____best_____ is colored purple.

8. It has a tail over _____twenty_____ feet long.

9. I have to use two _____strings_____ to fly it.

10. I pull on the strings to make it do _____tricks_____.

11. It's _____possible_____ to make it loop and dive.

12. I can make it _____brush_____ against the ground and go back up.

13. One kite we made has wings and looks like a _____butterfly_____.

14. It flies best in a quiet, _____gentle_____ breeze.

Long Vowels

Name _____

Read the words and name the pictures. Write each word below the picture it names.

page	skate	cube
spider	nine	globe

spider	skate	cube

globe	nine	page

Read the sentences and the word choices. Circle the word that makes sense in each sentence.

1. Last year everyone in our class (wrote) write) a book.

2. We could write about whatever we (chase, (chose)).

3. Someone's book was about rock (make, (music)).

4. My best friend wrote about the homes of ((snakes), spokes).

5. I wrote about the care of ((bikes), bakes).

6. I also wrote some safety (ropes, (rules)) that bikers should follow.

7. My book had ten ((pages), poles).

8. I ((like), lake) to ride my bike, and I enjoyed writing my book.

Long Vowels

Name _____

Read each word below and listen to its vowel sound. Write the word under the picture whose name has the same vowel sound.

vase	shape	cone	June
hive	cute	note	huge
bike	tune	code	lime
close	flame	tame	ripe
blade	dive	chose	rude

Words may be listed in any order.

vase	hive
blade	bike
shape	dive
flame	lime
tame	ripe

close	cute
cone	tune
note	June
code	huge
chose	rude

Long Vowels

Name _____

In each sentence, complete the unfinished word by writing the missing vowel or vowels. The word you form must make sense in the sentence.

1. My uncle dr__i__v__e__s one of the city buses.

2. He leaves for work at f__i__v__e__ o'clock every morning.

3. He m__a__k__e__s the first stop on his route at six o'clock.

4. M__o__st of his passengers are going to work.

5. Uncle Dave w__a__v__e__s to the passengers as they leave the bus.

6. They usually sm__i__l__e__ and tell him to have a good day.

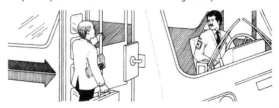

Read the paragraph below. Complete each unfinished word by writing the missing vowel or vowels. The word you form must make sense in the paragraph.

The hills in the West are filled with old silver and gold m__i__n__e__s. Some of them are very small, but others are h__u__g__e__. Mice and sp__i__ders now live in most of them. P__i__n__e__ trees grow in front of many mines. Some of the mines look like deep c__a__v__e__s. At one t__i__m__e__, miners worked in all these mines. All of them h__o__p__e__d to str__i__k__e__ it rich. Some did, but many went br__o__k__e__.

OLD and IND

Name _____

The letter **o** followed by **ld** usually stands for the long-**o** sound. The letter **i** followed by **nd** usually stands for the long-**i** sound.

c**old**
k**ind**

Read each sentence. In the blanks below the sentence, write the words from the sentence that have the long-**o** sound.

1. I thought it was cold inside, but it was even colder outside.

   cold   _colder_

2. We saved a lot of very old things, such as this tin candle mold.

   old   _mold_

3. I put the papers in a folder and asked my mom to hold them.

   folder   _hold_

4. The workers told us they had found a gold mine in the hills.

   told   _gold_

5. The people at the shop just sold the last candle holder.

   sold   _holder_

Read each sentence. In the blank, write the word from the sentence that has the long-**i** sound.

1. We visited a place where dogs are trained to help blind people.

   blind

2. This old mill used to grind wheat and corn into flour. _grind_

3. This morning our sister couldn't find her shoe. _find_

4. It was very kind of you to remember his birthday. _kind_

5. You can solve this puzzle if you put your mind to it. _mind_

OLD and IND

Name _____

Words to use: older, coldest, folded, holding, old, wind, grind, mind, kind, find

Read each sentence and the words beside it. Write the word that makes sense in each sentence.

1. They _told_ us that the movie begins at six o'clock. — unfold / told
2. The paper had gotten wet and was hard to _unfold_ . — sold
3. The chest full of _gold_ was hidden by the lake. — gold / bold
4. My brother is three years _older_ than you. — older
5. Do you _mind_ if I watch you put that toy together? — find / grinding
6. The machine was _grinding_ the wheat into flour. — mind
7. We made candle _holders_ from empty paper tubes. — holders / cold
8. It almost never gets very _cold_ in Florida. — sold
9. How much water do you think this pan will _hold_ ? — hold / told
10. The jacket I was hoping to buy has already been _sold_ — sold
11. The headlights of the car _blinded_ me for a moment. — find / kind
12. I'm going to try to _find_ another way to get home. — blinded
13. Can we _fold_ the tent and fit it back into the bag? — oldest / fold
14. Our apartment building is the _oldest_ one in the city. — told

---

OLD and IND

Name _____

Words to use: unfold, binder, grinding, kinder, finding, binding, kindest, holders, cold, blinded, oldest

Read each sentence. Complete the unfinished word by writing **old** or **ind.** The word you form must make sense in the sentence.

1. How long will it take you to w_ind_ up all that string?
2. I'm teaching my dog to walk on his h_ind_ legs.
3. It's usually c_old_er in Canada than in Mexico.
4. After you complete the order form, f_old_ it in half.
5. No one t_old_ me that there was no school today.
6. Thinking is a good exercise for your m_ind_ .
7. The fancy watch was made of g_old_ .
8. Did you ever f_ind_ the key that was missing?
9. My dad has a tool h_old_er he wears on his belt.
10. Please pull the bl_ind_ on the window to keep the sunshine out.
11. I caught two bad c_old_s last winter.
12. Please h_old_ the flashlight higher so I can see better.
13. I forgot to put the bread away, and now there's m_old_ on it.
14. The store owner s_old_ fruit and vegetables.
15. "Be k_ind_ to animals" is a good thought to remember.
16. I left the f_old_er on my desk, but now I can't find it.
17. The kitchen is the c_old_est room in the house.
18. The teacher is h_old_ing the word cards.

PROGRESS CHECK

Long Vowels

Name _____

Read each sentence and the words beside it. Write the word that makes sense in each sentence.

1. Sometimes I like to lie on my back and _gaze_ at the clouds. — gaze / quite / whole
2. It's an enjoyable way to rest my _mind_ for a while. — mind / old / make
3. I _told_ my best friend about all the pictures I can see. — shape / tape / told
4. One time I saw a whole group of _pine_ trees. — pine / joke / find
5. The clouds looked like a _huge_ forest in the sky. — huge / take / find
6. There was even a winding stream and a tiny _lake_ . — whole / lake / fold
7. People's _faces_ are fun to look for, too. — faces / finds / times
8. Some of them have big _noses_ or funny ears. — names / lakes / noses
9. Some of them seem to be laughing and telling _jokes_ . — jokes / places / homes
10. The _shapes_ of the clouds are always changing. — shapes / lakes / holds
11. There are always new pictures to _find_ . — huge / joke / find

---

172

Read the words and look at the pictures. Write each word below the picture it tells about.

can	hat	tape	van
plate	note	slide	cap
mat	cape	rip	cane

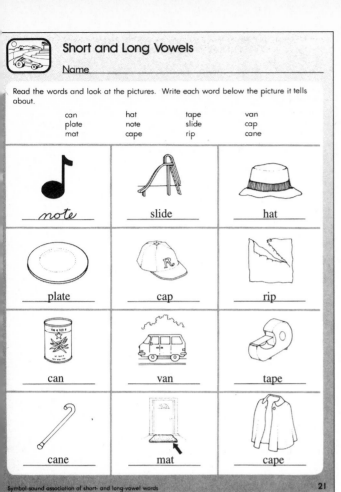

note   slide   hat

plate   cap   rip

can   van   tape

cane   mat   cape

Read the words and name the pictures. Circle the word that names each picture.

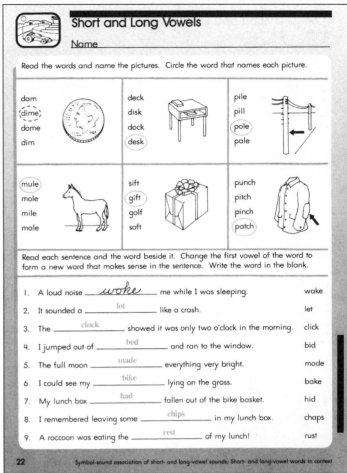

dam	deck	pile
(dime)	disk	pill
dome	dock	(pole)
dim	(desk)	pale

(mule)	sift	punch
mole	(gift)	pitch
mile	golf	pinch
male	soft	(patch)

Read each sentence and the word beside it. Change the first vowel of the word to form a new word that makes sense in the sentence. Write the word in the blank.

1. A loud noise _woke_ me while I was sleeping.   wake
2. It sounded a _lot_ like a crash.   let
3. The _clock_ showed it was only two o'clock in the morning.   click
4. I jumped out of _bed_ and ran to the window.   bid
5. The full moon _made_ everything very bright.   mode
6. I could see my _bike_ lying on the grass.   bake
7. My lunch box _had_ fallen out of the bike basket.   hid
8. I remembered leaving some _chips_ in my lunch box.   chaps
9. A raccoon was eating the _rest_ of my lunch!   rust

In each sentence, complete the unfinished word by writing the missing vowel or vowels. The word you form must make sense in the sentence.

1. Cal and Kate h_o_p_e_d to be in the school play.
2. It was going to be about bold knights and dr_a_gons.
3. They had noticed a sign that t_o_ld about the first practice.
4. They w_e_nt to Miss Blanco's room after school to sign up.
5. There was a h_u_g_e_ crowd of boys and girls with Miss Blanco.
6. "I can f_i_nd something for each of you to do," she said.
7. Miss Blanco had everyone read a p_a_g_e_ from the play book.
8. Then she told everyone to come b_a_ck the next day.
9. The n_e_xt afternoon everyone hurried to Miss Blanco's room.
10. She started by reading the n_a_m_e_s of the queen and the king.
11. Next she read the names of each of the t_e_n knights.
12. Kate was going to be one of th_e_m.
13. Th_e_n she read the names of the three dragons.
14. Cal g_o_t to be a dragon.
15. It would be a l_o_t of fun to put on a play.
16. But it would also t_a_k_e_ a lot of hard work.
17. Kate would have to study her l_i_n_e_s every night.
18. Cal would have to pretend to blow sm_o_k_e_ and fire.
19. Cal and Kate ran all the way h_o_m_e_ to tell the family the news.

Read each sentence and the words beside it. Write the word that makes sense in each sentence.

1. My little sister is wearing blue pants and a _pink_ skirt.   pin / pine / pink
2. After I took a short nap, I felt _fine_.   find / fine / fin
3. Last year my family flew on a jet _plane_ for the first time.   plate / plane / plans
4. We must guess the answer after he gives us a _clue_.   club / clock / clue
5. When Tat runs out of the house, he will _grab_ his backpack.   grass / grab / grape
6. Would you _mind_ carrying these boxes to the closet?   mine / mint / mind
7. When will the _next_ city bus stop at this corner?   next / need / nest
8. His uncle taught him how to _fold_ a flag.   fog / fond / fold
9. Small brown birds are a _common_ sight in our backyard.   common / cot / cold
10. Alma _hugs_ her puppy every time it runs to her.   hugs / huge / hum
11. I was able to fix the bookshelf that I _broke_.   bold / box / broke

Hard and Soft C and G

Name _____

The letters **c** or **g** followed by **e, i,** or **y** usually stand for their soft sounds, as in **cent** and **page.** The letters **c** or **g** followed by any other letters stand for their hard sounds, as in **can** and **wagon.**

cent (soft **c**)   pa**ge** (soft **g**)

Read the words and name the pictures. Draw a line from each word to the picture it names.

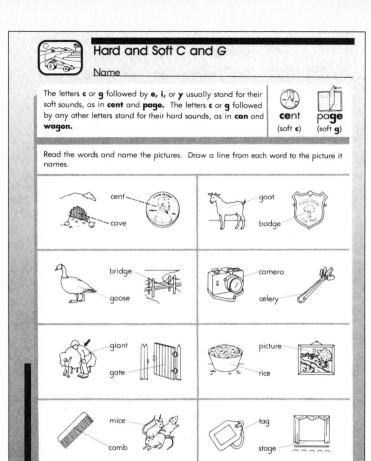

cent
cave

goat
badge

bridge
goose

camera
celery

giant
gate

picture
rice

mice
comb

tag
stage

Hard and Soft C and G

Name _____

Read the sentences. In the blanks below each sentence, write the words that have the soft **c** or **g** sound.

cent (soft **c**)   pa**ge** (soft **g**)

1. My Uncle Antonio gets to wear a shiny badge on his coat.
   badge

2. He works on a big bridge in the middle of the city.
   bridge _____ city _____

3. He is in charge of raising and lowering it when a barge comes by.
   charge _____ barge _____

4. He knows all the police who work nearby.
   police _____

5. He says it's nice to work in a place outdoors.
   nice _____ place _____

Read the sentences. Circle the words in each sentence that have the hard **c** or **g** sound.

1. (Gary) and Angela decided to plant a (garden.)
2. They wanted to raise (corn,) (carrots,) peas, and other vegetables.
3. They thought maybe they (could) (can) some of what they raised.
4. They (began) to (dig) in the dirt and gently put the seeds in.
5. When the work was (completed,) they decided they had done a (good) job.
6. The (gardeners) tried to (guess) how long it would be before their (crops) would (grow.)
7. They didn't want to wait until they (could) eat the vegetables from their (garden.)

Hard and Soft C and G

Name _____

Read each clue. Write **c** or **g** to complete the word that matches the clue.

cent (soft **c**)   pa**ge** (soft **g**)

1. something that can be pinned on a coat or shirt   bad _g_ e
2. a piece of bread   sli _c_ e
3. someone who prepares food in a kitchen   _c_ ook
4. red, blue, green, and yellow   _c_ olors
5. how a dog's tail moves   wa _g_ s
6. something to keep a tiger in   ca _g_ e
7. not noisy   pea _c_ eful
8. something that is usually red and has wheels   wa _g_ on

Read each sentence and the words beside it. Write the word that makes sense in each sentence.

1. Put your horn in its carrying _case_ .   cage / circus / case
2. It's just about time to leave for the ___circus___ .

3. There's a book of directions that tells how to play the ___game___ .   game / page / gave
4. But the book is missing the ___page___ that tells about scoring.

5. Check in the kitchen to see if there is any ___rice___ left.   cup / cent / rice
6. Then please get me a ___cup___ of flour from under the counter.

7. We have two ___goats___ that we milk every day.   giant / goats / gown
8. We put the milk into a ___giant___ can and keep it cool.

REVIEW   Hard and Soft C and G

Name _____

Read the list of words. Notice the sound that **c** or **g** stands for in each word. Then write each word under the correct heading.

given   giant   copper   center
guide   costume   city   stage
forgot   gentle   picnic   fog
fierce   gaze   peace   became
curl   certain   judge   badge

Words may be listed in any order.

Hard **g** as in **wagon**	Soft **g** as in **page**
given	giant
guide	gentle
forgot	judge
gaze	stage
fog	badge

Hard **c** as in **can**	Soft **c** as in **cent**
curl	fierce
costume	certain
copper	city
picnic	peace
became	center

Page 29

Hard and Soft C and G

Name _____

Read each sentence and the words beside it. Write the word that makes sense in each sentence.

1. My family likes to go *Camping* when it is warm.

   camping
   cashing
   circling

2. Some of the best stories I've ever read begin with the words, "_____ Once _____ upon a time."

   Once
   Organ
   Office

3. We need to have seven people to play this _____ game _____.

   game
   germ
   gave

4. My aunt enjoys her job as a _____ judge _____.

   juice
   judge
   jug

5. A giant _____ flag _____ is flying above our city building.

   flag
   face
   fancy

6. The guide knows the way through the dark _____ cave _____.

   cave
   cent
   cape

7. The zoo just built a bigger _____ cage _____ for its tigers.

   came
   cage
   cities

8. Look at the _____ price _____ tag and tell me the jacket's cost.

   price
   prince
   piece

9. After the play was over, the actors left the _____ stage _____.

   stage
   strange
   stack

10. Begin by having partners stand in the _____ center _____ of the room.

    cellar
    center
    circus

11. All of the _____ candles _____ were burning brightly.

    camera
    certain
    candles

Assessment of hard- and soft-c and g words in context

29

Page 30

Reading and Writing Wrap-Up

Name _____

Seeds and Plants

Inside every seed is a tiny plant waiting to grow. What does the little seed need to grow into a plant?

Seeds

Seeds come in many shapes and sizes. Some seeds are round, and some are long and thin. Some seeds are as tiny as grains of sand; others are bigger than golf balls.

Inside every seed is a tiny plant and stored food to help the seed grow. The food part of the seed is much larger than the plant part.

What Makes Seeds Grow?

A seed needs water and heat to grow. Most seeds grow best in the spring when there is a lot of rainfall and the weather is warm. After the seed begins to grow, it is called a seedling. The little seedling needs water, air, sunlight, and food to grow.

The Parts of a Plant

Most plants have roots, stems, leaves, and flowers. The roots hold the plant in the ground and take in water and food from the soil. The stems help water travel up to the leaves and flowers. They also help the plant stand up. The leaves make and store food. The flowers of the plant make seeds for new plants to grow.

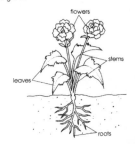

1. List the two things that are found inside every seed. _____ a plant _____ food

2. When does a seed become a seedling? _____

   A seed becomes a seedling after it begins to grow.

30

Application of reading and comprehension skills in a science context

---

Page 31

Name _____

Science

3. List the four most important things a seedling needs to grow into a plant.

   water   air   sunlight   food

4. List the four major parts most plants have.

   roots   stems   leaves   flowers

5. Tell what you think would happen if you planted a seed in a cold, dark basement. Give reasons for your answer.

   Answers may vary but should include the idea that the seed would not grow

   because it would not receive enough heat and light.

   _____

6. Write a story about how a seed becomes a plant. You might decide to write your story in the form of a newspaper story. Or you might pretend to be a seed and write your story as if the seed is telling how it became a plant.

   Answers will vary.

   _____
   _____
   _____
   _____
   _____
   _____
   _____
   _____

Application of comprehension, thinking, and writing skills in a science context

31

Page 32

Two-Letter Blends

Name _____

In some words, two consonants appear together. To say these words, blend the sounds of the two consonants together.

stop   **tw**in
blue   **sq**ueeze
tree

Read the words and name the pictures. Draw a line from each word to the picture it names.

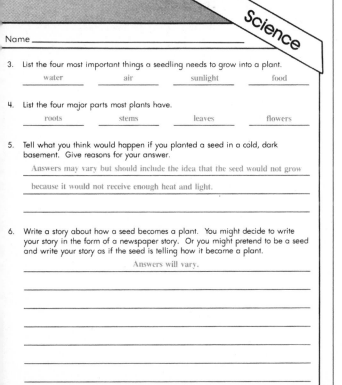
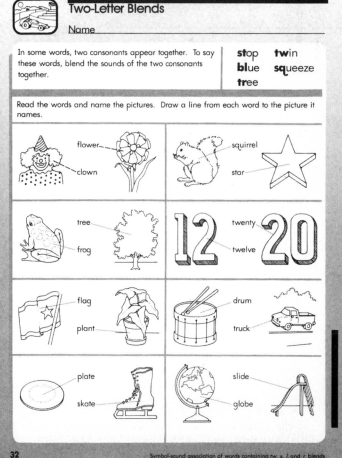

flower
clown
squirrel
star

tree
frog
twenty
twelve

flag
plant
drum
truck

plate
skate
slide
globe

32

Symbol-sound association of words containing tw, s, l, and r blends

---

175

Two-Letter Blends

Name _____

Read each set of sentences and its list of words. Find the word in the list that matches the clue. Write the word next to the clue.

1.	something used on a bed	*blanket*	plant
2.	something fluffy in the sky	cloud	blanket
3.	happy, pleased	glad	fly
4.	to put seeds into the ground	plant	blend
5.	what birds do to stay in the air	fly	squeak
6.	a toy to use in the snow	sled	blue
7.	a sharp noise or cry	squeak	place
8.	the color of a clear sky	blue	glad
9.	grain that has been ground into powder	flour	sled
			cloud
			flour

1.	a small stream	brook	greet
2.	a large bird that is black	crow	crow
3.	doesn't cost any money	free	draw
4.	to make a picture on paper	draw	grab
5.	to say hello	greet	tracks
6.	how much something costs	price	dream
7.	what trains run on	tracks	price
8.	something to catch a mouse in	trap	trap
9.	an idea that may never come true	dream	free
			brook
			tree

Words containing tw, s, l, and r blends   **33**

Two-Letter Blends

Name _____
Words to use: blend, plug, slowly, breeze, twine, twist, grab, crab, spy, sneeze, frown, swim, sting, twig, twenty.

In each sentence, complete the unfinished word by writing **s** or **t**. The word you form must make sense in the sentence.

1. My _t_win brother and I have a lot of fun together.
2. We both like to go roller _s_kating and swimming.
3. In the winter we go _s_ledding down steep slopes.
4. Mom says we get into _t_wice as much trouble together.
5. One time the two of us ate _t_welve cookies.
6. They tasted good, but we didn't _s_leep very well that night.

In each sentence, complete the unfinished word by writing **l** or **r**. The word you form must make sense in the sentence.

1. Some of my friends and I have started a c_l_ub.
2. We meet after school under a big pine t_r_ee.
3. Sometimes all we do is p_l_ay games or tell stories.
4. Other times we go for walks or swing from tree b_r_anches.
5. One time we helped a neighbor cut her g_r_ass and rake it.
6. Tomorrow we are all going to help clean up the p_l_ayground.

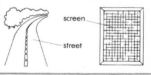
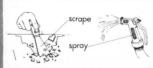

34   Words containing tw, s, l, and r blends in context

REVIEW   ## Two-Letter Blends

Name _____

Read each sentence and the words beside it. Write the word that makes sense in each sentence.

1. This oak tree is already _twenty_ feet tall.   twice / twenty / twig
2. Each of the tree's branches began as just a little _twig_.

3. Let's make a swing out of this _square_ piece of wood.   snap / sting / square
4. We'll also need a strong piece of rope that won't _snap_.

5. Someday this tadpole will grow into a big _frog_.   creek / frog / croak
6. Then it will sit by the _creek_ and catch flies.

7. My aunt and uncle just had a set of _twins_.   twins / twig / twice
8. They say it's _twice_ as much work but a lot more fun.

9. My grandmother has a _brick_ fireplace in her new house.   break / brick / broom
10. She uses a _broom_ to keep the ashes off the rug.

11. A little green _snake_ lives under our back porch.   slide / swim / snake
12. It likes to _slide_ through the grass in the backyard.

13. Last summer we visited another _state_.   state / still / steam
14. I can _still_ remember all the exciting things we saw.

Review of words containing tw, s, l, and r blends in context   **35**

Three-Letter Blends

Name _____
Words to use: sprint, stripe, street, scrub, splinter, scrap, scroll, strain, splatter, strange.

In some words, three consonants appear together. To say these words, blend the sounds of the three consonants together.

spring **spl**it
scream **str**ip

Read the words and look at the pictures. Draw a line from each word to the picture it tells about.

spread
split

string
spring

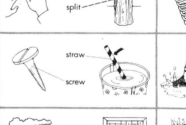

straw
screw

splash
strap

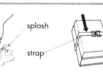

screen
street

stream
scream

scrape
spray

sprain
splinter

36   Symbol-sound association of words containing three-letter blends. spr, scr, spl, str

176

Three-Letter Blends

Name _____

Words to use: scrape, splendid, strike, scratch, strap, spray, sprout, spruce, screwdriver

Read each clue. Write **scr** or **spl** to complete the word that matches the clue.

1. to yell loudly .... _*scr*_ eam
2. to break something into pieces .... _spl_ it
3. something used to fasten boards together .... _scr_ ew
4. to rub hard while washing .... _scr_ ub
5. to scatter water in all directions .... _spl_ ash
6. a very thin piece of wood .... _spl_ inter
7. something used on doors and windows
   to keep bugs out .... _scr_ een
8. a piece of something that is left over .... _scr_ ap

Read each clue. Write **str** or **spr** to complete the word that matches the clue.

1. a person you do not know .... _*str*_ anger
2. to make something longer by pulling .... _str_ etch
3. to lightly cover with tiny drops of water .... _spr_ ay
4. a wide, straight line .... _str_ ipe
5. a small river .... _str_ eam
6. the season that comes after winter .... _spr_ ing
7. how butter is put on bread .... _spr_ ead
8. without any curves or corners .... _str_ aight
9. a road .... _str_ eet

Words containing three-letter blends: spr, scr, spl, str

37

Three-Letter Blends

Name _____

Words to use: scramble, spree, strength, split, straw, spruce, stream, strong, scratch, sprain

In each sentence, complete the unfinished word by writing **spr** or **scr.** The word you form must make sense in the sentence.

1. We clean and _*scr*_ ub everything in our apartment every spring.
2. I gather all the window _scr_ eens and take them outside.
3. I use a hose to _spr_ ay off all the dirt and dust.
4. When they're clean, we fasten the screens to the windows with _scr_ ews.
5. I have to be careful not to _scr_ atch myself while I'm working.
6. I like _spr_ ing better than any other time of year.

In each sentence, complete the unfinished word by writing **spl** or **str.** The word you form must make sense in the sentence.

1. At summer camp, we learned how to build a bridge over a _*str*_ eam.
2. First, we had to _spl_ it some big logs for the bridge.
3. One of the campers got a _spl_ inter in her hand doing this.
4. Then we _str_ etched a rope across the water.
5. It took a lot of _str_ ength to move the logs into place.
6. We made the bridge very _str_ ong so it would last a long time.

38

Words containing three-letter blends in context: spr, scr, spl, str

---

REVIEW

Three-Letter Blends

Name _____

Read each sentence and the words beside it. Write the word that makes sense in each sentence.

1. The batter _*struck*_ the ball so hard that it went over the wall.

   strain / strip / struck

2. I had to _strain_ my eyes to see it.

3. We had to _scrape_ the old paint off the door before we could repaint it.

   screws / scrape / scream

4. Then we put new _screws_ in the corners.

5. Today I got out the hose to _spray_ the flower garden.

   spring / spray / sprained

6. But I tripped over the hose and _sprained_ my arm.

7. When my brother and I swim in the lake, we _splash_ each other.

   split / splash / splinter

8. After swimming, we rest and _split_ a sandwich.

9. I couldn't find a _strap_ to fasten around the broken crate.

   strange / strap / strong

10. I tried to use string, but it wasn't _strong_ enough.

11. I'll need some help repairing the _screen_ door.

    screen / spring / stripe

12. I have to patch some holes, and it needs a new _spring_

13. I got a _splinter_ in my hand when I climbed the tree.

    stray / splinter / scrap

14. I was trying to rescue a _stray_ kitten that climbed up there.

Review of words containing three-letter blends in context: spr, scr, spl, str

39

Ending Blends

Name _____

Words to use: bend, drink, cent, wind, faint, wolf, part, sand, went, dunk, risk, pump, band, plant, help, think, rent, elf, hurt, find, pink, mint, cart, sent, thank

At the end of some words, two consonants appear together. To say these words, blend the sounds of the two consonants together.

last	ba**nk**	wo**lf**
de**sk**	fe**lt**	art
ha**nd**	sta**mp**	gi**ft**

Read the words and look at the pictures. Draw a line from each word to the picture it tells about.

hand — heart

gift — golf

dirt — desk

cent — coast

skirt — skunk

pond — pump

shirt — quilt

cast — sink

40

Symbol-sound association of words containing final blends: st, sk, nd, nk, lt, mp, rt, ft

177

Ending Blends

Name

Read each clue. Write **nd, nk,** or **nt** to complete the word that matches the clue.

1. part of a minute — seco_nd_
2. to put seeds into the ground — pla__nt__
3. to close one eye — wi__nk__
4. a kind of bed — bu__nk__
5. to look for something — hu__nt__
6. a small lake — po__nd__
7. a place to save money — ba__nk__
8. to color a picture with brushes — pai__nt__
9. to turn grain into flour — gri__nd__

Read each clue. Write **lf, lt,** or **rt** to complete the word that matches the clue.

1. to have pain — hu_rt_
2. soil — di__rt__
3. something to put books on — she__lf__
4. an outdoor game played with clubs and a small ball — go__lf__
5. to begin — sta__rt__
6. something used to change the taste of food — sa__lt__
7. a tiny make-believe person — e__lf__
8. a piece of clothing a girl might wear — ski__rt__
9. pumps blood through your body — hea__rt__

Words containing final blends: nd, nk, nt, lf, lt, rt — 41

Ending Blends

Name

In each sentence, complete the unfinished word by writing **sk** or **st**. The word you form must make sense in the sentence.

1. I have a li_st_ of contests I'd like to enter.
2. I enter a new contest ju__st__ about every week.
3. All I ri__sk__ is the price of a stamp.
4. I enter so many that I have a de__sk__ full of entry forms.
5. The fir__st__ contest I entered was run by a radio station.
6. Another one was run by a company that sells breakfa__st__ food.
7. One time I wrote a short song and won a monster ma__sk__.
8. Another time I had to guess how fa__st__ a tiger could run.
9. I guessed carefully, but I lo__st__ that contest.

In each sentence, complete the unfinished word by writing **mp** or **ft**. The word you form must make sense in the sentence.

1. Have you ever floated down a river on a rubber ra_ft_?
2. Where the river is slow, you can just dri__ft__ along.
3. If you fall into the river, your clothing will be da__mp__ all day.
4. Sometimes you can see frogs ju__mp__ from the river bank.
5. The ride gets more exciting where the river is swi__ft__.
6. Then you bu__mp__ into rocks and logs as you race along.
7. At night you can ca__mp__ along the shore.
8. Then you can fall asleep while listening to the so__ft__ river sounds.

42 — Words containing final blends in context: st, sk, mp, ft

---

Ending Blends

Name

Read each sentence and the words beside it. Write the word that makes sense in each sentence.

1. Many birds and animals live in the _forest_. — must / forest / dust
2. You may see their footprints in the _dust_.

3. Yuji's _shirt_ has a rip in the back. — hurt / lift / shirt
4. I think he _hurt_ himself when he fell.

5. I always do my homework at the _desk_ in my bedroom. — ask / desk / mask
6. If I need help, I can _ask_ my mom or dad.

7. We have a large _tank_ of fish in our living room. — tank / honk / pink
8. There are _pink_ stones on the bottom of the tank.

9. When we go camping, we _rent_ everything we need. — rent / tent / spent
10. We get sleeping bags, a stove, and a big _tent_.

11. We lit an oil _lamp_ when the lights went out. — lump / bump / lamp
12. We had to be careful not to _bump_ into it and break it.

13. Someone left a box in the _sand_. — sand / bend / hand
14. Someone had tried to _bend_ the lid.

15. The cans of paint are on the top _shelf_. — yourself / wolf / shelf
16. Be careful not to spill any of them on _yourself_.

Review of words containing final blends in context: st, sk, nd, nk, nt, mp, lf, rt, ft — 43

Blends

Name

Read each set of sentences and its list of words. Write a word from the list that makes sense in each sentence.

1. There is a bicycle _club_ in the town where we live.
2. There were only ten members when the club _started_.
3. Now, almost one hundred people _crowd_ into our meeting room. — speed / pleased / club / strong / started / dreaming / crowd / twelve / practice
4. Sometimes the members _practice_ for bicycle contests.
5. One of these contests tests the rider's _speed_.
6. There were _twelve_ of us who rode in that race last year.
7. These people had very _strong_ legs to pedal quickly.
8. We were _pleased_ that our club took second place in the contest.
9. Now some of those riders are _dreaming_ of a world race.

1. People enjoy saving many _different_ things as a hobby. — sent / think / stamp / drink / left / shelf / different / best / sift
2. My oldest sister has a very large _stamp_ book.
3. She keeps the stamp book on a _shelf_ in her bedroom.
4. My uncle says it is the _best_ book he's ever seen.
5. I _think_ I'd like to save stamps when I get older.
6. I just hope there will still be some good ones _left_.

44 — Assessment of words containing initial and final consonant blends in context

178

Silent Consonants: *KN, WR,* and *SC*

Name _____

In some words, two consonants together stand for one sound. The letters **kn** usually stand for the sound of **n**, as in **kn**ot. The letters **wr** usually stand for the sound of **r**, as in **wr**ite. The letters **sc** sometimes stand for the sound of **s**, as in **sc**issors.

knot
write
scissors

Read the words and name the pictures. Draw a line from each word to the picture it names.

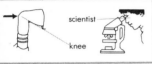
wrist — knife

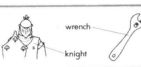
wrench — knight

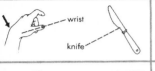
scientist — knee

scissors — wrap

Read each clue and the list of words. Find the word in the list that matches the clue. Write the word next to the clue.

1. to put letters and words on paper __*write*__
2. not right __wrong__
3. to understand a fact __know__
4. to hit a door with the hand __knock__
5. a nice smell __scent__
6. a person who does science experiments in a lab __scientist__

wrong
know
scent
wreck
scissors
write
knight
scientist
knock

45

Silent Consonants: *KN, WR,* and *SC*

Name _____

Read the riddles and the list of answers. Find the answer that matches each riddle. Write the answer next to the riddle.

a doorknob · a square knot · a flowery scent · sewing scissors
knee socks · a butter knife · a pulled muscle · a mountain scene
a pipe wrench · writing paper · wrapping paper · knitting needles

1. You'll be unhappy if you feel me. What am I? __a pulled muscle__
2. I can be used to help fix a leak under a sink. What am I? __a pipe wrench__
3. You use me and send me away. What am I? __writing paper__
4. You can use me to cut thread or cloth. What am I? __sewing scissors__
5. You may see me on a postcard or when you travel. What am I? __a mountain scene__
6. I can help you get from one room to another room. What am I? __a doorknob__
7. You may wear me to keep your feet and legs warm. What am I? __knee socks__
8. I can be made out of rope or string. I am good at holding things together. What am I? __a square knot__
9. I can cover a gift or a package. What am I? __wrapping paper__
10. You might use me when you have a piece of bread. What am I? __a butter knife__
11. You smell me when you walk through a garden. What am I? __a flowery scent__
12. I'll help you make a sweater or a scarf. What am I? __knitting needles__

46

Silent Consonants: *KN, WR,* and *SC*

Name _____

In each sentence, complete the unfinished word by writing **kn**, **wr**, or **sc**. The word you form must make sense in the sentence.

1. Shelly hurt her __wr__ist in the basketball game.
2. The doctor said she had bent it the __wr__ong way.
3. Shelly said her __kn__ee was also sore.
4. She did not __kn__ow how she had hurt it.
5. The doctor __wr__ote some directions on a piece of paper.
6. Then the doctor used __sc__issors to cut a bandage.
7. She showed Shelly how to __wr__ap her wrist and knee.
8. She also showed her how to tie a special __kn__ot.
9. The doctor wanted to make sure Shelly __kn__ew what to do.

1. My family and I stopped to look at the beautiful __sc__ene in the valley.
2. The __sc__ent of wild mountain flowers filled the air.
3. We had taken the __wr__ong road to camp.
4. My older brother said, "I thought I __kn__ew the way."
5. Then Dad said, "If you had __kn__own the right road, we might have missed this beautiful spot."
6. Everyone agreed, and then we got out the sandwiches Dad had __wr__apped for supper.
7. I started to __wr__ite a note on the map about this "wrong road."
8. On the map at this very spot, I saw the words "__sc__enic lookout."

47

Silent Consonants: *CK, MB, GN,* and *GH*

Name _____

In some words, two consonants together stand for one sound. The letters **ck** usually stand for the sound of **k**, as in **du**ck. The letters **mb** usually stand for the sound of **m**, as in **lamb**. The letters **gn** usually stand for the sound of **n**, as in **sign**. The letters **gh** are usually silent, as in **night**.

du**ck** · si**gn**
la**mb** · ni**ght**

Read the words and look at the pictures. Circle the word that tells about each picture.

dump / (duck) / luck / lump	limb / (lamb) / lamp / limp	flight / sight / (night) / tight
fight / (light) / might / right	crash / trash / (track) / crack	dumb / thump / dump / (thumb)
(comb) / crumb / chest / chick	dock / deck / (check) / clock	sick / (sign) / sigh / sock
crack / crown / combs / (crumbs)	(back) / brick / bright / bake	sight / flight / right / (knight)

48

179

In each sentence, complete the unfinished word by writing **ck** or **mb.** The word you form must make sense in the sentence.

1. Our family drove to my aunt's farm in our pickup tru___ck___.

2. Mom said that Aunt Ella had some baby pigs and a newborn la___mb___.

3. She also had a swing hanging from a tree li___mb___.

4. The pigs were kept in a building in ba___ck___ of the barn.

5. It was funny to watch the lamb su___ck___ milk from a bottle.

6. We remembered to lo___ck___ the barn when we were finished.

7. I almost pinched my thu___mb___ when I locked the door.

8. We hid the key under a ro___ck___ before we left.

In each sentence, complete the unfinished word by writing **ck, mb, gn,** or **gh.** The word you form must make sense in the sentence.

1. Bill was making a si___gn___ for the bird house.

2. The new house was going to hang from the li___mb___ of the oak tree.

3. Bill had painted the house with bri___gh___t yellow paint.

4. He wanted the birds to be able to find the house at ni___gh___t.

5. Bill also had painted a flower desi___gn___ on the front of the house.

6. Bill hoped the large birds wouldn't pe___ck___ at the wood.

7. He said that would wre___ck___ the house.

8. When Bill was finished, he put cru___mb___s of bread in a small dish for the house's first visitors.

Read each sentence and the words beside it. Write the word that makes sense in each sentence.

1. I could find only one blue ___sock___ this morning. — luck / sock / neck

2. Manny kept his ___comb___ in his pocket. — comb / lamb / crumb

3. We watched the bird ___peck___ at the small piece of bread. — pest / part / peck

4. My ___flight___ in the small airplane was very smooth. — bright / flight / tight

5. Please ___sign___ your name at the bottom of the letter. — sign / design / assign

6. Our neighbor usually raises a ___lamb___ each spring. — comb / lamb / thumb

7. The house was a ___wreck___ after the bad storm. — wrap / wrist / wreck

8. The brave ___knight___ fought the terrible dragon. — knight / known / knock

9. Troy ___might___ visit us next month. — might / tight / night

10. The giraffe has the longest ___neck___ of any animal. — check / neck / tuck

---

Read the list of words below. Then read the sentences that follow. Write a word from the list that makes sense in each sentence.

knife	scissors	sign	lambs
wrench	light	crumbs	track
check	knot	written	delighted

1. Please ___check___ each answer carefully before you hand in your paper.

2. We left some bread ___crumbs___ on the lawn for the birds.

3. I was ___delighted___ with the gift you sent.

4. The barber used a pair of ___scissors___ and a comb to cut my hair.

5. A spoon and ___knife___ go on the right side of the plate.

6. This story was ___written___ by a woman who lived long ago.

7. We wrote a colorful ___sign___ that said "Happy Birthday."

8. Sally used a ___wrench___ to tighten the pipe.

9. Don't forget to turn off the ___light___ before you leave.

10. Two of our ___lambs___ have black, fuzzy faces.

11. Railroad trains don't use this ___track___ anymore.

12. You'll need a tighter ___knot___ to tie the ribbon on the package.

Read each sentence and the words beside it. Write the word that makes sense in each sentence.

1. My grandmother ___knitted___ the sweater for my birthday. — known / knitted / knew

2. This blanket has a beautiful ___design___ on it. — design / signing / assigned

3. I think my answer to the question was ___wrong___. — wrist / wrong / wring

4. Last ___night's___ storm blew a lot of sticks into our yard. — night's / light's / fight's

5. Please hold your ___thumb___ on this ribbon while I tie it. — crumb / thumb / number

6. Grandfather likes to ___snack___ on raw vegetables. — snack / smack / stack

7. A well-known ___scientist___ will teach us about the planets. — scene / scientist / sciences

8. The three shirts I packed in the trunk are ___wrinkled___. — wreck / wrinkled / wrapping

9. We saw beautiful ___scenery___ when we were in Maine. — scenery / sciences / scent

10. Our apartment building is the ___highest___ one in the city. — highest / tighter / brightly

11. We will watch the workers build a new ___brick___ wall. — chick / brick / sticker

In some words, two vowels together stand for one vowel sound. The letters **ay** and **ai** usually stand for the long-**a** sound, as in **hay** and **train.** The letters **ei** sometimes stand for the long-**a** sound, as in **eight.**

h**ay**   **ei**ght
tr**ai**n

Read the words and name the pictures. Draw a line from each word to the picture it names.

— sprain

spray —

tray

— trail

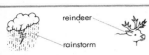

reindeer

rainstorm

sail

sleigh

Read each clue and the list of words. Find the word in the list that matches the clue. Write the word next to the clue.

1. a color ___ *gray*
2. a number ___ eighty
3. a path through the woods ___ trail
4. someone in charge of a city ___ mayor
5. water that falls from clouds ___ rain
6. blood runs through these ___ veins
7. to lift up something ___ raise
8. perhaps ___ maybe

trail
mayor
pay
veins
eighty
say
maybe
raise
rain
pail
gray

Read each set of sentences and its list of words. Write a word from the list that makes sense in each sentence.

1. Last summer we took a ___ *train* ___ ride on our vacation.
2. It took two ___ days ___ from beginning to end.
3. We had a little room where we ___ stayed ___ on the train.
4. The room had a closet and drawers where we could put our clothes ___ away ___
5. I couldn't ___ wait ___ to have supper in the dining car.
6. One of the train cars was used to carry freight and ___ mail ___
7. Riding on a train is a great ___ way ___ to travel.

sail
wait
mail
way
sleigh
train
stayed
playing
days
away

1. My brother and I lift ___ weights ___ to exercise our bodies.
2. In one exercise we ___ raise ___ the weights over our heads.
3. My brother can lift ___ eighty ___ pounds with just one arm.
4. Weight lifting helps your heart to pump blood through your ___ veins ___
5. If we try to lift too much, we get ___ pains ___
6. Then we have to ___ wait ___ a while before exercising again.
7. Someday I hope I can lift as much as I ___ weigh ___

veins
eighty
trail
wait
weights
sleigh
pains
rain
weigh
raise

Read the list of words below. Then read the sentences that follow. Write a word from the list that makes sense in each sentence.

train	clay	weight	weighed
may	rained	sleigh	afraid
eight	trail	spray	playground

1. When I was very young, I was ___ *afraid* ___ of the dark.
2. The fire fighters used four hoses to ___ spray ___ water on the fire.
3. I took my brother to the ___ playground ___, where there were new swings and a sliding board.
4. I think it would be fun to take a ___ sleigh ___ ride through the snow.
5. We can follow this ___ trail ___ made by the deer through the forest.
6. In some parts of the desert, it hasn't ___ rained ___ for three years.
7. I ___ weighed ___ all the fish I caught.
8. My brother's dog had ___ eight ___ puppies yesterday.
9. The puppet's head is made from hardened ___ clay ___
10. We ___ may ___ travel to another state next summer.
11. When I go to the doctor, she always checks my ___ weight ___
12. We'll have to wait at the crossing until the ___ train ___ goes by.

In some words, two vowels together stand for one vowel sound. The letters **ee** usually stand for the long-**e** sound, as in **bee.** The letters **ea** can stand for the long-**e** sound, as in **bean,** or the short-**e** sound, as in **bread.** The letters **oa** and **ow** often stand for the long-**o** sound, as in **coat** and **window.**

b**ee**   c**oa**t
b**ea**n   wind**ow**
br**ea**d

Read the words and name the pictures. Draw a line from each word to the picture it names.

soap

— sheep

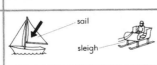

boat

bowl

— bread

beach —

beetle

beaver

window

wheel

seeds

seal

toast

— toad

road

row

Vowel Pairs: *EE, EA, OA,* and *OW*

Name _____

Read each set of sentences and its list of words. Write a word from the list that makes sense in each sentence.

1. We like to walk on the _____*beach*_____ in the summer.
2. We also like to play in the sand or swim in the _____*sea*_____.
3. The water gets very _____*deep*_____ when waves come in.
4. Sometimes, pieces of _____*seaweed*_____ wash up onto the sand.
5. Usually we take a picnic lunch along to _____*eat*_____.
6. We also bring a large jug of iced _____*tea*_____ to drink.
7. We all _____*agree*_____ that we have a good time at the beach.

please
seaweed
agree
beach
peace
eat
deep
free
sea
tea

---

1. My grandfather will be sixty years old _____*tomorrow*_____.
2. Our whole family will _____*show*_____ up at our house for dinner.
3. My sister is cooking a giant _____*roast*_____ to feed everyone.
4. My aunt and uncle are bringing four _____*bowls*_____ of vegetables.
5. My brother has baked a _____*loaf*_____ of special bread.
6. I get to look out the _____*window*_____ to watch for Grandfather.
7. I'll be able to see him when he drives down our _____*road*_____.

bowls
road
bow
window
tomorrow
boat
roast
show
loaf
soap

Vowel Pairs: *EE, EA, OA,* and *OW*

Name _____

Read the sentences. Circle the key word that has the sound of **ea** heard in the underlined word.

1. Our basketball <u>team</u> won all of its games this year.   (bean) bread
2. I had a <u>dream</u> about my summer vacation.   (bean) bread
3. I need a needle and <u>thread</u> to put this button on.   bean (bread)
4. Please <u>spread</u> butter on each slice of bread.   bean (bread)
5. Bob and Joyce spent some time <u>cleaning</u> their messy rooms.   (bean) bread
6. The painting is so good, you can almost count the <u>feathers</u> on the duck.   bean (bread)

Read each sentence and words beside it. Write the word that makes sense in the sentence.

1. Where is the _____*soap*_____ to clean the dishes?
2. I put it on the shelf under the kitchen _____*windows*_____.

soap
windows
sleep

3. Our _____*teacher*_____ didn't give us any homework tonight.
4. He said we _____*needed*_____ to have an evening off.

needed
team
teacher

5. See if this purple hat fits your _____*head*_____.
6. Then try on that _____*coat*_____ with the yellow trim.

heel
coat
head

Vowel Pairs: *OO, AU, AW,* and *EW*

Name _____

In some words, two vowels together stand for one sound. The letters **oo** can stand for the sound you hear in the middle of **moon** or **book.** The letters **au** and **aw** usually stand for the sound you hear in **auto** and **saw.** The letters **ew** usually stand for the sound you hear in the middle of **news.**

m**oo**n   **au**to
b**oo**k   s**aw**
n**ew**s

Read the words and look at the pictures. Write each word below the picture it tells about.

claw   foot   broom
balloon   jewel   launch
screw   jaw   hook

jaw

hook

jewel

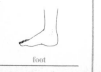
balloon

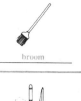
claw

broom

foot

screw

launch

Vowel Pairs: *OO, AU, AW,* and *EW*

Words to use: boot, broom, foot, haul, caught, crawl, claw, drew

Name _____

Read each clue. Write **oo** or **au** to complete the word that matches the clue.

1. an animal that has a pouch   kangar_*oo*
2. a building where you go to learn   sch_*oo*_l
3. to send a rocket into space   l_*au*_nch
4. what people eat   f_*oo*_d
5. a person who prepares food   c_*oo*_k
6. where you can swim   p_*oo*_l
7. the kind of hair a sheep has   w_*oo*_l
8. to carry or to pull   h_*au*_l
9. another word for car   _*au*_to

Read each clue. Write **aw** or **ew** to complete the word beside it to match the clue.

1. how a baby gets around   cr_*aw*_ls
2. the feet of dogs and cats   p_*aw*_s
3. a thick soup with meat in it   st_*ew*
4. not old   n_*ew*
5. something to drink through   str_*aw*
6. the time of day when the sun rises   d_*aw*_n
7. a group of people who work on a ship   cr_*ew*
8. not very many   f_*ew*
9. a cutting tool   s_*aw*

Vowel Pairs: OO, AU, AW, and EW

Name

Read each sentence and the words beside it. Write the word that makes sense in the sentence.

1. Please get the dustpan and ___broom___, and help me clean this mess.
   - too
   - broom
   - noon

2. I'm going to ___draw___ a picture of this pretty flower.
   - claw
   - saw
   - draw

3. Gina and I ___knew___ each other in second grade.
   - dew
   - few
   - knew

4. Put up your ___hood___ before going outside in the snow.
   - hood
   - look
   - good

5. One of our best players ___caught___ the ball to win the game.
   - auto
   - caught
   - because

6. Which of these ___tools___ will you need to do the repair work?
   - tools
   - cool
   - roof

7. We'll have to stand ___because___ there aren't enough chairs.
   - taught
   - auto
   - because

8. We built our house with ___wood___ from this forest.
   - look
   - wood
   - good

9. Very ___few___ people showed up for the meeting.
   - few
   - knew
   - dew

10. A ___hawk___ flew high above our heads.
    - hawk
    - dawn
    - jaw

Vowel Pairs

Name

Read the list of words below. Then read the sentences that follow. Write a word from the list that makes sense in each sentence.

balloon	spread	below	books	caught
paw	gray	wheel	sleighs	news
toad	teaching	maid	stream	bloom

1. Ms. Holly has been ___teaching___ us about Mexico.
2. Our dog can open the screen door with her ___paw___.
3. Do these flowers ___bloom___ early in the summer?
4. My sister has a summer job as a hotel ___maid___.
5. One ___wheel___ of my bicycle has a very noisy squeak.
6. Did you know that a brown ___toad___ lives in our flower garden?
7. Mom and Dad like to listen to the ___news___ on television.
8. This little ___stream___ looks like a good place to go fishing.
9. The sky got dark and very ___gray___ just before the storm.
10. My shirt got ripped when I ___caught___ it on a nail.
11. People used to travel in ___sleighs___ in the wintertime.
12. The library has more ___books___ than I could ever read.
13. We put the bowl in the cabinet ___below___ the sink.
14. Use this knife to ___spread___ the peanut butter on the bread.
15. Have you ever had a ride in a hot-air ___balloon___?

Vowel Pairs: IE

Name

In some words, two vowels together stand for one vowel sound. In the word **tie,** the letters **ie** stand for the long-i sound. In the word **shield,** the letters **ie** stand for the long-e sound.

tie   shield

Read the list of words. Notice the sound that **ie** stands for in each word. Then write each word under the correct heading.

died	cries	field	duties
movie	piece	untie	relief
berries	chief	believe	dried
lie	pie	skies	cities
tried	thief	flies	fried

Order of words may vary.

Long **i** as in **tie**	Long **e** as in **shield**
died	movie
lie	berries
tried	piece
cries	chief
pie	thief
untie	field
skies	believe
flies	duties
dried	relief
fried	cities

Vowel Pairs: IE

Name

Read each clue and the list of words. Find the word in the list that matches the clue. Write the word next to the clue.

1. a kind of dog ___collie___
2. something a knight used to protect himself ___shield___
3. to join pieces of rope or string together ___tie___
4. small flying insects ___flies___
5. very large towns ___cities___
6. something to eat ___pie___
7. an open area of land ___field___
8. a person who steals ___thief___

- dried
- field
- shield
- chief
- collie
- pie
- thief
- piece
- cities
- tie
- flies

Read the sentences. In the blank beside each sentence, write the word that has the letters **ie.** Then circle the key word that has the sound of **ie** heard in the word you wrote.

1. Have you ever eaten fried grasshoppers? ___fried___   (tie) shield
2. Would you like dried apples or bananas? ___dried___   (tie) shield
3. Do you think you'd like berries and honey? ___berries___   tie (shield)
4. These are some of the unusual foods people have tried.
   ___tried___   (tie) shield
5. Some cities have stores that sell unusual foods.
   ___cities___   tie (shield)
6. Just remember to start with a small piece of any food that's new to you. ___piece___   tie (shield)

Vowel Pairs: IE

Name _____

Read each sentence and the words beside it. Write the word that makes sense in each sentence.

1. I had **berries** on my pancakes this morning.
2. They grow wild in the _____field_____ behind our house.

shield
field
berries

3. My uncle ____flies____ a big jet airplane.
4. Sometimes he takes ____supplies____ to other countries.

flies
dried
supplies

5. Do you need any help trying to ____untie____ that rope?
6. We ____tried____ to untie it yesterday.

thief
untie
tried

7. The tribe picks the wisest person to be its ____chief____
8. They ____believe____ that person will guide them well.

believe
chief
collie

9. We had blueberry ____pie____ for dinner today.
10. Dad spilled some of it on his best ____tie____

pie
dried
tie

11. We watched a very sad ____movie____ last night.
12. At the end, the hero got sick and ____died____

died
movie
flies

13. I helped Ned cut some potatoes into thin ____pieces____
14. Then we ____fried____ them until they were crisp.

pieces
fried
movie

15. My ____nieces____ helped me bake turnovers.
16. We used the ____cherries____ that we had bought and frozen last summer.

duties
cherries
nieces

Vowel Pairs: OU

Name _____

In some words, two vowels together stand for one vowel sound. The letters **ou** can stand for the vowel sounds you hear in **soup**, **touch**, **doughnut**, and **should**.

s**ou**p   d**ou**ghnut
t**ou**ch   sh**ou**ld

Read the words and look at the pictures. Circle the word that tells about each picture.

(boulder) route shoulder bought	trouble through (touchdown) tough	soul sound should (soup)
double touch (dough) though	should (shoulder) south soup	(doughnut) dough through though

Read each clue and the list of words. Find the word in the list that matches the clue. Write the word next to the clue.

1. yourself _____you_____
2. very well-known ____famous____
3. uneven; not smooth ____rough____
4. something bread is made from ____dough____
5. a very large rock ____boulder____
6. a spoon is used to eat this ____soup____
7. where the arm joins the body ____shoulder____
8. eager to find out about things ____curious____

rough
dough
would
you
famous
through
curious
soup
shoulder
youth
boulder

Vowel Pairs: OU

Name _____

Read the list of words. Notice the sound that **ou** stands for in each word. Then write each word under the correct heading.

though	curious	although	famous	would
rough	you	boulder	country	through
youth	could	group	shoulder	

Words may be listed in any order.

ou as in doughnut	ou as in soup	ou as in touch
though	youth	rough
although	you	curious
boulder	group	famous
shoulder	through	country

ou as in should
could
would

Read each clue. Find the word in the list that matches the clue. Write the word next to the clue.

1. just the right amount **enough**
2. not easy to cut or chew ____tough____
3. not old ____young____
4. small cakes shaped like rings ____doughnuts____
5. three or more persons or things ____group____
6. a word that means "ought to" ____should____

group
young
trouble
tough
soup
should
shoulder
doughnuts
enough

Vowel Pairs: OU

Name _____

Read each sentence and the words beside it. Write the word that makes sense in each sentence.

1. Dad and I were going to make homemade **doughnuts**
2. First I had to be sure we had ____enough____ flour.
3. Then Dad said we ____could____ begin working.

enough
doughnuts
could

4. A huge ____group____ of people showed up for our garage sale.
5. Many of them were just ____curious____ about the sale.
6. I knew many of the people ____would____ not buy anything.

group
would
curious

7. We saw a baby camel that is ____younger____ than my little sister.
8. The baby camel seemed ____nervous____ and hid behind its mother.
9. Not even the zookeeper could ____touch____ it.

younger
touch
nervous

10. Can ____you____ help me carry this heavy log?
11. It will be easier if you can get it on your ____shoulder____
12. Be careful not to hurt your hand on the ____rough____ bark.

shoulder
you
rough

13. I'm making something to eat I think you ____should____ like.
14. We have to roll this ____dough____ into little balls.
15. Then we will put them into this special ____soup____

soup
dough
should

184

Vowel Pairs

Name _____

Read each sentence and the words shown below the blank. Write the word that makes sense in each sentence.

1. Carmen and Juan are newspaper carriers with a ___*tough*___ job.
   (tough, though)

2. At first, the papers came ___tied___ in a big bundle.
   (tied, tried)

3. The children ___would___ untie the papers and put them into the bag.
   (would, young)

4. Now the bundle comes with ___enough___ plastic bags for each paper.
   (although, enough)

5. The papers stay dry even if they ___lie___ in a puddle.
   (fried, lie)

6. Carmen and Juan have always ___tried___ to do a good job.
   (tried, dried)

7. They ___should___ win an award.
   (should, shoulder)

---

1. On Saturdays, I go to a cooking class for ___young___ people.
   (through, young)

2. Last week we learned to bake apple ___pie___.
   (pie, berries)

3. Two weeks ago we made a big pot of vegetable ___soup___.
   (should, soup)

4. Perhaps you ___would___ like to join the class, too.
   (would, curious)

5. Next week our ___group___ is planning to make pizza.
   (ground, group)

Two Sounds of Y

Name _____

When **y** comes at the end of a word that has no other vowel, the **y** usually stands for the long-**i** sound. When **y** comes at the end of a word that has another vowel, the **y** usually stands for the long-**e** sound.

fl**y**   pon**y**

Read the list of words. Notice the sound that **y** stands for in each word. Write the words that have the long-**i** sound under the word **fly**. Write the words that have the long-**e** sound under the word **pony**.

sky	twenty	city	fry
sticky	fly	any	pry
easy	sly	try	many
happy	berry	carry	why
by	very	cry	dry

Order of words may vary.

long **i** as in **fly**	long **e** as in **pony**
sky	sticky
by	easy
fly	happy
sly	twenty
try	berry
cry	very
fry	city
pry	any
why	carry
dry	many

Two Sounds of Y

Name _____

Read each clue and the list of words. Find the word in the list that matches the clue. Write the word next to the clue.

1. a green vegetable	*celery*	celery
2. a store that sells food	grocery	slowly
3. an insect with wings	fly	grocery
4. not wet	dry	carry
5. afraid to talk to people	shy	dry
6. not ill	healthy	shy
		my
		fly
		healthy

Read the list of words below. Then read the sentences that follow. Write the word from the list that makes sense in each sentence.

why	very	firefly	snowy
my	carry	Try	easy

1. Did you ever catch a ___*firefly*___ in a glass jar?

2. First, punch some ___very___ small holes in the lid.

3. Then ___carry___ the jar outside in the evening.

4. It will be ___easy___ to see the fireflies when they flash.

5. ___Try___ to scoop one out of the grass with the jar.

6. Then you can try to guess ___why___ they flash their lights.

Two Sounds of Y

Name _____

Read each sentence. Circle the key word that has the sound of **y** heard in the underlined word.

1. I just finished writing a <u>scary</u> story.	fly	(pony)
2. I thought about it a lot before I wrote <u>any</u> words.	fly	(pony)
3. I decided I wanted the story to have a <u>happy</u> ending.	fly	(pony)
4. When I was <u>ready</u> to write, I sat down at my desk.	fly	(pony)
5. The first time I wrote the story, I wrote it too <u>quickly</u>.	fly	(pony)
6. Mom said I should change some parts and <u>try</u> again.	(fly)	pony
7. I wrote the whole <u>story</u> two more times.	fly	(pony)
8. Each time I wrote it, <u>my</u> story got better.	(fly)	pony
9. One <u>tricky</u> part was hard to write.	fly	(pony)
10. The people had to fight a dragon that flew through the <u>sky</u>.	(fly)	pony

1. My birthday is in the month of <u>February</u>.	fly	(pony)
2. My friend <u>Danny</u> has his birthday in June.	fly	(pony)
3. It's usually <u>icy</u> when I have my birthday.	fly	(pony)
4. But it's always <u>very</u> hot for my friend's birthday.	fly	(pony)
5. <u>Why</u> couldn't he and I trade for one year?	(fly)	pony
6. Then he could get gifts for cold, <u>snowy</u> days.	fly	(pony)
7. <u>My</u> gift could be a great big kite to fly.	(fly)	pony
8. I wonder if he would like to <u>try</u> my idea?	(fly)	pony

Read each sentence and the words beside it. Write the word that makes sense in each sentence.

1. This is the biggest pine _tree_ I have ever seen.

2. I wonder why it is growing in the middle of this _field_.

field
tree
bead

3. The team members are having _soup_ and sandwiches for lunch.

4. I hope there are enough _spoons_ for everyone.

soup
should
spoons

5. Last night we had to _clean_ the basement.

6. I bumped my _head_ on an old pipe.

head
clean
scream

7. Bananas don't _grow_ well in this country.

8. They used to be sent here on large _boats_.

boats
snow
grow

9. It _rained_ all day long yesterday.

10. Our _eight_ ducks had a great time at the pond.

play
rained
eight

11. My grandfather _taught_ me how to use his tools safely.

12. He said that I can't use the power _saw_ until I'm older.

saw
taught
claw

13. The weather was very _dry_ last summer.

14. Everything in our garden grew very _slowly_.

dry
slowly
heavy

15. My little cousin _drew_ that picture with her new crayons.

16. It shows a horse eating _hay_ in a barn.

drew
took
hay

Your Bones

Have you ever broken a bone in your body? If you have, you know how important healthy bones are to a healthy body.

Bones are made of living cells. Blood runs through tiny vessels in your bones and supplies your bones with food to help them grow. Bones also have nerves in them. Nerves are what cause feeling. When you break a bone, the nerves in the bone make you feel pain.

Your bones also protect parts of your body. Your ribs protect your heart and lungs. The bones in your back protect many nerves that run through them.

Your bones are a frame that helps hold up your body. Your muscles are connected to your bones. Between your bones are joints so you can bend. Your bones, muscles, and joints work together. They help you walk, run, swim, roller skate, ride a bicycle, and do many other things.

A. Name the three parts of your body that work together to help you move.

bones   _muscles_   _joints_

B. What does blood do for your bones?

Blood supplies your bones with food to help them grow.

Health

Name _____

C. Check each group of words that describes a job your bones do.

_____ feed your body   _____ help you sleep

_✓_ protect parts of your body   _✓_ support your body

D. Finish each sentence with the correct word or words.

1. Bones are made of _living cells_.

2. A broken bone hurts because of the _nerves_ inside it.

E. Draw a line from each word on the left to the word or words on the right that have the same meaning.

protect ——— keep safe
support ⟋ joined
connected ⟋ hold up

F. If you broke a rib, what other part of your body might be hurt? _lungs or heart_

G. Imagine that you have broken a bone in your left arm. Tell why it hurts. Explain how you would have to change your way of doing certain things because of your broken bone.

Answers will vary.

_____

_____

_____

_____

Two consonants together can stand for one sound. Some consonants that stand for one sound are **sh, th,** and **wh.** At the beginnings of some words, three consonants together stand for special sounds, as in **three** and **shrug.**

shoe	**thr**ee
thin	**shr**ug
wheel	

Name the pictures. Write the letters that stand for the beginning sound of each picture name.

thr one	_wh_ istle	30 ___ th ___ irty
shr ug	_sh_ eep	_thr_ ead

Read each clue. Write **sh, th, wh, thr,** or **shr** to complete the word that matches the clue.

1. not fat   _th_ in

2. to get smaller   _shr_ ink

3. to talk very quietly _wh_ isper

4. you swallow with this _thr_ oat

5. a place for books   _sh_ elf

6. what you do with your mind _th_ ink

7. a tool used for digging _sh_ ovel

8. a bicycle has two of them _wh_ eels

186

Ending Consonant Pairs

Name _____

Two or three consonants together can stand for one sound. Some consonants that stand for one sound are **sh, th,** and **ng.**

wi**sh**   ri**ng**
wi**th**

Name the pictures. Write the letters that stand for the ending sound of each picture name.

tee **th**

fi **sh**

bru **sh**

ri **ng**

mou **th**

swi **ng**

Read each clue. Write **sh, th,** or **ng** to complete the word that matches the clue.

1. something to put food on — di**sh**
2. a loud noise — ba**ng**
3. what a shirt is made of — clo**th**
4. a trail — pa**th**
5. how a bee can hurt you — sti**ng**
6. able to lift heavy things — stro**ng**
7. unwanted things that are thrown away — tra**sh**
8. not stale — fre**sh**

Consonant Pairs

Name _____

Read each sentence and the list of words. Write the word from the list that makes sense in each sentence.

1. My dad owns a bicycle repair *shop* .
2. Sometimes I get to help _____ *with* _____ some of the work.
3. I use a _____ *brush* _____ to clean off the workbench.
4. One time Dad let me oil all the squeaky bicycle _____ *wheels* _____
5. There were no noisy bicycles when I was _____ *through* _____ working.
6. One time I made a mistake and put a pair of handlebars on _____ *wrong* _____
7. They looked really funny, but I was able to fix _____ *them* _____ .

| path |
| with |
| through |
| wrong |
| wish |
| brush |
| them |
| flight |
| wheels |
| shop |

Read the list of words below. Then read the paragraph that follows. Write the word from the list that makes sense in each sentence.

three	health	spring	shrugged
thread	shrubs	wishes	pushed
shovel	with	them	which

We planted new *shrubs* around our house yesterday. We placed _____ *three* _____ small ones on each side of the front door. I used a _____ *shovel* _____ to dig the holes. We decided _____ *which* _____ shrub should go into each hole. Then, using a hoe, Mom _____ *pushed* _____ dirt around the trunk of each shrub. I watered each one _____ *with* _____ the garden hose. Then we gave _____ *them* _____ all some special plant food. We'll give them more plant food in the _____ *spring* _____ . When we were done, I _____ *shrugged* _____ my shoulders and said, "What do we do now?"

Consonant Pairs

Name _____

Two or three consonants together can stand for one sound. The letters **ch** and **tch** usually stand for the sound you hear at the beginning of **chair** and the end of **catch.** The letters **ch** sometimes stand for the sound of **k,** as in **chemist.** The letters **ch** can also stand for the sound of **sh,** as in **chef.**

chair   **ch**emist
ca**tch**   **ch**ef

Read the key word shown at the left of each sentence. Then read the sentence. Circle the word in the sentence that has the same sound of **ch** as the key word.

chair   1. Look at the (chart) that shows the parts of the new machine.

catch   2. Yoko and Cheryl stayed up late to (watch) a scary movie on television.

chef   3. Can you teach me how to (parachute) from an airplane?

chemist   4. I ate too much, and now my (stomach) hurts.

chair   5. The chef served us a plate of (cheese) and fruit.

chef   6. Could you teach me how to use this new (machine)?

catch   7. The chemist lit the (match) to heat the oil.

chemist   8. Chad and I have parts singing in the (chorus) for our next music show.

Consonant Pairs

Name _____

Read each clue and the list of words. Find the word in the list that matches the clue. Write the word next to the clue.

1. something used to light a fire — *match*
2. something that tells the time — *watch*
3. the part of the face beside your nose and mouth — *cheek*
4. a person who prepares food — *chef*
5. a pain — *ache*
6. a meal that is eaten at noon — *lunch*
7. a large box or trunk — *chest*
8. a farm on which sheep, cattle, or horses are raised — *ranch*
9. to look or hunt for something — *search*

| chain |
| lunch |
| match |
| chef |
| ranch |
| search |
| ache |
| cheek |
| chemist |
| watch |
| chest |
| latch |

Read the sentences and the word choices. Circle the word that makes sense in each sentence.

1. My uncle works in a place in which wooden (benches, each) are made.
2. When he started working, his job was to clean up the wood (chips, chef).
3. That is quite a (chose, chore) in a big place.
4. Now he has a job as a (chose, mechanic).
5. He repairs any of the (catch, machines) that break down.
6. Sometimes he has to (watch, chorus) a machine very carefully.
7. Then he can find out (couch, which) part isn't working.
8. One time a machine kept making (aches, scratches) on the benches.
9. Someone had left a (cheese, each) sandwich inside it.

Page 81

Words to use: chorus, chalk, scratch, chase, match, chat, ache, chef, chore, search

Read the sentences. Circle **yes** or **no** to tell whether the letters **ch** and **tch** in the underlined words stand for the same sound.

1. Isn't it your turn to <u>choose</u> where we go for <u>lunch</u>? (yes) no

2. I sunburned my <u>stomach</u> while I was at the <u>beach</u> yesterday. yes (no)

3. This <u>machine</u> slices <u>peaches</u> and puts them into cans. yes (no)

4. I had to <u>watch</u> my baby sister while Dad fixed <u>lunch</u>. (yes) no

5. We used to raise <u>chickens</u> when we lived on a <u>ranch</u>. (yes) no

6. <u>Which</u> movie would you and <u>Chris</u> like to watch tonight? yes (no)

7. We have only one <u>match</u> left to light the <u>torch</u>. (yes) no

8. The <u>mechanic</u> said he could <u>change</u> the tires on our car. yes (no)

9. The <u>coach</u> was <u>cheering</u> louder than anyone else for the team. (yes) no

10. How <u>much</u> will a new <u>couch</u> and chair cost? (yes) no

11. We can <u>chop</u> the <u>branches</u> off this dead <u>birch</u> tree. (yes) no

12. The <u>chef</u> used just a <u>pinch</u> of salt in this soup. yes (no)

13. I was trying to <u>catch</u> <u>each</u> <u>cherry</u> that fell from the tree. (yes) no

Page 82

Two consonants together can stand for one sound. The letters **gh** sometimes stand for the sound of **f**, as in **laugh**. The letters **ph** usually stand for the sound of **f**, as in **elephant**.

lau**gh**
ele**ph**ant

Read the words and look at the pictures. Write each word below the picture it tells about.

cough elephant telephone photo trophy laugh

elephant

laugh

telephone

trophy

photo

cough

Read each clue and the list of words. Find the word in the list that matches the clue. Write the word next to the clue.

1. a picture taken with a camera _photo_
2. a very large animal _elephant_
3. what you do when something is funny _laugh_
4. a prize for winning a contest _trophy_
5. not easy to cut or break _tough_
6. not smooth _rough_

elephant
photo
enough
laugh
telephone
rough
cough
trophy
tough

Page 83

Read each sentence. In the blank that follows the sentence, write the word that contains the sound of **f** spelled by **gh** or **ph.**

1. I like to watch the tigers and the elephants at the zoo.
elephants

2. The tigers walk around their cages, looking mean and tough.
tough

3. Sometimes they'll reach through the bars with their rough paws.
rough

4. The elephants never look very mean, though. _elephants_

5. I took a photo of them the last time we were there. _photo_

6. I laughed when one tried to grab my camera with its trunk.
laughed

7. I think I'll go back next week if I have enough money. _enough_

8. Maybe this time I will look at the dolphins, too. _dolphins_

Page 84

Read each sentence and the words beside it. Write the word that makes sense in each sentence.

1. A _microphone_ makes your voice sound much louder.
2. A _telephone_ lets you hear people who are far away.

microphone
telephone
trophy

3. The _elephant_ is one of the largest animals.
4. Its skin is very _rough_ and thick.

rough
cough
elephant

5. I won a silver _trophy_ in the bicycle race today.
6. Mom took a _photo_ of me holding it beside my bike.

photo
trophy
nephew

7. I learned the _alphabet_ when I was young.
8. My parents have a _photo_ of me studying the letters.

laughter
alphabet
photo

9. This wood was very _rough_ when I began sanding it.
10. Is it smooth _enough_ now for us to use?

enough
phone
rough

11. My little brother had a very bad _cough_.
12. My father _phoned_ the doctor about it.

photo
cough
phoned

13. This piece of meat is so _tough_, I can't chew it.
14. Maybe I should give it to my _nephew's_ dog.

graph
nephew's
tough

Read the sentences. Choose and write the letters needed to complete the unfinished word in each sentence. The word you form must make sense in the sentence.

1. We planted some new trees and __*shr*__ubs in our yard. — shr, thr

2. Have you ever made a wi__sh__ and had it come true? — th, sh

3. Mom says I cook so well I should become a ___ch___ef. — shr, ch

4. The whistle made a very ___shr___ill sound. — th, shr

5. Did you know that ___wh___ales are not really fish? — th, wh

6. Will there be enou___gh___ chairs for everyone at the party? — gh, ng

7. The person who just called had the wro___ng___ number. — ng, gh

8. I don't think the piano will fit ___thr___ough that door. — shr, thr

9. Does this pa___th___ go to the beach or to the woods? — th, sh

10. Mom needed only one ma___tch___ to light the campfire. — tch, sh

11. I keep some paper and a pencil by the tele___ph___one. — th, ph

12. My legs a___ch___e from running so hard in that race. — sh, ch

13. I'm trying to ___th___ink of the answer to your question. — th, wh

---

Read each set of sentences and its list of words. Write a word from the list that makes sense in each sentence.

1. Do you think we __*should*__ wait here any longer?
2. I scraped my __chin__ when I fell on the ice.
3. How far can you __throw__ a football?
4. I forgot to __wash__ my hands before coming to dinner.
5. We had to __patch__ the hole in our tent to keep the bugs out.
6. The cat in the pet store window has a black nose and long white __whiskers__.
7. This sidewalk is too __rough__ for roller skating.
8. My cousin raises horses on a __ranch__.

patch
square
should
ranch
match
throw
chin
bush
whiskers
wash
rough

1. The puppies are still too __young__ to leave their mother.
2. There were over __thirty__ people at the family picnic.
3. My throat was so sore, I could only __whisper__.
4. I hope this shirt doesn't __shrink__ when I wash it in warm water.
5. The __chorus__ is going to practice singing on Friday afternoon.
6. The dentist checked my __teeth__ during my last visit.
7. The __machine__ that makes peanut butter is broken.
8. The nearest __telephone__ booth is on the next corner.

whale
teeth
whisper
machine
elephant
shrink
telephone
chorus
thirty
young
thief

A vowel that is followed by **r** stands for a special sound that is neither long nor short.

j**ar**	h**or**n
f**er**n	b**ur**n
b**ir**d	

Name the pictures and read the sentences. Circle the word in each sentence that has the same vowel sound as the picture name.

 fork
1. The farmer is going to plow the (corn) field today.

 barn
2. We will study about the (stars) later this month.

 horse
3. There will be a (short) meeting here on Thursday.

 shirt
4. The windows have (dirt) on them from the dust storm.

 turtle
5. The clown was wearing an orange wig with (curls).

 horn
6. My friends and I made a snow (fort) in the park.

 jar
7. Adela has a small (part) in the school play.

 bird
8. Tat used a long fork to (stir) the vegetable stew.

Read each clue and the list of words. Find the word in the list that matches the clue. Write the word next to the clue.

1. a person who cuts hair __*barber*__
2. to break open __burst__
3. soft hair on an animal __fur__
4. not tall __short__
5. an animal that flies __bird__
6. a meal that is eaten in the evening __supper__
7. a round shape __circle__
8. the outside covering of a tree __bark__

fur
short
sir
barber
circle
hurt
burst
bark
tar
supper
bird

Read the sentences. Choose and write the letters needed to complete the unfinished word in each sentence. The word you form must make sense in the sentence.

1. Our neighbors painted their p__or__ch last week. — ar, or
2. F__ir__st, they got paint, brushes, and rags. — ir, or
3. Then they borrowed our ladd__er__ to climb to the roof. — ar, er
4. I helped Jack carry the ladder into their y__ar__d. — ar, ur
5. We had to be careful not to h__ur__t any of the shrubs. — or, ur
6. Jack's mother painted the really h__ar__d parts. — ar, er
7. His younger brother helped st__ir__ each can of paint. — ir, or
8. Because Jack and I are short, we painted the bottom p__ar__t of the door. — ar, ur

Read each sentence and the words beside it. Write the word that makes sense in each sentence.

1. My best friend is very _smart_ in math and reading. — her, horn, **smart**
2. She finishes _her_ homework before anyone else. — smart
3. Try to ride your bicycle along this _curved_ line. — curved, first, carved
4. You will win _first_ prize if you can do it.
5. The store was having a sale on _purses_. — part, purses, first
6. It was the _first_ sale I've been to this year.
7. This is the _third_ bath I've given my dog today. — porch, third, perch
8. He chased a skunk under the back _porch_ last night.
9. The artist drew many _circles_ in the pattern. — paper, sort, circles
10. Then she glued the design onto a heavy piece of _paper_.
11. The knives we use in the kitchen are very _sharp_. — shirt, sharp, hurt
12. We are careful not to _hurt_ ourselves when we use them.
13. My _alarm_ clock didn't wake me up this morning. — alarm, cord, car
14. Mom had to bring me to school in the _car_.
15. We don't have any photos of Tom's _birthday_ party. — camera, birthday, border
16. Judy forgot to bring her new _camera_.

Read each sentence and the words beside it. Write the word that makes sense in each sentence.

1. I take my dog to the _park_ to exercise. — park, pork, perk
2. The _person_ in the photo looks like my cousin. — purse, part, person
3. My brother is too _short_ to reach the table. — sharp, shirt, short
4. Our cat always gets stickers caught in his _fur_. — far, for, fur
5. We watched a woman _carve_ a bird out of wood. — carve, curve, curl
6. I'm trying to find the brightest _star_ in the sky. — star, stir, store
7. We saw a _herd_ of buffalo out West. — herd, hard, horn
8. Do you like to play any _sports_ besides basketball? — spurts, sports, sparks
9. I haven't been able to wash all the _dirt_ off myself. — dark, dart, dirt
10. Yesterday we chopped wood to _burn_ in our fireplace. — born, burn, barn

---

Read the list of words below. Then read the sentences that follow. Write a word from the list that makes sense in each sentence.

forest	birds	hard	before	for
driver	teacher	orange	march	harp
shirt	river	turtle	burn	circle

1. Mr. Campa is the best _teacher_ I've ever had.
2. The dancers joined hands and formed a _circle_.
3. I caught a _turtle_ in the pond behind our house.
4. In the winter, we put seeds out for the _birds_.
5. I have to finish my homework _before_ I can play.
6. Our high-school band will _march_ in the parade.
7. Our school bus _driver_ is always very careful.
8. The ice isn't _hard_ enough to skate on yet.
9. Be careful not to _burn_ your fingers on the hot stove.
10. The bright _orange_ flowers in the yard are very pretty.
11. I enjoy watching the big ships sail up the _river_.
12. Have you seen the man who is wearing a gray hat and orange _shirt_?
13. I would like to learn to play the flute and the _harp_.
14. Our scout troop took a hike through the _forest_.
15. Have you ever sent away _for_ something from a catalog?

The letters **oi** and **oy** stand for the vowel sounds in **coin** and **toys**. The letters **ou** and **ow** often stand for the vowel sounds in **cloud** and **cow**.

| c**oi**n | cl**ou**d |
| t**oy**s | c**ow** |

Read the words and look at the pictures. Write each word below the picture it tells about.

point   oil   cow   boy   mouse   mouth

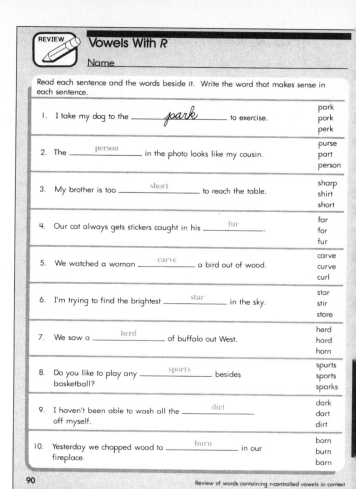

boy   _point_   _mouse_

cow   _mouth_   _oil_

Read each clue. Write **oi** or **ou** to complete the word that matches the clue.

1. dirt — s _oi_ l
2. a place where people live — h _ou_ se
3. a piece of furniture to sit on — c _ou_ ch
4. a round piece of money — c _oi_ n
5. to make water very hot — b _oi_ l
6. sixty minutes — h _ou_ r
7. a small animal — m _ou_ se
8. what you speak with — v _oi_ ce

OI, OY, OU, and OW

Name _____

Read the sentences and the word choices. Circle the word that makes sense in each sentence.

1. I enjoy spring and summer in our (**town**, proud).
2. It's fun to do things (**outdoors**, powder) when the weather is nice.
3. I (join, **enjoy**) going for a hike in the forest.
4. Swimming is fun when the weather is (**boiling**, boy) hot.
5. Sometimes I like to just watch the (**clouds**, clowns) float by.
6. In the spring we plant (choice, **flowers**) all around our house.
7. I like to read under a tree for an (**hour**, joy) sometimes.
8. In the evening we can listen to the (toys, **owls**) in the forest.
9. There are so many things to do, it's sometimes hard to make a (loud, **choice**).

Read each clue. Write **oy** or **ow** to complete the word that matches the clue.

1. a male child — b**oy**
2. something a queen wears — cr**ow**n
3. something to play with — t**oy**
4. a large bird that hoots — **ow**l
5. a dark color — br**ow**n
6. to like something; to have a good time — enj**oy**
7. a large group of people — cr**ow**d
8. something to dry yourself with — t**ow**el
9. a farm tool — pl**ow**

Words containing diphthongs in context: oi, oy, ou, ow; Words containing diphthongs: oi, oy, ou, ow

93

OI, OY, OU, and OW

Name _____

Read each sentence and the words shown below the blank. Write the word that makes sense in each sentence.

1. A new boy _*joined*_ our class today.
   (joined, joy)
2. Ping dropped some __coins__ on her way to buy a toy.
   (coins, coiled)
3. Some oil had leaked into the __soil__ and spoiled the grass.
   (soybean, soil)
4. The chef served __oysters__ to the royal family.
   (oily, oysters)
5. This __poison__ will destroy the bugs that are in the house.
   (pointed, poison)
6. The farmer keeps the cows in that __mountain__ field.
   (mountain, mounds)
7. The quick rain __shower__ cooled off the hot ground.
   (show, shower)
8. It took the __clown__ an hour to get ready for the show.
   (clown, crown)
9. The owl made a __loud__ noise as it swooped down.
   (loyal, loud)
10. Behind that board is where the __brown__ mouse lives.
    (brown, bought)
11. As the clouds covered the moon, Kenji heard a dog __howl__
    (howl, hour)
12. Be careful not to get the white __powder__ on your eyebrows.
    (powder, pound)
13. You have the __choice__ of any of the blouses on this rack.
    (coil, choice)
14. We enjoyed looking at the city from the top of the __tower__
    (towel, tower)

94

Words containing diphthongs in context: oi, oy, ou, ow

REVIEW

OI, OY, OU, and OW

Name _____

Name the pictures and read the sentences. Circle the word in each sentence that has the same vowel sound as the picture name.

 mouse
1. Can you (**bounce**) the basketball and throw it through the hoop?

 boy
2. I think you'll (**enjoy**) this movie about a tiger.

 cow
3. From this (**tower**), we can see corn growing in the farthest fields.

 coin
4. My first (**choice**) is the blue blouse, but I also like the green one.

 oil
5. My father saves (**coins**) from all over the world.

 house
6. We could put the new (**couch**) by the big window.

 crown
7. I'm not (**allowed**) to play in the snow unless I wear boots.

 clown
8. Let's look for a rainbow when this rain (**shower**) stops.

Review of sound-symbol association of words containing diphthongs: oi, oy, ou, ow

95

PROGRESS CHECK

OI, OY, OU, and OW

Name _____

Read each sentence and the words beside it. Write the word that makes sense in the sentence.

1. The Indians built huge _*mounds*_ of dirt in a circle.
2. They were far from any cities or __towns__.

   mounds
   towns
   round

3. First, we need to __boil__ this kettle of water.
4. Then we'll put the __oysters__ in and let them cook.

   oysters
   boil
   point

5. I want to buy a __toy__ lawn mower for my brother.
6. He can use it __outdoors__ when we work in the yard.

   towel
   outdoors
   toy

7. I kept hearing a strange scratching __noise__ all night long.
8. In the morning I found a __mouse__ in the drawer.

   moist
   noise
   mouse

9. Our garden has the best __soil__ anywhere around.
10. It's dark __brown__ and doesn't have many stones.

   soil
   spoil
   brown

11. Floating along in the hot-air balloon was very __enjoyable__
12. But coming back __down__ to earth was a good feeling, too.

   brown
   enjoyable
   down

96

Assessment of words containing diphthongs in context: oi, oy, ou, ow

191

Endings: -ED and -ING

Words to use: rush, talk, fry, stop, play, snap, wash, smile, cook, bounce, block, whistle, wink, tag, toss

When a word ends with one vowel followed by a consonant, double the consonant before adding **-ed** or **-ing**. When a word ends in **e**, drop the **e** before adding **-ed** or **-ing**. When a word ends in a consonant followed by **y**, change the **y** to **i** before adding **-ed**.

snap	snap**ped**
save	sav**ing**
hurry	hurr**ied**

Read the words below. Add **-ed** and **-ing** to each word. Write the new words in the blanks.

		Add -ed	**Add -ing**
1.	whistle	*whistled*	*whistling*
2.	try	tried	trying
3.	watch	watched	watching
4.	skip	skipped	skipping
5.	bake	baked	baking
6.	copy	copied	copying

Read the list of words below. Then read the sentences that follow. Add **-ed** or **-ing** to a word from the list to complete each sentence. Write the new word in the blank. The word you form must make sense in the sentence.

wash   use   tape   stir   lean   carry   search   plan

1. Joyce was *planning* to paint a picture of the park.
2. The student artist _carried_ her paper, paint, and brushes with her.
3. When she arrived, she began _stirring_ her paint.
4. Joyce _taped_ the paper onto a board to keep it from moving.
5. She then _leaned_ her homemade easel against a large tree.
6. The artist _used_ the park bench to hold the paint and brushes.

Adding -ed and -ing to verbs in isolation and in context

97

Endings: -S and -ES

Words to use: stare, yell, clean, bake, skip, rest, carry, study, wish, shop, try, cash, use, boil

Often new words can be formed by adding **-s** or **-es** to other words. To change many words, add the ending **-s**. When a word ends in **s, ss, sh, ch, x,** or **z,** add **-es**. When a word ends in a consonant followed by **y,** change the **y** to **i** and add **-es.**

laugh	laugh**s**
rush	rush**es**
copy	cop**ies**

Read each sentence and the word beside it. Add **-s** or **-es** to the word to complete the sentence. Write the new word in the blank.

1. Mei *hurries* through breakfast every morning. — hurry
2. She _catches_ the bus on the corner at eight o'clock. — catch
3. On the way to school, she _enjoys_ talking to friends and classmates. — enjoy
4. Mei always _tries_ to do her best in school. — try
5. She _passes_ most of the tests and quizzes. — pass
6. One of her friends _switches_ schools often because her family moves often. — switch
7. Mei _says_ that she would not like to change schools. — say
8. Whenever she is ill, she _misses_ her classes and her friends. — miss
9. Mei _wants_ to catch up on the work she misses. — want

98

Adding -s or -es to verbs in context

Base Words and Endings

Words to use: arranging, behaved, drifts, begged, leads, ordered, arriving, coaches, failed, notices, tried, hurries, matches, kisses, carried, learned, nibbling, caused

A word to which an ending can be added is called a base word.

roasting   **watch**es

Read the words below. Write the base word for each one.

1.	learned	*learn*	7.	swinging	swing
2.	buzzes	buzz	8.	hurried	hurry
3.	raking	rake	9.	writes	write
4.	planned	plan	10.	fixes	fix
5.	teaches	teach	11.	swimming	swim
6.	fries	fry	12.	cried	cry

Read the list of base words below. Then read each sentence that follows. Add the ending shown beside each sentence to a word from the list. Write the new word in the blank. The word you form must make sense in the sentence.

cook   join   scrape   play   watch
think   toss   teach   win   study

1. Lucy *joined* the soccer team this year. — -ed
2. Her team is _winning_ every game they play. — -ing
3. The coach _teaches_ the players the correct ways to kick the soccer ball. — -es
4. Lucy has _studied_ the rule book the coach gave each team member. — -ed
5. The team _plays_ at five o'clock every Monday and Thursday. — -s
6. Sometimes Lucy's brother _watches_ the games and cheers from the sidelines. — -es
7. He is _thinking_ about starting another soccer team in the neighborhood. — -ing

Identifying base words; Adding endings to verbs in context

99

Endings: -ER and -EST

Words to use: dark, flat, wise, cute, large, silly, early, warm, friendly, busy

In many words, the ending **-er** means "more." It is used to compare two things. The ending **-est** means "most." It is used to compare three or more things.

| deep | deep**er** |
| deep | deep**est** |

Read each sentence and the word beside it. Add **-er** or **-est** to the word to complete the sentence. Write the new word in the blank.

1. Selma is *older* than I am. — old
2. It is _warmer_ today than it was yesterday. — warm
3. The kitchen is the _brightest_ of all the rooms in our apartment. — bright
4. The freight train was _longer_ than the last train. — long
5. The road runner is one of the _fastest_ animals in the world. — fast
6. Pedro is the _tallest_ player on the team. — tall
7. The bowl filled with noodles was much _lighter_ than the platter of meat. — light
8. The blue package is the _smallest_ birthday gift on the table. — small
9. This winter weather is _colder_ than the weather we had last winter. — cold
10. Casey is the _youngest_ boy in our class. — young
11. The hill in Forest Park is _steeper_ than the one near school. — steep
12. The knot on that package was the _tightest_ knot I've ever untied. — tight
13. The sky was _clearer_ in the morning than it was in the afternoon. — clear

100

Adding -er or -est to adjectives in context

Endings: -ER and -EST

Name _____

When a word ends with one vowel followed by a consonant, double the consonant before adding **-er** or **-est.** When a word ends in **e,** drop the **e** before adding **-er** or **-est.** When a word ends in a consonant followed by **y,** change the **y** to **i** before adding **-er** or **-est.**

wet	wet**test**
wise	wis**er**
cloudy	cloud**ier**

Read the words below. Add **-er** and **-est** to each word. Write the new words in the blanks.

		Add **-er**	Add **-est**
1.	pretty	*prettier*	*prettiest*
2.	short	shorter	shortest
3.	fat	fatter	fattest
4.	funny	funnier	funniest
5.	fine	finer	finest

Read the list of words below. Then read the sentences that follow. Add **-er** or **-est** to a word from the list to complete each sentence. Write the new word in the blank. The word you form must make sense in the sentence.

friendly   dark   thick   few   funny   close   wide   sticky

1. I think this is the _____*funniest*_____ show on television.

2. Because our doctor's office is _____closer_____ to home than our dentist's office, it takes less time to get there.

3. The shade of blue in your coat is _____darker_____ than the shade of blue in your hat.

4. We had _____fewer_____ than thirty people at the party.

5. The white cat is the _____friendliest_____ of the three cats.

Adding -er or -est to adjectives in isolation and in context   101

Endings: -ER and -EST

Name _____

Words to use: sunnier, roughest, noisier, biggest, finer, thickest, calmer, thinnest, dirtiest, fancier, greediest, lazier, fresher, liveliest, lovelier

Read the paragraph below. Complete each sentence by adding **-er** or **-est** to the base word shown below the blank.

Shiny Wax is _____*easier*_____ to use than the
(easy)

best-selling wax. It is the _____smoothest_____ wax you can buy,
(smooth)

and it makes your floors look _____cleaner_____ and
(clean)

_____shinier_____ than other waxes did. Hurry to the
(shiny)

_____closest_____ supermarket! Buy Shiny Wax and enjoy
(close)

having the _____brightest_____ floors in town.
(bright)

Read each sentence and the word beside it. Add **-er** or **-est** to the word to complete each sentence. Write the new word in the blank.

1. Last week my family went to the _____*greatest*_____ parade I have ever watched.   great

2. Because we were _____earlier_____ than most of the crowd, we had a good view.   early

3. The floats were _____bigger_____ than the ones in last year's parade.   big

4. One float carried the _____meanest_____ dragon I have ever seen.   mean

5. Some of the _____finest_____ marching bands in the country took part in the parade.   fine

6. The clowns were the _____silliest_____ I've seen in a long time.   silly

7. Because we were having a good time, my family went home at a _____later_____ time than we had planned.   late

102   Adding -er or -est to adjectives in context

REVIEW

Endings

Name _____

Read each sentence and the endings shown beside it. Add the correct ending to the word shown below the blank in each sentence. Write the new word in the blank.

1. The Nile River _____*stretches*_____ north for many miles through Africa.
(stretch)   -s, -es

2. The Amazon River is not as long as the Nile, but it is _____wider_____ in parts.
(wide)   -er, -est

3. The Mississippi River is the _____longest_____ river in the United States.
(long)   -er, -est

4. It flows south and _____carries_____ much river traffic.
(carry)   -s, -es

5. Many people are _____living_____ near the banks of these three rivers.
(live)   -ing, -ed

6. People have _____settled_____ near rivers for many years.
(settle)   -ing, -ed

7. A river bank _____supplies_____ farmers with good soil for their crops.
(supply)   -s, -es

8. Farmers have _____shipped_____ their crops to markets by using many kinds of boats.
(ship)   -ing, -ed

9. Some of these boats have been _____flatter_____ than others.
(flat)   -er, -est

10. Many of the world's _____busiest_____ cities are built near rivers.
(busy)   -er, -est

11. Many people in these cities have _____used_____ the rivers for swimming and boating.
(use)   -ing, -ed

Review of adding endings to base words in context   103

Plurals: -S and -ES

Name _____

Words to use: blouse, tree, class, watch, fox, puppy, story, country, buggy, jelly, bike, room, peach, glass, match

A word that stands for one of something is a singular word. A word that stands for two or more of something is a plural word. Most plurals are formed by adding **-s** to a singular word. When a word ends in **s, ss, sh, ch,** or **x,** add **-es** to form its plural. When a word ends in a consonant followed by **y,** change the **y** to **i** and add **-es.**

plant	plant**s**
dish	dish**es**
penny	penn**ies**

Read each sentence and the word beside it. Write the plural form of the word to complete the sentence. Write the new word in the blank.

1. Making _____*lunches*_____ for our family can be quite a job.   lunch

2. In some _____families_____, each person makes his or her own lunch.   family

3. However, we take _____turns_____ working in pairs.   turn

4. Last week, I made all the _____sandwiches_____.   sandwich

5. I used ten _____pieces_____ of bread each day.   piece

6. My brother cut each sandwich into two _____parts_____.   part

7. My _____parents_____ like us to put a piece of fruit in each lunch.   parent

8. Sometimes my dad reads _____stories_____ to us while we are working.   story

9. He once read us a story about a worker who made lunch _____boxes_____.   box

10. I enjoy making the lunches, but I don't like doing the _____dishes_____ when I am done.   dish

104   Forming plurals in context: -s and -es

193

Plurals: Changing *F* to *V*

Words to use: half, leaf, life, loaf, self, shelf, wife, calf, knife, wolf, elf

Name _____

To form the plural of most words that end in **f** or **fe,** change the **f** or **fe** to **v** and add **-es.**

cal**f**	cal**ves**
kni**fe**	kni**ves**

Read each sentence and the words beside it. Write the plural form of one of the words to complete the sentence, according to the rule given above. The word you write must make sense in the sentence.

1. Ms. Thomas put the dishes on *shelves* so the shoppers could see them.
   self
   shelf

2. Kim and her friends made two *loaves* of bread and a dozen rolls for the party.
   loaf
   leaf

3. Joe traced *leaves* on bright paper and cut them out to use as bookmarks.
   life
   leaf

4. The tale about tiny *elves* and their lives in the forest was delightful.
   shelf
   elf

5. Matt wanted to read about the *lives* of world leaders.
   life
   loaf

6. Please cut the small pizzas into *halves* before you put them into the oven.
   shelf
   half

7. The farmer fed the hungry *calves* early every morning.
   knife
   calf

8. We watched the wildlife program about *wolves* and learned how they travel in packs.
   loaf
   wolf

9. The doctor checked the horse's legs and *hooves* after it came back to the stable.
   hoof
   half

Irregular Plurals

Words to use: teeth, children, women, geese, mice, men, feet, sheep, fish, moose

Name _____

The plurals of some words are formed by changing the spellings of their singular forms.

   tooth—teeth   child—children   woman—women   goose—geese
   mouse—mice   man—men   foot—feet

The plural forms of some words can be the same as their singular forms.

   deer   sheep   fish   moose

Read each sentence and the word beside it. Write the plural form of the word to complete the sentence. Write the new word in the blank.

1. The *sheep* had thick coats of wool.
   sheep

2. It was so cold that my *teeth* would not stop chattering.
   tooth

3. Please feed the guppies and the other *fish (fishes is also acceptable)* in the tank.
   fish

4. *Moose* belong to the deer family and live in the northern fields.
   Moose

5. Many women and *men* work in this building.
   man

6. Beth's *feet* hurt after the trail walk yesterday.
   foot

7. Most of the *children* who went on the walk enjoyed the day.
   child

8. Beth liked seeing the chipmunks and tiny field *mice* running about.
   mouse

9. Their guide pointed out two tall *deer (deers is also acceptable)* with antlers that were hidden behind the trees.
   deer

10. The group stopped to throw bread to the ducks and *geese* swimming on the lake.
    goose

Showing Ownership

Name _____

To make most words show ownership, add an apostrophe (') and **s.** To make a plural word that ends in **s** show ownership, add just an apostrophe.

cat**'s** dishes
cats**'** dishes

Rewrite each group of words below, adding ' or 's to the underlined word to show ownership.

1. the hat that Judy wears   *Judy's hat*
2. the pencils that the pupils use   *pupils' pencils*
3. the tent that belongs to Jill   *Jill's tent*
4. the windows of a store   *store's windows*
5. the toys of the babies   *babies' toys*
6. the pennies that Matt has   *Matt's pennies*

Read each sentence and the words beside it. Add 's or s' to one of the words to complete the sentence. The word you form must make sense in the sentence.

1. The *workers'* glasses protect their eyes.
   worker
   world

2. The *mayor's* speech was very long.
   matter
   mayor

3. My oldest *brother's* friends live near us.
   brush
   brother

4. All the *neighbors'* driveways have been repaired.
   neighbor
   nickel

5. All the team *players'* shirts stayed clean during the game.
   plate
   player

6. The *book's* print is large.
   book
   boat

Showing Ownership

Name _____

To make a plural word that does not end in **s** show ownership, add an apostrophe (') and **s.**

mice**'s** cheese
children**'s** game

Rewrite each group of words below, using 's to form words that show ownership.

1. the cage for the mice   *mice's cage*
2. the toys for the children   *children's toys*
3. the feathers of the geese   *geese's feathers*
4. the coats that the men have   *men's coats*
5. the shoes that belong to the women   *women's shoes*
6. the food for the geese   *geese's food*

Read each sentence and the words shown below the blank. Write the word that completes the sentence. The word you form must make sense in the sentence.

1. The *students'* desks are arranged in rows.
   (student's, students')

2. The *mouse's* tail was very long.
   (mouse's, mice's)

3. We will have the two *children's* birthday parties this month.
   (child's, children's)

4. My *mother's* award was hanging on her office wall.
   (mother's, mothers')

5. The three nearest *towns'* schools were closed during the storm.
   (town's, towns')

6. Did you see *Juan's* new bike?
   (Juan's, Juans)

7. The *geese's* pond, where they usually swam, was frozen.
   (goose's, geese's)

Showing Ownership

Name _____

Words to use: men, visitors, geese, son, snakes, elf, sailors, knives, President, woman, queen, passengers, chief, husband, heroes, giant

Read each sentence and the words shown below the blank. Write the word that completes the sentence. The word you write must make sense in the sentence.

1. My favorite _____*aunt's*_____ dog sometimes stays at our house.
   (aunt's, aunts')

2. The zoo keeper cleaned all the _____animals'_____ cages.
   (animal's, animals')

3. The _____country's_____ President spoke on TV and radio.
   (countries', country's)

4. The _____children's_____ noses were red from the wind.
   (child, children's)

5. I gave _____Fred's_____ ticket to him yesterday.
   (Fred's, Freds')

Read each sentence and the words beside it. Add **'s** or **s'** to one of the words to complete the sentence. The word you form must make sense in the sentence.

1. After the four _____*campers'*_____ boxes were unpacked, they began to set up the tents. — carton / camper

2. The library _____book's_____ cover was bright and colorful. — base / book

3. The two bridge _____workers'_____ hats were hanging in their lockers. — worker / whistle

4. My oldest _____sister's_____ friend works for the mayor. — stamp / sister

5. The _____cups'_____ handles are all broken. — cup / cut

6. The _____children's_____ playground has a new sliding board. — chalk / children

Using singular and plural possessives in context; Forming singular and plural possessives in context   109

Plurals and Showing Ownership

Name _____

Read each sentence and the singular word beside it. Change the singular word to its plural form to complete the sentence. Write the new word in the blank.

1. Ted enjoyed the story about the _____*elves*_____ and the shoemaker. — elf

2. Please put the _____dishes_____ in the sink. — dish

3. Joyce has visited many _____cities_____. — city

4. Your _____feet_____ will get wet if you step in the puddles. — foot

5. Uncle Steve heard the _____puppies_____ barking in the pet shop. — puppy

6. She made the sock puppets look like woolly _____sheep_____. — sheep

7. We packed the books in _____boxes_____ to ship to another school. — box

8. There were many cars and _____trucks_____ in the parking lot. — truck

Rewrite each group of words below, adding **'** or **'s** to the underlined word to show ownership.

1. the frame for the <u>photo</u> _____*photo's frame*_____

2. the parents of the <u>children</u> _____children's   parents_____

3. the watch that belongs to <u>Don</u> _____Don's   watch_____

4. the windows of the <u>stores</u> _____stores'   windows_____

5. the colors of the <u>rainbow</u> _____rainbow's   colors_____

6. the gift for <u>Jessica</u> _____Jessica's   gift_____

7. the pupils of the <u>teachers</u> _____teachers'   pupils_____

8. the maps of the <u>student</u> _____student's   maps_____

110   Review of forming plurals in context; Forming singular and plural possessives

---

Endings and Plurals

Name _____

Read each sentence and the word beside it. Add one of the endings shown below to the word to complete each sentence. The word you form must make sense in the sentence.

-ed   -ing   -s   -es   -er   -est

1. Bill _____*hurried*_____ to catch the train yesterday. — hurry

2. Sally _____watches_____ TV after she does her homework. — watch

3. Lisa used the _____longest_____ ribbon in the box to tie the bow. — long

4. The child was _____flipping_____ the pages of the book. — flip

5. The twins _____dried_____ the dishes and set them on the table. — dry

6. Mom came home at a _____later_____ time than she usually does. — late

7. My brother _____calls_____ me every morning and talks for a few minutes. — call

8. Many people were _____skating_____ on the frozen pond. — skate

9. Sue's joke was _____funnier_____ than Terry's. — funny

10. Andy was _____inviting_____ all his friends to the party. — invite

Read the sentences below. Complete each sentence by changing the singular word shown below the blank to its plural form. Write the new word in the blank.

1. I enjoyed watching the _____*puppies*_____ in the pet show. (puppy)

2. The _____mayors_____ will meet on Monday. (mayor)

3. We watched the _____foxes_____ leave their den. (fox)

4. The _____leaves_____ on the trees are bright orange. (leaf)

5. The backpackers saw the tracks of two _____deer (deers is also acceptable)_____ (deer)

6. Tess painted the set of _____benches_____ (bench)

Assessment of adding endings; Forming plurals   111

Showing Ownership

Name _____

Read each sentence and the words beside it. Write the word that makes sense in the sentence.

1. My youngest _____*sister's*_____ cat is brown and white. — sister's / sisters'

2. The _____writer's_____ pencil broke while she was taking notes. — writer's / writers'

3. The five _____friends'_____ clubhouse was made with logs and stones. — friend's / friends'

4. _____Rosa's_____ bike is being repaired in the shop. — Rosa's / Rosas'

5. We listened to the _____President's_____ speech on the radio. — President's / Presidents'

6. Before Frank cleaned his _____hamsters'_____ cage, he put them in a large box. — hamster's / hamsters'

7. My _____parents'_____ birthdays are both on the same day. — parent's / parents'

8. I found _____Mike's_____ ruler on the classroom floor. — Mike's / Mikes'

9. The pet _____store's_____ large sign flew in the air during the storm. — store's / stores'

10. The three _____workers'_____ lunches were locked in the closet. — worker's / workers'

11. The _____clown's_____ wig fell when she took off her pointed hat. — clown's / clowns'

12. Our _____plane's_____ pilot arrived late at the airport. — plane's / planes'

112   Assessment of forming singular and plural possessives in context

Compound Words

Name _____ Words to use: workbook, bookcase, notebook, schoolhouse, classroom, playground, chalkboard, lunchbox, textbook, hallway, schoolbag, classmate, lunchroom

A compound word is formed by joining two smaller words together.	rain + bow = rainbow

Read each compound word and write the two words that form it.

1. homework   *home*   *work*
2. something   some   thing
3. notebook   note   book
4. birthday   birth   day
5. upstairs   up   stairs
6. downtown   down   town
7. sidewalk   side   walk

Read the sentences below. Circle the compound words in each sentence.

1. Grandmother and I went to the beach last weekend.
2. I took suntan oil in my backpack.
3. We looked for seashells and made footprints in the sand.
4. We stopped to watch the lifeguards pull in a rowboat.
5. Then we found a starfish covered with seaweed.
6. We stayed to watch the beautiful sunset beyond the lighthouse.
7. On the way home, we munched on homemade popcorn we had brought.

Forming compound words; Identifying compound words in context   113

Compound Words

Name _____ Words to use: anyhow, footprints, everybody, rainbow, anyone, somebody, skyline, rainstorm, everything, storeroom, steamboat, mailroom, storyteller, lifeboat, handbag

Read the words in each list below. Draw lines to match the words that form compound words.

wheel	meal		book	berry
any	noon		blue	book
oat	barrow		wind	case
tooth	body		fire	place
after	brush		school	mill

Read the list of compound words below. Then read the sentences that follow. Write the word from the list that makes sense in each sentence. Then draw a line under the other compound word in the sentence.

footsteps   everyone   runway   highway   newspaper
rainfall   sunrise   airport   suitcases   pancakes

1. Last month my grandparents and I went to the _____ *airport* .
2. There was hardly anyone on the _____ highway _____ , so it did not take us long to get there.
3. When we arrived, we stopped downstairs to eat and I had pancakes _____ .
4. When we went upstairs, I could see a plane arriving on the runway _____ .
5. My grandfather then asked me to go to the gift shop to buy him a newspaper _____ .
6. As I was walking into the shop, I heard _____ footsteps _____ behind me.
7. I turned to see my cousin Jean and my grandparents carrying her suitcases _____ .
8. Then _____ everyone _____ laughed, and Jean took a snapshot of my surprised look.

114   Forming compound words; Using compound words in context

---

Compound Words

Name _____ Words to use: dustpan, someone, anywhere, sometime, anything, everywhere, grownups, upstairs, housework, windmill, somewhere, necktie, fireplace, sunburn, firewood

Read each sentence below. Use two words from the sentence to form a compound word. Write the compound word in the blank.

1. A boat that tugs other boats is a *tugboat*
2. A brush that is used to clean each tooth is a toothbrush
3. A box where mail is put is called a mailbox
4. An area of ground where children play is a playground
5. A person who tells a story is called a storyteller
6. A book that tells people how to cook is a cookbook
7. A place where a fire burns is called a fireplace
8. A house made for a dog is a doghouse
9. A coat that a person wears in the rain is called a raincoat

Read the list of words below. Then read the paragraph that follows. Complete each sentence by writing one of the compound words from the list. The word you write must make sense in the sentence.

snowstorm   sidewalks   somewhere   sunshine   airplane
snowplows   downtown   railroad   snapshot   highway

The _____ *snowstorm* _____ hit the city very quickly. The people who were _____ downtown _____ were quite surprised. Shoppers had a hard time walking on the snow-covered _____ sidewalks _____ . People had to stand in long lines at the _____ railroad _____ station. Some cars were stopped on the _____ highway _____ because of high winds and drifting snow. The city's _____ snowplows _____ tried to remove as much snow as possible. Most people had not prepared for the snow because the weather forecasters had said there would be _____ sunshine _____ all week.

Forming compound words; Using compound words in context   115

Contractions

Name _____ Words to use: he will, they have, I would, they will, it is, he is, had not

A contraction is a short way to write two words. It is written by putting two words together and leaving out a letter or letters. An apostrophe (') takes the place of the letters that are left out. The word **won't** is a special contraction made from the words **will** and **not**.	was + not = **wasn't** I + have = **I've** will + not = **won't**

Read the list of contractions below. Then read the word pairs that follow. Write a contraction from the list for each word pair.

I've   he'd   I'm   let's   hasn't
she's   there's   we're   aren't   we'll

1. has not   *hasn't*   6. let us   let's
2. we are   we're   7. she is   she's
3. there is   there's   8. I have   I've
4. he would   he'd   9. are not   aren't
5. we will   we'll   10. I am   I'm

Read each sentence and the pair of words shown below the blank. Complete the sentence by writing the contraction that stands for the word pair.

1. Larry thinks _____ *we'll* _____ win the basketball game.
(we will)
2. _____ We're _____ going to practice this morning.
(We are)
3. Nina _____ won't _____ be able to play because she is ill.
(will not)
4. The coach said that she _____ isn't _____ worried.
(is not)
5. _____ I've _____ never been so excited about a game.
(I have)
6. _____ You've _____ got to come and watch the best game of the season.
(You have)

116   Forming contractions in isolation and in context

Contractions

Name _____

Read each contraction below. Then write the two words for which each contraction stands.

1. didn't
   did not

2. that's
   that is or that has

3. they've
   they have

4. here's
   here is

5. won't
   will not

6. I'd
   I had or I would

7. hadn't
   had not

8. he'll
   he will

9. I'm
   I am

10. they're
    they are

Read each sentence and the contraction shown below the blank. Complete the sentence by writing the two words for which the contraction stands.

1. Judy: _We will_ have to listen for your brother on the radio.
   (We'll)

2. Gary: Yes, _he is_ going to read ads for many different stores.
   (he's)

3. Judy: _I will_ have to listen to the ads more closely.
   (I'll)

4. Gary: _I am_ quite proud that Dan is doing the ad for The Record Storeroom.
   (I'm)

5. Judy: Well, _you have_ every reason to be proud of him.
   (you've)

6. Gary: _Let us_ turn on the radio to listen to the ten o'clock ad.
   (Let's)

Identifying words from which contractions are formed   117

Contractions

Name _____

Read each sentence and find the two words that can be made into a contraction. Draw a line under the two words and write the contraction in the blank.

1. Dawn does not mind going to her trumpet lessons. _doesn't_

2. She is really enjoying learning how to play the trumpet. _She's_

3. Her teacher said he would like Dawn to try out for the school band. _he'd_

4. Dawn's parents think that it is a good idea. _it's_

5. Dawn wonders if she will play well in front of people. _she'll_

6. Her teacher told her, "You have no reason to worry." _You've_

Read the sentences and the list of contractions. Write a contraction from the list to complete each sentence.

1. Our car _wouldn't_ start this morning.

2. _There's_ a stop sign at the corner.

3. Luis says that _he's_ coming home at five o'clock.

4. _We'll_ be leaving for school soon.

5. I _haven't_ seen you in a long time.

6. The twins have saved most of the money _they've_ earned together.

7. _It's_ not a good idea to leave during a storm.

8. Our neighbors told us that _they're_ going to be gone for a week.

We'll
won't
wouldn't
they're
There's
It's
haven't
they've
he's
I'm

118   Forming contractions in context; Using contractions in context

---

REVIEW   Compound Words and Contractions

Name _____

Read the clues below. Use two words from each clue to form a compound word. Write the compound word in the blank.

1. the bud of a rose _rosebud_
2. work that is done in school _schoolwork_
3. a box where mail is put _mailbox_
4. a cloth that is put on a table _tablecloth_
5. a flat pan that is used to pick up dust _dustpan_
6. work that is done at home _homework_
7. a tie that is worn around the neck _necktie_
8. a boat that uses steam _steamboat_
9. a pot used to hold tea _teapot_
10. a burn that is caused by sitting in the sun for too long _sunburn_

Read the word pairs below. Then write the contraction that stands for each word pair.

1. were not _weren't_
2. I would _I'd_
3. she is _she's_
4. did not _didn't_
5. you have _you've_
6. I am _I'm_
7. he will _he'll_
8. you are _you're_
9. has not _hasn't_
10. they have _they've_
11. will not _won't_
12. it is _it's_

Review of forming compound words; Forming contractions   119

PROGRESS CHECK   Compound Words and Contractions

Name _____

Read the rows of words below. Then read the sentences that follow. Use a word from Row A and a word from Row B to form a compound word to complete each sentence. The word you form must make sense in the sentence.

A.	book	home	bed	any	every	with
B.	where	case	one	out	work	room

1. Has _anyone_ seen my notebook?
2. I thought I left it on my desk in my _bedroom_ at home.
3. I've looked _everywhere_ in the apartment.
4. I can't go to school _without_ it.
5. Will someone look on the top shelf of my _bookcase_?
6. The book has all my math notes and _homework_ in it.

Read each sentence and the pair of words beside it. Complete the sentence with a contraction that stands for the word pair.

1. I _haven't_ been to the dentist since my last checkup.   have not
2. Dr. Lake is very nice, and _she's_ always pleasant.   she is
3. She usually has a story to tell _that's_ interesting.   that is
4. _I'll_ probably have to sit in the waiting room for a while.   I will
5. _You'd_ be surprised at the number of people who go to Dr. Lake's office.   You would
6. I guess _they've_ heard that Dr. Lake is a good doctor.   they have

120   Assessment of forming compound words in context; Forming contractions in context

Prefixes: UN-, DIS-, RE-, and PRE-

Name _____

Words to use: unopened, disliked, rewash, unhurt, recook, rewrite, unlucky, distrust, prepaid, pretest

A prefix is a letter or group of letters that can be added to the beginning of a word. The prefixes **un-** and **dis-** usually mean "not" or "the opposite of." For example, the word **untie** means "the opposite of tie." The word **dislike** means "not like."

The prefix **re-** usually means "again," so the word **rewrite** means "write again." The prefix **pre-** means "before," so the word **prepay** means "pay before."

un + tie = **un**tie
dis + like = **dis**like

re + write = **re**write
pre + pay = **pre**pay

Read each sentence and the word beside it. Add **un-** or **re-** to the word to complete the sentence. Write the new word in the blank. The word you form must make sense in the sentence.

1. Matt _unpacked_ his bags after he arrived.   packed
2. We can read the story when the newspaper _reprints_ it.   prints
3. The building is _unsafe_ for people to use.   safe
4. The manager will _unroll_ the carpet so we can see it.   roll
5. We saw the _replay_ of the touchdown.   play

Read each sentence and the word beside it. Add **dis-** or **pre-** to the word to complete the sentence. Write the new word in the blank. The word you form must make sense in the sentence.

1. Do you _distrust_ the story you heard yesterday?   trust
2. When making bread, first _preheat_ the oven.   heat
3. The dog _disobeyed_ its owner when she told it to sit.   obeyed
4. Marta _dislikes_ weeding the flower garden.   likes
5. Our school's band played during the last _pregame_ show. game

---

Prefixes: IN-, OVER-, MIS-, and POST-

Name _____

Words to use: season (postseason), game (postgame), lead (mislead), trust (mistrust), spell (misspell), sleep (oversleep), pay (overpay), direct (indirect), correct (incorrect), active (inactive).

The prefix **in-** often means "not." The word **incomplete** means "not complete." The prefix **over-** means "too much" or "more than usual." The word **overeat** means "to eat too much."

The prefix **mis-** means "badly" or "wrongly." The word **mistreat** means "to treat badly." The prefix **post-** means "after." The word **postwar** means "after a war."

in + complete = **in**complete
over + eat = **over**eat

mis + treat = **mis**treat
post + war = **post**war

Read each sentence and the word beside it. Add **in-** or **over-** to the word to complete the sentence. Write the new word in the blank. The word you form must make sense in the sentence.

1. The bus took an _indirect_ route to the park.   direct
2. During the summer I ate too much, and I became _overweight_. weight
3. Five of my test answers were _incorrect_.   correct
4. She is wearing an _oversized_ shirt today.   sized
5. After the storm, the river _overflowed_ its banks.   flowed

Read each sentence and the word beside it. Add **mis-** or **post-** to the word to complete the sentence. Write the new word in the blank. The word you form must make sense in the sentence.

1. Yuji _misread_ the price on the package.   read
2. The pilot wrote the _postflight_ report.   flight
3. I try not to _mispronounce_ people's names.   pronounce
4. Many of the drivers were at the _postrace_ party.   race
5. The child was _misbehaving_ in the store.   behaving

Prefixes

Name _____

Words to use: misread, overload, unhappy, dislike, rewrite, incomplete, untie, disconnect, reheat, incorrect, mistreat, overweight.

Read each sentence and the prefixes beside it. Complete each sentence by adding one of the prefixes to the word shown below the blank. Write the new word in the blank. The word you form must make sense in the sentence.

1. The workers will _disconnect_ the pipes.   dis-
   (connect)   over-

2. We'll go in as soon as you _unlock_ the door.   post-
   (lock)   un-

3. Benito _rebuilt_ the bookcase so the library   mis-
   (built)   re-
   could use it.

4. I couldn't find a seat because the room was _overcrowded_. over-
   (crowded)   re-

5. I corrected the _misspelled_ words in my story.   mis-
   (spelled)   post-

6. The trip's fees were _prepaid_ before we left town. dis-
   (paid)   pre-

7. Lin was going to buy an _inexpensive_ plant because in-
   (expensive)   over-
   she didn't have much money.

8. After flying the plane, Rena finished a _postflight_ post-
   report.   un-
   (flight)

9. The spoiled cheese had an _unpleasant_ smell.   un-
   (pleasant)   post-

10. Beth will be _displeased_ if we don't visit her. re-
    (pleased)   dis-

Suffixes: -FUL, -LESS, -Y, and -LY

Name _____

Words to use: colorful, curly, truthful, thoughtful, harmful, thirsty, dreamy, frosty, fairly, shortly, painless, careful, softly, cheerful, stormy, snowy, fearless, quietly.

A suffix is a letter or group of letters that can be added to the end of a word. The suffix **-ful** usually means "full of." For example, the word **restful** means "full of rest." The suffix **-less** usually means "without." The word **useless** means "without use."

The suffixes **-y** and **-ly** can be added to some words. For example, a car that has **rust** on it is a **rusty** car. A person who talks in a **loud** way talks **loudly.**

rest + ful = rest**ful**
use + less = use**less**

rust + y = rust**y**
loud + ly = loud**ly**

Read each sentence and the word beside it. Add **-ful** or **-less** to the word to complete the sentence. Write the new word in the blank. The word you form must make sense in the sentence.

1. The bridge across the wide bay seemed _endless_.   end
2. We had a calm and _restful_ time at the beach.   rest
3. The sun was shining and the sky was _cloudless_.   cloud
4. The _wonderful_ day was just what each of us needed.   wonder
5. I was _forgetful_ and left our lunches at home.   forget

Read each sentence and the word beside it. Add **-y** or **-ly** to the word to complete the sentence. Write the new word in the blank. The word you form must make sense in the sentence.

1. We cleaned the house _quickly_ before the guests arrived. quick
2. We were busy and had not done our _weekly_ jobs.   week
3. Jan used oil to fix the _squeaky_ front door.   squeak
4. Chung cleaned and polished the _dusty_ tables.   dust
5. Mom stacked the newspapers _neatly_.   neat

Suffixes: -ABLE, -ISH, -MENT, and -NESS

Name _____

Words to use: tax (taxable), agree (agreeable), child (childish), baby (babyish), yellow (yellowish), excite (excitement), arrange (arrangement), good (goodness), weak (weakness)

The suffix **-able** means "can be" or "able to be." For example, the word **breakable** means "can be broken." The suffix **-ish** can mean "like" or "somewhat." The word **childish** means "like a child."

The suffixes **-ment** and **-ness** can be added to some words. For example, if you **enjoy** reading books, reading brings you **enjoyment**. If you are feeling **ill**, you have an **illness**.

break + able = break**able**
child + ish = child**ish**

enjoy + ment = enjoy**ment**
ill + ness = ill**ness**

Read each sentence and the word beside it. Add **-able** or **-ment** to the word to complete the sentence. Write the new word in the blank. The word you form must make sense in the sentence.

1. These bus seats are not very _comfortable_ — comfort
2. The flower _arrangement_ was pretty. — arrange
3. Are the books on the top shelf _reachable_? — reach
4. The new wallpaper is _washable_. — wash
5. We are going to study our city _government_. — govern

Read each sentence and the word beside it. Add **-ish** or **-ness** to the word to complete the sentence. Write the new word in the blank. The word you form must make sense in the sentence.

1. The _soreness_ in my hurt arm has gone away. — sore
2. The cat was _selfish_ and would not share its treat. — self
3. The new rug is a _greenish_ color. — green
4. Bart has been absent because of a long _illness_. — ill

Suffixes

Name _____

Words to use: arrangement, forgetful, quickly, cloudless, squeaky, wonderful, weekly, comfortable, restful, dusty, spotless, neatly, government, sharpness, illness

Read each sentence and the suffixes beside it. Complete each sentence by adding one of the suffixes to the word shown below the blank. Write the new word in the blank. The word you form must make sense in the sentence.

1. Preparing for the school play was _enjoyable_ — -able / -ish
   (enjoy)
2. Miss Norton told us to read our lines _loudly_ — -able / -ly
   (loud)
3. Some days, our play practice seemed _endless_ — -y / -less
   (end)
4. I played a _clownish_ person and had to practice — -able / -ish
   (clown) falling without hurting myself.
5. My costume was striped and very _colorful_. — -ful / -able
   (color)
6. I also wore a _curly_ wig. — -y / -ment
   (curl)
7. All the actors were _friendly_ — -ly / -y
   (friend)
8. Everyone was _cheerful_ on opening night. — -ful / -ness
   (cheer)
9. The _brightness_ of the stage lights made it easy for — -ness / -less
   (bright) the people in the back rows to see us.
10. The _excitement_ of the actors filled the stage. — -able / -ment
    (excite)

Prefixes and Suffixes

Name _____

Read the list of prefixes and suffixes below. Then read the clues that follow. Add one of the prefixes or suffixes to the underlined word to form a word that matches the clue.

un-   dis-   re-   pre-   -ful   -less   -y   -ly   -ness

1. the opposite of continue _discontinue_
2. without color _colorless_
3. every year _yearly_
4. to view before _preview_
5. to do again _redo_
6. full of care _careful_
7. having thirst _thirsty_
8. not planned _unplanned_
9. a state of being weak _weakness_

Read the list of prefixes and suffixes below. Then read the clues that follow. Add one of the prefixes or suffixes to the underlined base word to form a word that matches the clue.

post-   in-   mis-   over-   -able   -ish   -ment

1. somewhat warm _warmish_
2. not complete _incomplete_
3. to pronounce wrongly _mispronounce_
4. the act of agreeing _agreement_
5. able to be trained _trainable_
6. like a child _childish_
7. after the season _postseason_
8. pay too much _overpay_

Prefixes and Suffixes

Name _____

Read the list of words below. Circle the prefix or suffix in each word.

treat(able)	care(less)	sleep(y)	(dis)appear
(pre)school	(re)play	(un)tie	(mis)behave
thank(ful)	dust(y)	good(ness)	home(less)
agree(ment)	(post)war	(over)load	teach(able)
(dis)trust	baby(ish)	(in)correct	sweet(ly)

Read the list of words below. Then read the sentences that follow. Write the word from the list that makes sense in each sentence.

pretest   mistaken   cloudy   overpaid   lightness
unlocked   rewrite   tightly   tasteless   grayish

1. I think it might rain, because the sky looks gray and _cloudy_
2. Because the soup had too much water, it was almost _tasteless_
3. The _lightness_ of the box made it easy to carry.
4. I must _rewrite_ the letter I wrote yesterday.
5. The suit was _grayish_ blue.
6. Harry is often _mistaken_ for his twin brother, Barry.
7. The bank teller _unlocked_ the safe.
8. Mario held the bike's handlebars _tightly_ as he raced down the hill.
9. The math _pretest_ had five problems.
10. The job was so easy that I felt I was _overpaid_

Panel 1 (page 129)

Syllables

Words to use: syllable, trees, telephone, iron, matter, cup, follow, magazine, helping, porch, benches, daisy, jar, tunnel, tomato, bears, market, library, rug

Name

Words are made of small parts called syllables. Because each syllable has one vowel sound, a word has as many syllables as it has vowel sounds. The word **desk** has one vowel sound, so it has one syllable. The word **cabin** has two vowel sounds, so it has two syllables.

Look at the pictures and read the picture names. Write the number of syllables you hear in each picture name.

2 candle	3 butterfly	2 jelly
1 kite	2 sixteen	2 banjo
3 calendar	2 window	1 leaf
2 camel	1 bench	3 potato

Panel 2 (page 130)

Syllables

Words to use: became, downstairs, eyelid, beehive, highway, sidewalk, bathroom, cardboard, somewhere, earthquake, oatmeal, playmate

Name

A compound word should be divided into syllables between the words that make it compound.

high/way

Read the words below. Circle each compound word. Then write each compound word and draw a line between the syllables.

1. (bookcase) *book/case*
2. (downtown) down/town
3. running
4. (rainbow) rain/bow
5. replay
6. (notebook) note/book
7. (airplane) air/plane
8. (driveway) drive/way
9. pencil
10. (sunshine) sun/shine
11. (into) in/to
12. (mailroom) mail/room
13. (steamboat) steam/boat
14. camper
15. blend

16. (someone) some/one
17. (footprint) foot/print
18. (greenhouse) green/house
19. soapy
20. place
21. (rainfall) rain/fall
22. (snowplow) snow/plow
23. sprinkle
24. (cookbook) cook/book
25. (birthday) birth/day
26. (railway) rail/way
27. (dustpan) dust/pan
28. school
29. tells
30. (oatmeal) oat/meal

Panel 3 (page 131)

Syllables

Words to use: unfold, pregame, dusty, careless, joyful, pretest, reheat, careful, foolish, childish, mistreat, slowly, replay, distrust, misplace, dislike, unwrap

Name

Many two-syllable words have prefixes or suffixes. These words can be divided into syllables by dividing the word between the prefix or suffix and the base word.

re/pay
cheer/ful

Read the list of words. Divide each word into syllables by drawing a line between the syllables. Then read the story and write a word from the list that makes sense in each sentence.

cloud/less   cheer/ful   dis/likes   harm/ful   re/mind
soft/ly   quick/ly   re/turned   snow/y   un/hook

It was a cold, _snowy_ day when my friends and I went sledding. The blue sky was _cloudless_. The white flakes had fallen slowly and _softly_ the night before. I had to carefully _unhook_ my sled from the hook on the basement wall. Then I listened to Dad _remind_ me of all the sledding rules that he and Mom had set last year.

All my friends were excited and _cheerful_ when I met them at the top of Spark's Hill. Even Jan, who _dislikes_ cold weather, was there. She and Jack had removed any _harmful_ things that might be in the path of our sleds. I guess I seemed fearless on my first ride down the hill, but I was a bit afraid. I had forgotten how steep the slope was! But when I reached the bottom of the hill, I _quickly_ forgot my fears. I _returned_ to the top of the hill for another fun-filled ride.

Panel 4 (page 132)

Syllables

Words to use: letter, hobby, winter, album, kitten, running, curtains, soccer, picture, parrot, carrots, humming, doctor, drummer, carpet, poster

Name

When a two-syllable word has two consonants between two vowels, the word usually is divided between the two consonants.

but/ter
VC/CV
pic/nic
VC/CV

Read the list of words. Write each word and draw a line between its syllables.

1. napkin *nap/kin*
2. corner cor/ner
3. worry wor/ry
4. dentist den/tist
5. mistake mis/take

6. whisper whis/per
7. tunnel tun/nel
8. contest con/test
9. invent in/vent
10. pencil pen/cil

Read each sentence and the word choices shown below the blank. Complete each sentence by writing the word that has the VC/CV pattern.

1. Yesterday Dad and I made the salad for _dinner_.
   (lunch, dinner)
2. We bought lettuce and pickles at the _corner_ vegetable stand.
   (closest, corner)
3. When we _arrived_ home, I was very hungry.
   (arrived, got)
4. I put some rolls in a large _basket_ while he tossed the salad.
   (basket, bowl)
5. I also put _napkins_, plates, and forks on the table.
   (spoons, napkins)
6. When Dad was finished, he set the salad bowl on the _center_ of the table.
   (center, end)
7. Then everyone helped themselves to the cool _summer_ salad.
   (crisp, summer)

Syllables

Name _____

Words to use: legal, manage, label, climate, siren, palace, lizard, honest, damage

Words that have one consonant between two vowels can be divided into syllables in two ways. When you see a word that has one consonant between two vowels, say the word. If the first vowel sound is long, divide the word after the first vowel. If the first vowel sound is short, divide the word after the consonant that follows the vowel.

1
fā/mous
V/CV
mū/sic
V/CV

2
wăg/on
VC/V
fĭn/ish
VC/V

Read the list of words. Write each word. Mark the first vowel of the word with ˘ if it stands for the short sound or ¯ if it stands for the long sound. Then draw a line between its syllables.

1. later _lā/ter_
2. broken brō/ken
3. tiger tī/ger
4. river rĭv/er
5. finish fĭn/ish
6. paper pā/per
7. punish pŭn/ish
8. robin rŏb/in
9. item ī/tem
10. closet clŏs/et

11. lemon lĕm/on
12. minus mī/nus
13. pedal pĕd/al
14. cozy cō/zy
15. pilot pī/lot
16. fever fē/ver
17. moment mō/ment
18. travel trăv/el
19. second sĕc/ond
20. motor mō/tor

Syllables

Name _____

Words to use: over, habit, second, closet, never, favor, hotel, pupil, lilac, climate, vacant

Read the list of words. Write each word and draw a line between its syllables. Then mark the first vowel of the word with ˘ if it stands for the short sound or ¯ if it stands for the long sound.

1. acorn _ā/corn_
2. planet plăn/et
3. petal pēt/al
4. spider spī/der
5. secret sē/cret

6. model mŏd/el
7. lemon lĕm/on
8. minus mī/nus
9. robot rō/bot
10. even ē/ven

Read the list of words and the sentences. Divide each list word into syllables by drawing a line between the syllables. Then write the word from the list that makes sense in each sentence.

e/vent
bro/ken
rob/in
dri/ver
riv/er
pal/ace
ta/ble
med/al
mo/ment
fla/vor

1. The _robin_ was making a nest in the tree in our backyard.
2. I can't decide what _flavor_ of oatmeal I would like for breakfast.
3. The last _event_ of the picnic was the potato sack race.
4. Ray won a _medal_ for swimming.
5. Ruth tried to fix the _broken_ chain on her bicycle.
6. The narrow _river_ gets a little wider at Cliff's Bend.
7. The _driver_ of the large truck needed a rest after his trip.
8. Will you please set ten places at the _table_?

REVIEW

Syllables

Name _____

Read the list of words. Write each word and draw a line between its syllables.

1. wagon _wag/on_
2. hotel ho/tel
3. doctor doc/tor
4. closet clos/et
5. retell re/tell
6. painless pain/less
7. open o/pen
8. airplane air/plane
9. tiger ti/ger
10. useful use/ful
11. pupil pu/pil
12. later la/ter
13. second sec/ond
14. unlike un/like
15. iron i/ron

16. favor fa/vor
17. thankful thank/ful
18. driveway drive/way
19. famous fa/mous
20. never nev/er
21. slowly slow/ly
22. blanket blan/ket
23. downtown down/town
24. into in/to
25. cabbage cab/bage
26. planet plan/et
27. toothbrush tooth/brush
28. normal nor/mal
29. preview pre/view
30. replace re/place

PROGRESS CHECK

Syllables

Name _____

Read the list of words. Write each word and draw a line between its syllables.

1. metal _met/al_
2. unripe un/ripe
3. kindly kind/ly
4. railroad rail/road
5. dislike dis/like

6. silent si/lent
7. carpet car/pet
8. cloudy cloud/y
9. invite in/vite
10. replay re/play

Read the list of words and the sentences. Divide each list word into syllables by drawing a line between the syllables. Then write the word from the list that makes sense in each sentence.

quick/ly
re/join
end/less
bor/der
re/play
help/ful
home/work
ti/ger
ba/ker
un/zip

1. The _border_ around the edge of the wallpaper was bright blue.
2. Lee puts away the dishes and is _helpful_ in many other ways.
3. The children of the city were asked to name the baby _tiger_ at the city zoo.
4. Our teacher gave us _homework_ in geography and spelling.
5. Last week seemed _endless_ to the workers who were tired.
6. The young child could not _unzip_ his new winter coat.
7. The runners started to race _quickly_ around the track.
8. The coach for the other team asked to see a film _replay_ of the swim meet.

Antonyms

Name _____

Words to use: fasten-unfasten, lead-follow, raise-lower, safe-unsafe, softly-loudly, loose-tight, below-above, comfortable-uncomfortable, excite-bore, fancy-plain, alike-different

An antonym is a word that has the opposite meaning of another word.	early—late

Read the words in each box below. Draw a line to match each word with its antonym (opposite).

strong	false	full	after	early	wide
true	weak	before	wild	over	late
loose	tight	tame	empty	narrow	under

win	spend	cool	warm	dirty	heavy
save	few	easy	dull	light	clean
many	lose	sharp	hard	young	old

Read the list of words below. Then read the sentences that follow. Write the word from the list that is an antonym (opposite) for the underlined word in each sentence.

correct	light	dry	never	thin
slowly	awake	deep	open	smiling

1. The water was <u>shallow</u> during the low tide. — *deep*
2. I wrote down the <u>wrong</u> telephone number. — correct
3. We <u>always</u> use this road to go to school. — never
4. Clara, why are you <u>frowning</u>? — smiling
5. The runner moved <u>swiftly</u> around the track. — slowly
6. The rug was <u>wet</u> after we cleaned it. — dry
7. Mark dropped the <u>heavy</u> box on the floor. — light
8. I was <u>asleep</u> in the softest chair. — awake
9. The pillows on the couch were <u>fat</u>. — thin
10. Please <u>close</u> the car windows. — open

Synonyms

Name _____

Words to use: hotel-inn, jelly-jam, meadow-field, rapid-fast, alive-living, funny-amusing, terrible-awful, started-began, boast-brag, cattle-cows, center-middle, correct-right

A synonym is a word that has the same or nearly the same meaning as another word.	rush—hurry

Read the words in each box below. Draw a line to match each word with its synonym (word that has the same meaning).

quiet	thin	raise	tell	ship	close
simple	easy	say	lift	near	yell
narrow	still	small	little	shout	boat

tale	story	stay	hear	chilly	cold
well	large	forest	remain	present	wash
big	healthy	listen	woods	clean	gift

Read the list of words below. Then read the sentences that follow. Write the word from the list that is a synonym (word that has the same meaning) for the underlined word in each sentence.

unload	skinny	sea	fix	begin
going	raw	cover	hurry	tall

1. Kara will <u>repair</u> the kitchen sink. — *fix*
2. I would like a <u>thin</u> slice of bread. — skinny
3. Don't <u>rush</u> through your homework. — hurry
4. Billy enjoyed the <u>uncooked</u> vegetables. — raw
5. The <u>ocean</u> was calm yesterday. — sea
6. Tess is unhappy that I am <u>leaving</u>. — going
7. We can <u>start</u> the game without Carlos. — begin
8. The workers wanted to <u>unpack</u> the truck. — unload
9. The cats were sitting on the <u>high</u> fence. — tall
10. Please put a <u>lid</u> on the box. — cover

Antonyms and Synonyms

Name _____

Words to use: (antonyms) narrow-wide, sick-healthy, smooth-rough, wise-foolish, true-false, deep-shallow, save-spend, sunrise-sunset, afraid-unafraid, everything-nothing; (synonyms) level-even, tearful-afraid, shout-yell, talk-speak, unhappy-sad, pals-friends, almost-nearly, raise-lift, stay-remain, glisten-sparkle

Read the words below. Circle the two words in each row that are antonyms (opposites).

1. (loose)　empty　(tight)　new　pretty
2. write　sing　(sell)　(buy)　mix
3. (receive)　tie　(send)　draw　clean
4. slow　tall　(noisy)　raw　(quiet)
5. in　buy　near　(after)　(before)
6. (slowly)　happily　fondly　(quickly)　carefully

Read each sentence and the words beside it. Write the word that is a synonym (word that has the same meaning) for the word shown below the blank.

1. There is a small __*tear*__ in the lamp shade. — tear / spot
   (rip)
2. Rita will __repair__ it tomorrow. — repair / sell
   (fix)
3. She knows about a special __glue__ that she can use to fix the shade. — patch / glue
   (paste)
4. Rita also wants to replace the __dull__ light bulb with one that burns more brightly. — dull / bright
   (dim)
5. She will probably go to the store __nearest__ her house. — farthest / nearest
   (closest)
6. Rita will __talk__ to the owner about which light bulbs to buy. — write / talk
   (speak)

REVIEW

Antonyms and Synonyms

Name _____

Read each pair of sentences. In the blanks, write a pair of antonyms (opposites) from the sentences.

1. The young children wanted to play baseball.
   They were going to use the old school's field. — *young* / *old*
2. It was a very warm day in the spring.
   Sam brought ice and water for cool drinks. — warm / cool
3. One team wore dark blue shirts.
   The other team's players wore light green shirts. — dark / light
4. Many people came to watch the first inning.
   Only a few stayed for the whole game. — Many / few

Read each pair of sentences. In the blanks, write a pair of synonyms (words that have the same meaning) from the sentences.

1. Have you heard The Tuners' new song?
   I listened to it ten times last night. — *heard* / *listened*
2. This poem tells a story about John Henry.
   The tale has been told in many different ways. — story / tale
3. Luke, you seem jolly today.
   Are you happy because it's your birthday? — jolly / happy
4. I have discovered a wonderful store.
   I've found many bargains in its basement. — discovered / found

Antonyms and Synonyms

Name _____

Read the list of words below. Then read the sentences that follow. Write the word from the list that is an antonym (opposite) for the underlined word in each sentence.

bright	short	asleep	light
ugly	boring	late	same

1. Tom was <u>awake</u> most of the night. — *asleep*
2. He was thinking about all the <u>beautiful</u> sights he and his parents would see. — ugly
3. They wanted to get an <u>early</u> start on the road. — late
4. Tom's parents didn't want to drive through <u>heavy</u> rush-hour traffic. — light
5. The Smiths were going to visit friends whom they had not seen in a <u>long</u> time. — short
6. Traveling to another city would be <u>exciting</u>. — boring

Read the list of words below. Then read the sentences that follow. Write the word from the list that is a synonym (word that has the same meaning) for the underlined word in each sentence.

waving	happy	shining	pretty
place	dull	like	tiny

1. The scene in the painting was <u>beautiful</u>. — *pretty*
2. The wings of butterflies were <u>fluttering</u> in the breeze. — waving
3. The drops of dew on the leaves were <u>sparkling</u> in the sunlight. — shining
4. Lidia was <u>pleased</u> that she had taken the picture. — happy
5. She decided to <u>put</u> the photo in a frame. — place
6. She thought her friends would <u>enjoy</u> looking at the butterflies and leaves. — like

---

Reading and Writing Wrap-Up

Name _____

Homes Around the World

What kind of house do you live in? Would your house be the same if you lived in a desert or in Alaska? Would your house be the same if you often had to travel from place to place?

Weather and Houses

In the hot, dry New Mexico desert, some people build their houses out of bricks made of mud, clay, straw, and water. These houses have very thick walls to keep out the heat in summer.

In the coldest parts of Alaska, some people build their houses out of thick blocks of ice. The thick walls of ice help to keep the people comfortable during the long, cold winters.

Building Supplies and Houses

When the first settlers came to America, they found large stretches of forests, so they built their houses out of wood.

In some parts of the world there is not much wood, but there are rocks and mountains. Some people in Turkey live in houses carved into the side of stone mountains.

Movable Houses

In some countries, people have one job in the summer and another job in the winter. These people like to have houses they can take with them. In the deserts of Africa, people often live in tents, which they can carry with them when they travel from one place to another.

In the United States and other countries, many people live in trailers. Such homes allow them to live in different places during the year in order to work at different jobs.

1. How are some houses in New Mexico and Alaska alike?
        They both have thick walls.

2. Name two kinds of movable houses. __tents__ __trailers__

Name _____

Social Studies

3. Check the sentence that tells the main idea.

   _____ Houses can be made of wood, brick, stone, or cloth.

   _____ Houses in deserts and mountains are different from houses in cities.

   ✓ Houses around the world are different because of weather, building supplies, and people's jobs.

4. One reason people live in houses is to protect themselves from the weather.

   What other reasons can you think of? Answers may vary but might include the following: People live in houses to protect themselves from insects and animals. People live in houses in order to have a place to keep their belongings. Some people live in houses so they can have a place to go to be by themselves.

5. Invent a new kind of house and draw a picture of it. Describe your house and tell how it will fit the weather and building supplies where you will build it.

   Answers will vary.

   _____
   _____
   _____
   _____
   _____
   _____
   _____

   Use the space below for your drawing.

Homophones

Words to use: haul-hall, horse-hoarse, meet-meat, not-knot, pain-pane, write-right, oar-or,
Name _____ wring-ring, wait-weight, led-lead, see-sea, break-brake

Homophones are words that sound the same but have different spellings and different meanings.

would—wood

Read the words in each box. Draw a line to match each word with its homophone.

nose	buy	son	here	knew	deer
bare	knows	break	brake	dear	sail
by	bear	hear	sun	sale	new

one	eight	weight	peace	see	hour
beat	beet	piece	pail	our	blew
ate	won	pale	wait	blue	sea

Read each pair of sentences. In the blanks, write a pair of homophones (words that sound the same) from the sentences.

1. The flower in the vase was bright yellow.
   Dad used whole wheat flour to make the bread. — *flower* *flour*
2. The heel of my shoe is loose.
   My sister's cuts should heal quickly. — heel / heal
3. Joe will write a letter to his grandparents.
   Make a right turn onto Hunter Street. — write / right
4. Her niece threw the last pitch of the inning.
   We couldn't find our way through the crowd. — threw / through
5. There was only one piece of pizza on the platter.
   Grandma won third prize in the bicycle race. — one / won
6. The road near the bridge is being repaired.
   Yesterday was the first time I rode in a jeep. — road / rode

Homographs are words that have the same spelling but different meanings. Sometimes they are pronounced differently.

The plumber checked the building's **lead** pipes.   The van will **lead** the group of cars.

Read each pair of sentences and circle the homographs (words that have the same spelling). Then draw a line from each sentence to the picture it tells about.

David will (wind) his new watch.
The winter (wind) was cold and biting.

A (tear) fell from the little boy's eye.
Lily will (tear) strips of newspaper for her project.

Mother stood (close) to the desk.
The last person to leave should (close) the door.

The square dancers will (bow) to each other.
Carlos made a large (bow) for the package.

Tracy touched the rough (bark) of our tallest tree.
Our neighbor's dog might (bark) at the squirrels.

Identifying homographs; Determining meanings of homographs   145

Homophones and Homographs

Words to use: (homophones) tale-tail, hear-here, sale-sail, deer-dear, peak-peek, seem-seam, beet-beat, our-hour (homographs) wind, close, lead, bow, bark

Name

Read the words below. In each row, circle two words that are homophones (words that sound the same).

1.	saw	(sea)	side	(see)	sound
2.	pass	(pail)	past	(pale)	part
3.	(meat)	made	(meet)	mess	mouth
4.	(brakes)	brings	(breaks)	bright	breeze
5.	west	weep	(week)	well	(weak)
6.	block	blast	(blew)	blade	(blue)

Read the list of homographs (words that have the same spelling) and their meanings below. Then read the sentences that follow. In each sentence, decide the meaning of the underlined homograph. Write the letter of the correct meaning in the blank.

wind A. to turn or twist   B. fast-moving air
close A. to shut   B. near
bark A. sound made by a dog   B. the covering of a tree

1. The <u>wind</u> blew all the leaves from the tree. — B

2. Ms. Watkins lives <u>close</u> to her office. — B

3. Connie will show us the piece of <u>bark</u> she found. — B

4. Please <u>close</u> the kitchen windows. — A

5. The new highway will <u>wind</u> around the mountain. — A

6. I called Jack when I heard Patches' <u>bark</u>. — A

7. The kites were tossed about in the <u>wind</u>. — B

146   Identifying homophones; Determining meaning of homographs

---

Read each pair of sentences. In the blanks, write a pair of homophones (words that sound the same) from the sentences.

1. Martín knew the answer to the difficult question.   *knew*

   The new airport is larger than the old one.   *new*

2. My parents chopped wood for the fireplace.   wood

   Karen said she would try to visit us soon.   would

3. Our cousins do not know us very well.   Our

   The hour hand of the clock is broken.   hour

4. Kenny will wait for the next bus.   wait

   She read the weight label on the turkey.   weight

5. I don't know who won the game last night.   won

   At one time, we lived in a small town.   one

Read the list of homographs (words that have the same spelling) below. Then read each pair of meanings. Write a homograph from the list that matches both meanings.

wind	lead	tear
close	bow	bark

1. A. near   B. to shut   *close*

2. A. a kind of metal   B. to guide; to be in front   lead

3. A. sound made by a dog   B. the covering of a tree   bark

4. A. a fancy knot made with ribbon   B. to bend the body at the waist   bow

5. A. water from the eye   B. to rip; to pull apart   tear

6. A. a stream of air   B. to turn or twist   wind

Review of identifying homophones; Determining meanings of homographs   147

Read each pair of sentences. Write a pair of homophones (words that sound the same) from the sentences.

1. I was walking by the store window when I saw the coat display.   *by*

   I went into the store to buy a warm winter coat.   *buy*

2. Jesse took the last piece of paper in the stack.   piece

   He asked for peace and quiet while he was working.   peace

3. The sail on the boat was bright blue and yellow.   sail

   She had bought the boat at a toy sale.   sale

4. Our telephone is not working.   Our

   The repair person will be here in an hour.   hour

5. Leo threw the old letters into the basket.   threw

   He had just gone through the week's mail.   through

Read the homographs (words that have the same spelling) and their meanings below. Then read the sentences that follow. In each sentence, decide the meaning of the underlined homograph. Write the letter of the correct meaning in the blank.

wind A. to turn or twist   B. a stream of air
close A. to shut   B. near
tear A. to rip; to pull apart   B. water from the eye

1. Jennifer, please <u>close</u> the front door.   *a*

2. As I peeled the onion, a <u>tear</u> fell from my eye.   B

3. The <u>wind</u> was blowing the snow across the street.   B

4. I'm glad I live <u>close</u> to school.   B

5. The road will <u>wind</u> around the steep hill.   A

6. The thin paper will <u>tear</u> easily.   A

148   Assessment of identifying homophones; Determining meanings of homographs

Guide Words

Words to use: gear, heart, jeep, jolly, invite, hero, dozen, fancy, crisp, dime, instead, doctor, cute, donkey, gift, grown, dirt, cord, deer, hush

Name _____

The two words at the top of a dictionary page are called guide words. The first guide word is the same as the first word listed on the page. The second guide word is the same as the last word listed on the page. To find a word in the dictionary, decide if it comes in alphabetical order between the guide words on a page. If it does, you will find the word on that page. For example, the word **home** falls between the guide words **hollow** and **hop.**

Read each pair of guide words and the words that are listed below them. Circle the words in each list that could be found on a page that has that pair of guide words.

deep / feast	gas / hole	ill / knot	melt / noise
dark	(grease)	ice	(meet)
(drip)	garage	(jar)	(mountain)
fog	(heart)	(kitchen)	(metal)
(false)	(hold)	know	(needle)
(different)	(guide)	(knife)	(nobody)
(fast)	hurry	(jelly)	notice

paint / pond	reward / search	telephone / town	water / yellow
(piano)	(rooster)	teach	(wisdom)
package	(sale)	taste	wash
(people)	silver	(ticket)	(wrap)
porch	special	(today)	wander
(paste)	(ruler)	(test)	(weak)
(pencil)	(ribbon)	(toast)	(yard)

Guide Words

Name _____

Read the lists of words below. Then read the guide words that follow. Write each list word below the correct pair of guide words. Then number each list of words to show how they would be listed in alphabetical order.

roast	cliff	power	brush	climb	sad
print	cheek	company	safe	remain	butter
cage	calf	rush	copy	quick	row
quack	rabbit	below	rose	cave	cabin

Order of words may vary.

1. **bell / camera**
cage	5
calf	6
below	1
brush	2
butter	3
cabin	4

2. **candle / curtain**
cliff	3
cheek	2
company	5
copy	6
climb	4
cave	1

3. **porch / right**
print	2
quack	3
rabbit	5
power	1
remain	6
quick	4

4. **ripe / sail**
roast	1
rush	4
safe	6
rose	2
sad	5
row	3

Guide Words

Name _____

Read the six pairs of guide words and their page numbers. Then read the lists of words that follow. Write the page number on which each list word would be found.

arm / bear—p. 8   **call / curl**—p. 11   **glove / heel**—p. 15
moon / ninety—p. 23   **pay / plow**—p. 29   **still / team**—p. 35

1.	basket	p. 8	14.	pleasant	p. 29
2.	peach	p. 29	15.	night	p. 23
3.	grain	p. 15	16.	carry	p. 11
4.	swallow	p. 35	17.	guest	p. 15
5.	coach	p. 11	18.	straw	p. 35
6.	tea	p. 35	19.	arrange	p. 8
7.	moose	p. 23	20.	tame	p. 35
8.	clever	p. 11	21.	heavy	p. 15
9.	pillow	p. 29	22.	sting	p. 35
10.	ax	p. 8	23.	contest	p. 11
11.	motor	p. 23	24.	napkins	p. 23
12.	half	p. 15	25.	pencil	p. 29
13.	beach	p. 8	26.	nickel	p. 23

Entry Words

Words to use: harmed, funnier, shoveling, dragged, angriest, warming, families, snapping, skipped, harder, poorest, easiest

Name _____

The word or phrase that you look up in a dictionary is called an entry word. An entry word shows the spelling of the word. It also shows the number of syllables in the word. A space is left between the syllables. Entry words are printed in dark type at the left of each column on a dictionary page. An entry word together with its meanings is called an entry.

cit y /sit′ ē/ n, pl **cit ies** a large town: *The city is a very busy place.*

di vide /də vid′/ v **di vid ed; di vid ing** to cut into parts or to separate: *Divide the apple into three pieces.*

When you look for a word in the dictionary, look for the base word. For example, if you want to know the meaning of the word **dividing**, look for the base word **divide.** If you want to know the meaning of **cities**, look for its base word **city.** Any spelling changes for the entry word are usually listed in the entry. In the example above, **divided** and **dividing** are listed in the entry for the word **divide.** **Cities** is listed in the entry for the word **city.**

Read the words below. Beside each word, write the entry word (base word) you would look for in the dictionary.

1.	baking	*bake*	10.	knives	knife
2.	foxes	fox	11.	beaches	beach
3.	saddest	sad	12.	steepest	steep
4.	walked	walk	13.	helped	help
5.	planned	plan	14.	happier	happy
6.	slipping	slip	15.	babies	baby
7.	passes	pass	16.	liked	like
8.	hurried	hurry	17.	laughing	laugh
9.	prettier	pretty	18.	faster	fast

Dictionary Meanings

Name

Many dictionary entry words have more than one meaning. Most dictionaries show the different meanings of a word by numbering them. Some dictionaries also give an example sentence for each meaning. These sentences help to make each meaning clear.

be long /bə lông'/ v **1** to be owned by someone or something: *Does that hat belong to Kelly?* **2** to be in the right place: *Your coats belong in the closet.*

clear /klir/ adj **1** with nothing in the way: *The road is clear now.* **2** not cloudy or foggy: *It looks as if it will be a clear day.* **3** easy to understand: *The directions on the map were clear.*

Read the sentences below. Use the entry words above to decide the meaning of each underlined word. In the blank, write the number of the correct meaning.

1. The forks and spoons <u>belong</u> in the top drawer. **2**
2. The puppies <u>belong</u> to Jose. **1**
3. The birthday gifts <u>belong</u> to Nancy Lopez. **1**
4. These folders <u>belong</u> in my school desk. **2**
5. I hope we have a <u>clear</u> day for the picnic. **2**
6. The driveway is <u>clear</u> of snow and ice. **1**
7. The dictionary lesson was <u>clear</u> to her. **3**
8. On a <u>clear</u> day, you can see for many miles out to sea. **2**
9. The driver wanted the car windows to be <u>clear</u>. **2**
10. Ron's plan was <u>clear</u> to his friends. **3**

Entry Words and Dictionary Meanings

Words to use: hurries, benches, invited, watches, longest, skating, calls, dried, flipping, foxes, puppies
Name

Read the words below. Beside each word, write the entry word you would look for in the dictionary.

1. weighing — *weigh*
2. happier — happy
3. waved — wave
4. laughs — laugh
5. wrapping — wrap
6. traveled — travel
7. tracks — track
8. climbing — climb

Read the dictionary entries. Then read the sentences that follow. Use the dictionary entries shown below to decide the meaning of each underlined word. In the blank, write the number of the correct meaning.

track /trak/ n **1** a line of metal rails for trains to travel on: *The engine pulls the train along the track.* **2** a place to run races: *I ran four miles on the track.* **3** a mark left by something that has passed by: *We saw a raccoon track near the tree.*

weigh /wā/ v **1** to have a certain weight: *I weigh 110 pounds.* **2** to find out how heavy something is: *Please weigh the grapes for me.*

1. The <u>track</u> was clear for the runners. **2**
2. The workers were loading fruit into the freight car on the <u>track</u>. **1**
3. The campers left a <u>track</u> from their tents to the river. **3**
4. The joggers used the park path as a <u>track</u>. **2**
5. I am going to <u>weigh</u> the potatoes. **2**
6. The apples <u>weigh</u> five pounds. **1**
7. The salesperson will <u>weigh</u> the corn. **2**

REVIEW

Guide Words, Entry Words, and Meanings

Name

Read each pair of guide words and the words that are listed below them. Circle the words in each list that could be found on a page that has that pair of guide words.

fear / give	keep / lean	name / one	trade / vine
face	(kind)	(old)	tire
(game)	(lap)	nail	(travel)
guide	joy	(nose)	(understand)
(front)	learn	(o'clock)	(tunnel)
(fur)	(lamb)	only	(valley)
(giant)	(knife)	(nobody)	visit

Read the dictionary entries below. Then read the sentences that follow. Use the dictionary entries to decide the meaning of each underlined word. In the blank, write the number of the correct meaning.

join /join/ v **1** to become a member of a group: *Lisa would like to join the record club.* **2** to bring together: *The two roads join at the bottom of the hill.*

spend /spend/ v spent **1** to use money to buy things: *Try not to spend too much when you're shopping.* **2** to pass time or stay: *We are going to spend our vacation at home.*

1. The artist will <u>join</u> the lines together to form a triangle. **2**
2. Russ might <u>spend</u> three hours on his homework. **2**
3. Janet <u>joined</u> the writing class yesterday. **1**
4. The farmer did not <u>spend</u> too much money for the plow. **1**
5. The new bridge <u>joins</u> the two large islands. **2**
6. I want to <u>join</u> the library because I like to read a lot. **1**

Pronunciation Key and Respellings

Words to use: /rīt'ər/, /flūt'/, /ə wāk'/, /kār/, /klos'ət/, /jen'təl/, /yū'chər/, /bēst/, /kŏm/, /akt/, /hūd/
Name

A dictionary can show you how words are pronounced. Each entry word is followed by a respelling. The respelling is made up of letters and special symbols. The words in the dictionary's pronunciation key show you how to pronounce each letter or symbol. By combining the sounds for each symbol and letter, you can pronounce the word.

Pronunciation Key

/a/ = apple, top	/k/ = kick, can	/th/ = thing, both
/ā/ = ate, say	/l/ = laugh, pail	/u/ = up, cut
/är/ = car, heart	/m/ = mouse, ham	/ü/ = soon, rule
/âr/ = hair, care	/n/ = nice, ran	/u/ = look, put
/b/ = bat, cab	/ng/ = ring, song	/v/ = vine, live
/ch/ = chain, chair	/o/ = father, hot	/w/ = wet, away
/d/ = door, sad	/ō/ = old, so	/y/ = yes, you
/e/ = get, egg	/ô/ = ball, dog	/yü/ = use, cute
/ē/ = even, bee	/oi/ = boy, oil	/yu/ = cure, pure
/f/ = fan, off	/ou/ = house, cow	/z/ = zoo, zero
/g/ = goat, big	/p/ = pan, nap	/zh/ = pleasure, beige
/h/ = her, happy	/r/ = ran, race	/ə/ = a (ground)
/hw/ = wheel, why	/s/ = sun, mess	e (better)
/i/ = is, fit	/sh/ = she, rush	i (rabbit)
/ī/ = ice, ride	/t/ = toy, mat	o (doctor)
/j/ = jump, gentle	/th/ = they, smooth	u (upon)

Read each respelling below. Write the words from the key that show how to pronounce the underlined letters.

1. /ch<u>ā</u>s/ — *ate, say*
2. /<u>th</u>ik/ — thing, both
3. /t<u>ō</u>ld/ — old, so
4. /sp<u>ü</u>n/ — soon, rule
5. /tre<u>zh</u>'ər/ — pleasure, beige
6. /<u>TH</u>əm/ — they, smooth
7. /r<u>ā</u>s/ — ate, say
8. /kl<u>a</u>m/ — apple, tap
9. /n<u>ou</u>/ — house, cow
10. /k<u>ē</u>/ — even, bee

Pronunciation Key and Respellings

Name _____ Words to use: /rut/, /mü′vér/, /kãp/, /rãs/, /let′es/, /skrach/, /nüz/, /throt/, /kõf/, /nã′chèr/, /kür/, /but′en/, /vurb/, /brij/, /nok/, /sok/, /kwes′chen/, /sät′te/, /kärt/

In most dictionaries, a short form of the pronunciation key can be found on each page.

Pronunciation Key

/a/ = apple, tap; /ā/ = ate, say; /ār/ = car, heart; /âr/ = hair, care; /ch/ = chain, chair; /e/ = get, egg; /ē/ = even, bee; /hw/ = wheel, why; /i/ = is, fit; /ī/ = ice, tie; /ng/ = ring, song; /o/ = father, hot; /ō/ = old, so; /ô/ = ball, dog; /oi/ = boy, oil; /ou/ = house, cow; /sh/ = she, rush; /th/ = they, smooth; /th/ = thing, both; /u/ = up, cut; /ü/ = soon, rule; /u̇/ = look, put; /yü/ = use, cute; /yu̇/ = cure, pure; /zh/ = pleasure, beige; /ə/ = a (ground), e (better), i (rabbit), o (doctor), u (upon)

Use the key to pronounce the symbol shown at the beginning of each row. Then read the words in the row. Circle each word that contains the sound for which the symbol stands.

1.	/ē/	(team)	bread	(sleep)	best	(shield)
2.	/ī/	(shine)	(my)	fish	rain	(tie)
3.	/ō/	(boat)	boil	took	(phone)	(flow)
4.	/ü/	(moon)	(tube)	rust	(to)	(stew)
5.	/ch/	(ranch)	chorus	(chair)	chef	(match)
6.	/ou/	soup	(plow)	(hour)	enough	(outside)

Use the pronunciation key shown above to pronounce the respelling shown at the beginning of each row. Then read the words in the row. Circle the word that matches the respelling.

1.	/nīf/	night	(knife)	kite	knight
2.	/skül/	scoop	skate	scale	(school)
3.	/plou/	play	pound	(plow)	proud
4.	/sāl/	said	(sail)	salt	seal
5.	/prīz/	price	prince	pies	(prize)
6.	/sent/	(scent)	scene	send	seat

Using a pronunciation key and respellings 157

Pronunciation Key and Respellings

Name _____ Words to use: /sud′ən/, /stär/, /welth/, /vin/, /trub′el/, /boil/, /kaf/, /är/, /ai′ik/, /ber′e/, /chō′zən/, /in sted′/, /hol′ō/, /jel′ē/, /pe les′/

Pronunciation Key

/a/ = apple, tap; /ā/ = ate, say; /ār/ = car, heart; /âr/ = hair, care; /ch/ = chain, chair; /e/ = get, egg; /ē/ = even, bee; /hw/ = wheel, why; /i/ = is, fit; /ī/ = ice, tie; /ng/ = ring, song; /o/ = father, hot; /ō/ = old, so; /ô/ = ball, dog; /oi/ = boy, oil; /ou/ = house, cow; /sh/ = she, rush; /th/ = they, smooth; /th/ = thing, both; /u/ = up, cut; /ü/ = soon, rule; /u̇/ = look, put; /yü/ = use, cute; /yu̇/ = cure, pure; /zh/ = pleasure, beige; /ə/ = a (ground), e (better), i (rabbit), o (doctor), u (upon)

Use the key shown above to help you pronounce the respelling shown at the beginning of each row. Then read the words in the row. Circle the word that matches the respelling.

1.	/hōz/	house	(hose)	home
2.	/rīt′ər/	(writer)	written	walker
3.	/pik/	(pick)	pitch	pit
4.	/chüz/	cheese	(choose)	shoes
5.	/fôl/	false	fail	(fall)
6.	/ə buv′/	about	(above)	aboard
7.	/yüth/	you	young	(youth)
8.	/spred/	spray	spend	(spread)

Use the key to pronounce each respelling in List A. Then read the words in List B. Write the word from List B that the respelling stands for.

	List A		**List B**
1.	/stāj/	_stage_	famous
2.	/ə genst′/	against	harm
3.	/laf/	laugh	stage
4.	/härm/	harm	laugh
5.	/fā′məs/	famous	oak
6.	/ōk/	oak	against

158 Reading dictionary respellings; Using a pronunciation key

---

Accent Marks

Name _____ Words to use: an noy′, car′rot, be side′, pup′py, a part′, of′fice, per fect′, own′er, to′tal, sil′ver, up′stairs, pud′dle, com′mon, at′tic, with out′, out doors′, de pend′, pump′kin, sixteen′

Some words have more than one syllable. The respellings of these words show the syllables with a space or mark between them. One syllable is usually said with more stress than the others. In the respelling /fin′ish/, the mark after the first syllable shows that **fin** is said with more stress than **ish.** The mark is called an accent mark.

/fin′ish/
fin′ ish
/traf′ik/
traf′fic
/ə gen′/
a gain′

Pronunciation Key

/a/ = apple, tap; /ā/ = ate, say; /ār/ = car, heart; /âr/ = hair, care; /ch/ = chain, chair; /e/ = get, egg; /ē/ = even, bee; /hw/ = wheel, why; /i/ = is, fit; /ī/ = ice, tie; /ng/ = ring, song; /o/ = father, hot; /ō/ = old, so; /ô/ = ball, dog; /oi/ = boy, oil; /ou/ = house, cow; /sh/ = she, rush; /th/ = they, smooth; /th/ = thing, both; /u/ = up, cut; /ü/ = soon, rule; /u̇/ = look, put; /yü/ = use, cute; /yu̇/ = cure, pure; /zh/ = pleasure, beige; /ə/ = a (ground), e (better), i (rabbit), o (doctor), u (upon)

Use the key to pronounce each respelling in List A. Then read the words in List B. Write the word from List B that matches each respelling. Leave a space between syllables. Then put an accent mark after the syllable that is said with more stress.

	List A		**List B**
1.	/wun′dər/	_won′der_	cac/tus
2.	/skam′pər/	scam′per	re/mem/ber
3.	/splen′dəd/	splen′did	neigh/bor
4.	/bi gan′/	be gan′	scam/per
5.	/kak′təs/	cac′tus	whis/tle
6.	/bi sīd′/	be side′	be/gan
7.	/ri mem′ bər/	re mem′ ber	won/der
8.	/pal′əs/	pal′ace	splen/did
9.	/hwis′ əl/	whis′ tle	pal/ace
10.	/nā′ bər/	neigh′ bor	be/side

Recognizing accented syllables and respellings 159

Accent Marks

Name _____

Some words have more than one syllable. In these words, the stress, or accent, often falls on the base word.

fish′ ing
care′ less

Read the words that have been divided into syllables below. Say each word and listen for the stressed syllable. Put an accent mark after the stressed syllable in each word.

1.	good′ness	6.	snow′y	11.	help′ing
2.	thank′ful	7.	push′ing	12.	home′less
3.	clown′ish	8.	fast′est	13.	help′ful
4.	test′ing	9.	dust′y	14.	smooth′est
5.	night′ly	10.	friend′less	15.	calm′ly

Read each word below. Say each word and listen for the stress. Write the word, leaving a space between syllables. Put an accent mark after the stressed syllable in each word.

1.	barking	_bark′ing_	9.	snapping	snap′ ping
2.	tightly	tight′ ly	10.	weekly	week′ ly
3.	careless	care′ less	11.	grayish	gray′ ish
4.	sleepy	sleep′ y	12.	strongest	strong′ est
5.	quicker	quick′ er	13.	cloudy	cloud′ y
6.	rusting	rust′ ing	14.	foolish	fool′ ish
7.	slowly	slow′ ly	15.	weakness	weak′ ness
8.	wanted	want′ ed	16.	friendly	friend′ ly

160 Recognizing accented syllables

207

Accent Marks

Name _____

Some two-syllable words that are spelled alike may have different respellings. They may be pronounced with the stress on different syllables. Read the entries below. Use the accent marks to help you say each word. Listen for the stressed syllable.

¹ob ject /ob′ jikt/ *n* a thing that can be seen or touched: *I removed the object from the table.*

²ob ject /əb jekt′/ *v* to be against the idea of something: *We object to the building of the new highway.*

¹pres ent /prez′ ənt/ *n* a gift: *I received a lovely present of flowers.*

²pre sent /pri zent′/ *v* to hand over or to give: *Mr. James will present the awards.*

¹rec ord /rek′ ərd/ *n* **1** something kept in writing for future use: *I keep a record of the books I read.* **2** a round phonograph disk: *I bought the group's latest record.*

²re cord /ri kôrd′/ *v* **1** to put into writing: *Record the names of the club members who are here.* **2** to put music or words on tape: *We will record the mayor's speech.*

Read each sentence below. In the blank, write the underlined word as it's shown above. Leave a space between syllables. Put an accent mark after the stressed syllable in each word. Use the entries above to help you.

1. There was a large <u>object</u> on the road. _____ *ob′ ject*

2. The artist will <u>present</u> his painting. _____ pre sent′

3. The <u>record</u> I'm listening to has an old song on it. _____ rec′ ord

4. Shelly might <u>object</u> to our picnic plans. _____ ob ject′

5. Will you <u>record</u> the school band's concert? _____ re cord′

6. Sam liked the <u>present</u> the twins gave to him. _____ pres′ ent

7. Keep a <u>record</u> of how much money you spend. _____ rec′ ord

8. Why do you <u>object</u> to our idea? _____ ob ject′

9. Maggie will <u>record</u> the runners' finishing times. _____ re cord′

REVIEW Pronunciation Key and Respellings

Name _____

Pronunciation Key

/a/ = apple, tap; /ā/ = ate, say; /âr/ = car, heart; /âr/ = hair, care; /ch/ = chain, chair; /e/ = get, egg; /ē/ = even, bee; /hw/ = wheel, why; /i/ = is, fit; /ī/ = ice, tie; /ng/ = ring, song; /o/ = father, hot; /ō/ = old, so; /ô/ = ball, dog; /oi/ = boy, oil; /ou/ = house, cow; /sh/ = she, rush; /ŦH/ = they, smooth; /th/ = thing, both; /u/ = up, cut; /ū/ = soon, rule; /u̇/ = look, put; /yū/ = use, cute; /yu̇/ = cure, pure; /zh/ = pleasure, beige; /ə/ = a (ground), e (better), i (rabbit), o (doctor), u (upon)

Use the key above to help you pronounce the respelling at the beginning of each row. Then read the words in the row. Circle the word that the respelling matches.

1. /tā′ bəl/   (table)   tasted   tablet

2. /ə pärt′/   appeal   appear   (apart)

3. /kan′ dəl/   castle   canned   (candle)

4. /min′ ət/   minus   (minute)   miner

5. /pen′ səl/   pedal   person   (pencil)

6. /sē′ zən/   second   secret   (season)

Use the key to help you pronounce each respelling in List A. Then read the words in List B. Write the word from List B that each respelling stands for.

	List A		**List B**
1.	/nēd′ əl/	*needle*	again
2.	/nir bī′/	nearby	planet
3.	/plan′ ət/	planet	person
4.	/pur′ sən/	person	along
5.	/ə gen′/	again	nearby
6.	/ə lông′/	along	needle

PROGRESS CHECK Dictionary Skills

Name _____

Read the sample entries below. Use them and the key to answer the questions that follow.

float /flōt/ *v* **1** to rest in or on the surface of water or liquid: *The toy boat will float in the tub of water.* **2** to move through the air: *I watched the clouds float across the sky.*

writ ing /rīt′ ing/ *n* **1** the way a person forms letters and words: *Your writing is easy to read.* **2** something that is written or printed, such as a book or a letter: *This story is an example of Mark Twain's writing.*

Pronunciation Key

/a/ = apple, tap; /ā/ = ate, say; /âr/ = car, heart; /âr/ = hair, care; /ch/ = chain, chair; /e/ = get, egg; /ē/ = even, bee; /hw/ = wheel, why; /i/ = is, fit; /ī/ = ice, tie; /ng/ = ring, song; /o/ = father, hot; /ō/ = old, so; /ô/ = ball, dog; /oi/ = boy, oil; /ou/ = house, cow; /sh/ = she, rush; /ŦH/ = they, smooth; /th/ = thing, both; /u/ = up, cut; /ū/ = soon, rule; /u̇/ = look, put; /yū/ = use, cute; /yu̇/ = cure, pure; /zh/ = pleasure, beige; /ə/ = a (ground), e (better), i (rabbit), o (doctor), u (upon)

1. Write the number of the meaning of <u>float</u> as it is used in each sentence.

   a. The plane seemed to <u>float</u> across the clear sky. _____ 2

   b. This inner tube should help me <u>float</u> on the lake. _____ 1

   c. I watched a leaf <u>float</u> from the tree to the ground. _____ 2

2. Write the number of the meaning of <u>writing</u> as it is used in each sentence.

   a. The <u>writing</u> on the chart is very clear. _____ 1

   b. The <u>writing</u> of E. B. White includes the story <u>Stuart Little</u>. _____ 2

3. Circle the pair of words that would be guide words for each dictionary entry shown in dark print.

   a. **float**   flake / flap   fleet / flick   (flip / flow)

   b. **writing**   wait / white   (wrap / wrong)   wrote / wrung

4. Write the words from the pronunciation key that show how to pronounce the letters shown in dark print.

   a. /fl**ō**t/ _____ old, so   b. /rīt′ **ing**/ _____ ring, song

---

Reading and Writing Wrap-Up

Name _____

Using Your Senses to Describe

How would you describe something you can't see?

Who Has Seen the Wind?

Who has seen the wind?
   Neither I nor you;
But when the leaves hang trembling
   The wind is passing through.

Who has seen the wind?
   Neither you nor I;
But when the trees bow down their heads
   The wind is passing by.
       —*Christina Rossetti*

The Wind

I saw you toss the kites on high
And blow the birds about the sky;
And all around I heard you pass,
Like ladies' skirts across the grass.
   O wind, a-blowing all day long,
   O wind, that sings so loud a song!

I saw the different things you did,
But always you yourself you hid;
I felt you push, I heard you call,
I could not see yourself at all.
   O wind, a-blowing all day long,
   O wind, that sings so loud a song!
       —*Robert Louis Stevenson*

1. In "Who Has Seen the Wind?" how does the author answer the question in the title? _____ She says that neither I nor you have seen the wind.

2. In "The Wind," what does the author say the wind is like?

   _____ a story   ✓ a song   _____ a storm

3. In "The Wind," which two senses does the author say the wind affects directly?

   _____ sight   ✓ sound   _____ smell   _____ taste   ✓ touch